MUSIC IN AMERICAN LIFE

A list of volumes in the series Music in American Life appears at the end of this book.

Goin' to Kansas City

Goin' to
Kansas City

Nathan W. Pearson, Jr.

University of Illinois Press
Urbana and Chicago

© *1987 by Nathan W. Pearson, Jr.*
Manufactured in the United States of America

C 5 4 3 2

This book is printed on acid-free paper.

Library of Congress Cataloging-in-Publication Data

Pearson, Nathan W., 1951-
  Goin' to Kansas City.

  (Music in American life)
  Discography: p.
  Bibliography: p.
  Includes index.
  1. Jazz music—Missouri—Kansas City.   I. Title.
II. Title: Goin' to Kansas City.   III. Series.
ML3508.8.K37P4   1987   785.42′09778′411   87-5987
ISBN 0-252-01336-0 (alk. paper)

Dedication

This book is dedicated to the countless musicians of the Midwest whose artistry and inspiration conspired to create glorious music, and great good times, in Kansas City before World War II, and in particular to the many musicians, politicians, booking agents, promoters, and others who graciously gave of their time and memories to create the oral histories that make up the bulk of this story.

Contents

Preface

Howard Litwak and I first discussed preparing an oral history of Kansas City jazz in 1975. Howard had a background in American studies and I in ethnomusicology; we had been college friends and shared personal and professional interests in jazz, history, and American culture. Howard had worked with Dr. Tamara Harevan of Clark University on an oral history of the Amoskeag (New Hampshire) woolen mills. My M.A. thesis was an oral history/biography of Mance Lipscomb, a Texas songster, and I was about to begin working for the Smithsonian Institution as an ethnomusicologist with the Festival of American Folklife.

We were both marginally employed in 1975 and looking for ways to use our talents in an interesting and creative way. Howard had the idea to join forces to conduct an oral history of a jazz "scene," exploring humanistic, political, and economic aspects of jazz culture as well as the music itself. We initially thought of studying New Orleans but were dissuaded by Martin Williams, head of the Smithsonian Institution's Jazz Program and a noted jazz scholar. Both he and Tom Vennum, ethnomusicologist for the Smithsonian Institution's Folklife Program, strongly encouraged us to study a less well known and potentially richer urban jazz center. Several possibilities existed, and among the four major centers of jazz's development — New Orleans, Chicago, New York, and Kansas City — we chose K.C. as the most fruitful and least explored.

After much hair-pulling over finding a way to pay for this project we obtained a National Endowment for the Humanities Youthgrant that provided our initial financial support. We left New York for Kansas City in February 1977 after conducting our first series of interviews with jazz and political figures in New York and Washington, D.C.

The grant provided us with eighty dollars each, weekly, so additional help was crucial to our survival. Jim and Betty Nicol, pillars of the Kansas City community, offered their hospitality on our arrival, and continued to provide much-appreciated home cooking, moral support, and introductions to key informants in K.C.

Our 1977 stay lasted six months, and during it Howard and I built the core of our oral history archive. We added to it over the course of several later trips through 1980. Most interviews were conducted by both of us, tape recorded, and each interviewee was paid fifty dollars for his participation (Count Basie graciously declined to accept his honorarium). Follow-up sessions were arranged if needed and possible. Most of the sessions were transcribed, many by the Smithsonian's Jazz Oral History Program, others by the University of Missouri, and the remainder by Howard and me. Copies of the interview tapes are now in public (but restricted) archives at the Institute for Jazz Studies, Rutgers University, Newark, New Jersey, and the Western Historical Manuscripts Collection of the University of Missouri, Kansas City, where written transcripts of many of the sessions are also stored.

Countless hours of often frustrating hunting for important sources, low pay, and comically poor living conditions aside, our work was an almost completely joyful experience, largely due to the people we encountered. K.C. became our home and our informants were immensely generous with their time. Many became close friends.

The roster of the sources who made this project possible is long and impressive: Don Albert, Bernard "Buddy" Anderson, Eddie Barefield, Bill "Count" Basie, Druie Bess, Congressman Richard Bolling, Arthur Bryant, Wilbur "Buck" Clayton, John Cooper, Ernest Daniels, Herman Davis, Lawrence Denton, Eddie Durham, Curtyse Foster, Bernard Gnefkow, Charles Goodwin, Sam Grievious, John Hammond, Walter Harrold, Torrence "T." Holder, Raymond F. Howell, George Jackson, Jimmy Jewell, Hugh Jones, William Kemper, Parris "Dude" Lankford, Clarence Love, Baby Lovett, Henry McKissick, Irene McLaurian, Jay McShann, Orville Minor, Ida and Edna Mintirn, Elmer Orrie, Edgar Allen and Marguerite Poe, Sam Price, Gene Ramey, John Sandusky, William Saunders, Roy Searcy, Henry "Buster" Smith, Jesse Stone, George "Buddy" Tate, Myra Taylor, John Tumino, Herman Walder, Woodie Walder, Booker Washington, Jerry Westbrook, Claude Williams, Ernie Williams, and Mary Lou Williams.

Others do not appear in the archives or in this text, but were no less important to our success and the pleasure we found in our effort. Among them are: Kathy Nicol, Philip Bowles and Jamie Nicol, Art and Mary Smith, Bill Crowley and Nancy Martin, Bob and Diane Suckiel, Luke Baldwin, Brian Morahan, Sam and Nadine Indyk, Sherron Stratton, Jerry Eisterhold and Anita Llewellyn, Edeen Martin and Tim Nichols, Jack Ralston, Trudi and John Nepsted, Bill, Cecile, Marilyn, Tom, Ann, and Matt Jones, Art Brisbane, Midge Nutman, and David Katzman. Many important friends, however, are neglected. Time, stolen address books, and confusion all take their toll. I trust they'll realize that they are only absent from ephemeral records, and not from the heart.

Toward the end of our NEH Youthgrant, in July 1977, we made contact with Bill Crowley, curator of history at the Kansas City Museum of History and Science. Through him we met Edeen Martin, project specialist at the Mid-America Arts Alliance, a multistate arts consortium. We all discussed possible products from the oral history research, and came up with a multimedia museum exhibit, to be built in K.C. and then sent on tour throughout the Midwest.

Howard and I had always intended that the research produce a book, but funds were scarce, and we were eager to find avenues to make our information more broadly available and keep the project alive. In the process we discovered a fruitful and rewarding world of creative expression in museum exhibitions.

After many grant applications, much internal controversy, and dedicated work with many friends and colleagues, "Goin' to Kansas City" came into being as a traveling museum exhibit. It was a compact thirty-seven-panel exhibit that included a descriptive catalog, a twenty-five-minute film, and audio supplements. The exhibit made both of us proud. The Mid-America Arts Alliance was the sponsor of the museum exhibit and made its creation and subsequent tour throughout the Midwest possible. Major funding came from the National Endowment for the Humanities; other support was provided by the Mobil Foundation, the American Folklife Center of the Library of Congress, Kansas City Parks and Recreation, and the Music Performance Trust Fund. We built the show at the Kansas City Museum, where Jerry Eisterhold became the third member of the Litwak and Pearson team. Jerry is an artist, graphic designer, and all-around exhibit whiz who helped translate concepts and recollections into meaningful images.

"Goin' to Kansas City" opened Saturday, May 24, 1980 in Kansas City. To kick it off we held a party and invited the city. The highlight of the day was a battle of bands, with groups chosen by a panel of local authorities and the winner to tour with the exhibit for a year. This allowed for both a delightful event and resonance with K.C.'s past—annual band battles had been major factors in determining the bands for choice gigs in the coming year. Pianist Jay McShann opened the show with an all-star band made up of blues shouter Big Joe Turner, Claude "Fiddler" Williams, saxophonist Eddie "Lockjaw" Davis, vocalist Priscilla Bowman, bassist LaVern Barker, and drummer Paul Gunther. The Scamps, strong local favorites, won the battle, five thousand people attended, and the exhibit earned rave reviews. Subsequently Howard and I worked on a series of television programs with Nebraska Educational Television that featured three of K.C.'s most important performers—Count Basie, Mary Lou Williams, and Jay McShann.

"Goin' to Kansas City" toured for nearly three years and returned to K.C. Though now in storage, it will be released to a permanent local site when one appears. Recent events in K.C. give hope that the Mutual Musician's Foundation, built from the old black musician's union, will create a K.C. jazz museum where the exhibit can be a tribute to the milieu from which it sprang.

As Howard and I pursued other livelihoods after our work in Kansas City ended, a wish to create a more complete, written exposition of the oral history remained in our minds. We knew that it wasn't likely that both of us would be able to take off several months and write it together, so we agreed that the first one who could, should. I now work with McKinsey and Company, an international management consulting firm that is generous of spirit and with leaves of absence, and my desire to write was stronger than Howard's. As a result, the book in your hands is my effort. From the beginning, however, *Goin' to Kansas City* was a partnership, and it is only due to the exigencies of careers that we are not joined now. Howard Litwak's presence is still everywhere in this work.

Throughout the writing my primary, and best, source of editorial advice and support has been my wife, Jane Wallace, and in its final stages the assistance of Judith McCulloh and Carol Betts of the University of Illinois Press has been invaluable.

Structurally, *Goin' to Kansas City* follows a roughly chronological progression in its chapters. The first two set the stage by describing some of the broad cultural, musical, and theatrical roots of the music, and by discussing ragtime and New Orleans jazz, two highly influential antecedents of the K.C. jazz style. (In these chapters and throughout, each commentator is introduced by a biographical sketch containing the following information where known: birth date, birthplace, death date, place of death, specialty, career highlights.)

Chapters 3 through 6 treat the proliferation of jazz in the Mid- and Southwest (the "Territories") during the 1920s. This section begins with accounts of several notable Territory bands of that era, continues with more detailed descriptions of two of the best known and most important, the T. Holder/Andy Kirk Twelve Clouds of Joy and Walter Page's Blue Devils. This section concludes with the Great Depression, and the decline of a once-profitable musical circuit of theaters, roadhouses, and dance halls.

Chapter 7 begins the Kansas City accounts with the political and economic environment dominated by Boss Tom Pendergast's administration. Chapters 8 and 9 describe the extraordinarily open, exotic, and corrupt K.C. nightlife of the twenties and thirties.

Kansas City jazz style is described in chapter 10, followed by histories of the most important K.C. jazz orchestras—Bennie Moten, Count Basie, George E. Lee, the Kansas City Rockets, and Jay McShann.

The coming of war coupled with civic reform signaled the end of K.C.'s heyday; chapter 16 discusses this process. Chapter 17 treats some of the most important musicians who carried the K.C. heritage into jazz's modern age—Buster Smith, Lester Young, and Charlie Parker. Although Kansas

City never regained its stature as a jazz center, it has retained an active core of musicians, and continues to make attempts at better preserving its musical heritage, as described in chapter 18.

The oral histories that tell the Kansas City jazz story are taken, with very few and noted exceptions, from Howard's and my research. They are arranged by theme and context rather than by speaker. Supplementary words, phrases, and explanations are occasionally added by me for clarity and are marked by brackets.

Throughout, the Kansas City story is carried by the musicians, dancers, agents, and politicians who made it happen. This is their book, too.

Introduction

I might take a plane, I might take a train,
but if I have to walk I'm goin' just the same.
I'm goin' to Kansas City, Kansas City here I come.
—Little Willie Littlefield
"Goin' to Kansas City"

Beginning in the mid-1920s and continuing through the late 1930s, jazz musicians from the central part of America were "goin' to Kansas City" in search of jobs, musical challenge, and good times. When they arrived they entered a musical community that was extraordinarily supportive, demanding, and artistically uplifting. These musicians brought together many different musical styles—strong-rhythmed blues-based dance music from Texas and Oklahoma, small-ensemble polyphony from New Orleans, brass band and theater orchestra sophistication from Missouri and Northern states, circus and carnival music from everywhere—and created a distinctive Kansas City jazz. The great bands of the K.C. era—the Blue Devils, Bennie Moten, Andy Kirk, the Kansas City Rockets, Count Basie, and Jay McShann—are among the greatest in jazz. They offered the finest expressions of swing and laid groundwork for the development of modern jazz.

Kansas City jazz prospered while most of America suffered the catastrophe of the Great Depression, largely because of the corrupt but economically stimulating administration of Boss Tom Pendergast. Through a combination of labor-intensive public works programs (many of which closely resembled later New Deal programs), deficit spending, and the tacit sanction of massive corruption, Pendergast created an economic oasis in Kansas City. Vice was a major part of this system and gave a strong, steady cash flow to the city. Jazz was the popular social music of the time, and the centers of vice— nightclubs and gambling halls—usually hired musicians to attract customers. The serendipitous result was plentiful, if low-paying, jobs for jazz musicians from throughout the Midwest and an outpouring of great new music.

Kansas City has long been recognized as having been a major jazz center, ranking in importance behind New York and with New Orleans and Chicago. As a consequence it has periodically been the subject of historians who have usually seen Kansas City from the viewpoint of the jazz specialist.[1] This book takes a different approach, and uses the development of jazz in Kansas City as the focal point for a social history set in the Midwest before World War II. In this history the forces of urban politics and the national economy intersect with talented individuals as they form a jazz community in K.C., and marvelous music results.

The social history of jazz in Kansas City is that of the growth, flowering, and decline of this community, and has elements in common with histories of other notable artistic communities, where creativity and innovation were fueled by more than individual inspiration. Some twentieth-century examples of these communities and their best recognized arts are: New Orleans in the teens, also for jazz; Paris in the twenties for literature; New York in the 1940s and 1950s for visual arts; and London and San Francisco in the 1960s for rock music. Each time and place is remembered and admired for both remarkable creative output and the strength and character of its communities. Each community was notorious for eccentricity in its day and each had serendipitous support from political and economic events. All have histories that lie beyond specific chronological details of artistic development and biographies of the artists. Their histories are enriched with stories of human interactions, as filtered through the memories of those who were there.

Kansas City musicians also lived in a community that enjoyed its own distinctive "scene," complete with its own legends of heroes and villains, triumphs and tragedies. *Goin' to Kansas City* tells the story of this community, primarily through the recollections of many who were active participants. It is the story of the times and lore of an important center of American music, of its development, of its great bands, and, most important, of the lives of some of the men and women who made it a thrilling place to be.

NOTE

1. Particularly important are Frank Driggs, in numerous articles, and Ross Russell, whose *Jazz Style in Kansas City and the Southwest* (which borrows heavily from Driggs) is the only previous book-length work on Kansas City jazz.

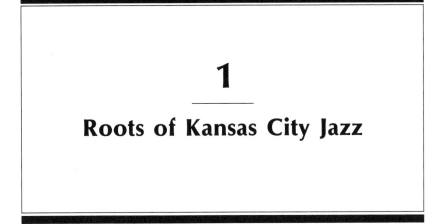

1

Roots of Kansas City Jazz

Jazz in the Midwest evolved from many sources, and developed in a territory with boundaries determined by economic, political, and cultural circumstances. Before jazz styles developed in the early 1920s musicians performed ragtime, brass band, and social dance music on village greens and in carnivals, minstrel shows, vaudeville theaters, and dance halls. In rural areas Saturday night suppers, roadhouses, and juke joints were arenas for blues, country ragtime, and string dance band musicians. And music "professors," usually pianists who were the most musically sophisticated members of their communities and were known for both performance and instruction, proliferated in the schoolroom and in local parlors. All these provided important roots for both the musical styles of jazz and the life styles of the entertainers. The first part of the "Goin' to Kansas City" story is the story of the musicians of these early days, from the turn of the century through the mid-1920s.

Saturday Night Suppers and Rural Music-Making

In the rural South, Saturday night was often the time for six-day-a-week farmers to relax and attend a supper put on by a local family. For a small admission charge, people ate, drank, gambled, sang, and danced to the music of the local songster—a musician who could satisfy nearly any song or dance request.[1] A similar versatility characterized most jazz bands of the twenties and thirties; their ability to play in a variety of styles enriched the music of the period and allowed the bands to find employment in a variety of settings.

The Saturday night supper was not only the main entertainment for many rural black families, it was also an economic necessity, earning crucial supplements to the meager income of the host family. The tradition of hosting a party for entertainment and income moved north with these families to urban areas, and became rent parties in the twenties, thirties, and forties.

JESSE STONE. *Born 11/16/1901, Atchison, Kansas. Piano and arranger. Led the Blues Serenaders, arranger and performer with T. Holder and Andy Kirk's Twelve Clouds of Joy, George E. Lee, Thamon Hayes's Kansas City Rockets, and for many recording sessions, including with Joe Turner. Generally considered to be, along with Buster Smith and Eddie Durham, among the most influential composers and arrangers of Midwestern jazz in the twenties, thirties, and forties.*

Most people did that [have Saturday night suppers] in bygone days; there was a financial necessity, because somebody was short on their rent, someone was ill and needed money for a doctor, or such as that. This was their way of accumulating money, because black people do love to have a good time and they don't mind congregating and spending money as long as they are having fun. If you asked them to put in a hat, you know, for such and such a cause, you wouldn't get near as much. . . .

In the very beginning [of these parties] they played a guitar. It was one instrument. [They had these parties] all over. They had it in the South everywhere. One guy playing the guitar and singing blues. That was the entertainment and the drawing card. I have a cousin that did it. One of his fortes was singing the blues and he used to make a lot of parties, singing and playing blues. His pay would be maybe a dollar or a dollar and a half for a whole night's work, and all the food and drink [he wanted]. . . . Harley Skyatt was his name. He was way ahead of the Beatles because he wore his hair down to here, in the teens. That was his Indian blood that caused him to do that. . . . He used a spike, a big heavy nail, or a glass tumbler, or sometimes just a switchblade knife, back of a knife . . . for a [guitar] slide.

ROY SEARCY. *Born 1913, Moorhead, Mississippi. Piano and vocal. Active in Kansas City from 1942 as solo performer and bandleader. Heads the Jason Royce Searcy Foundation, which accepts contributions.*

When I started playing [piano] . . . I was about twelve years old. They'd come and ask my Momma, "We have a fish fry." We called it a supper then, we didn't call it a fish fry. "We're having a supper tonight. Will you let your little boy come over and play for us?" She said, "Well, what you goin' to pay him?" "We'll give him fifty cents." "All right."

Now they didn't ask me a damn thing. She'd send me over there and I'd go in and play for fifty cents. They really didn't have to give me the fifty cents because I was so anxious to play. And then they'd give me a fish sandwich. . . .

We'd go out on the farm to the Saturday night supper. . . . We had a big plantation, maybe ten families, and this guy that owned the farm, a white guy named Cab DuPont, very nice guy, [would] make this whiskey and he'd hide it all out in the cotton fields. . . . If I'd find one of 'em I'd open it, get me a drink.

Some old guys, they was big shots, they had a horse to ride. They'd put me on a horse. I didn't weigh no more than ninety pounds at most and I'd ride around to this place. We'd get on a damn horse and I'm drunk and they're drunk. They'd take me from one Saturday night supper to the next, maybe ten miles, and that damn horse just flying, I'm sitting back there, no control, just goin' along for the ride. Get there and I'd play the piano and get drunk. . . . I went on over in Alabama on a Saturday night and I didn't have no salary. They would charge fifteen cents at the door, and whoever owns the house would split it. I had no way of countin' it, but I'd sit there and make a dollar and a half or two dollars, and hell, I'm rich.

EDDIE BAREFIELD. *Born 12/12/1909, Scandia, Iowa. Saxophones, clarinet, arranger. Featured with many bands including Bennie Moten, Count Basie, Cab Calloway, Zack Whyte, Don Redman, Benny Carter, and Duke Ellington.*

In Chicago I continued to play music, although I didn't know how to read. I started playing around there with a piano player at house parties and things. . . . House-rent parties [were] where people gave a party on the weekends, especially, and they served fried chicken and maybe chitterlings. Then maybe have a little gambling on the side, and dancing. They raised money to pay the rent. So people would come there and buy the food and dance, and they sold booze. They'd always have a piano player to play and like that. In my case, I used to play the saxophone with the piano player. . . . [We played] blues and different things, whatever it was, because most everybody in those days . . . just played what they knew.

Saturday night suppers and black rural music encompass many styles of music, but the blues was the most popular among them, and the most significant as a jazz source. If improvisation and swing are the grammar of jazz, then the blues is the music's basic vocabulary. The blues originated among rural blacks, probably as work songs — vocal music improvised to and fitting the rhythms of work — and social songs. Blues lyrics come from a vast body of well-known rhymes, slang expressions, homilies, and metaphors, from hymns and sermons, and from individual poetic inspiration. The style was rhythmically free and highly melismatic,[2] with the singer/composer altering notes in pitch and meter, or "worrying" them to best express himself.

The blues is also an instrumental music. Among the first instruments used by rural blacks in America were homemade drums (often banned because of their known use to transmit messages in Africa), fiddles, fretless banjos, jaw harps and mouthbows, pan pipes, and simple reed instruments. All these instruments are free from the chromatic limitations of fretted and fixed-pitch instruments. Many folk musicians use musical scales different from the tempered, diatonic system that began to be adopted in Western art music in the seventeenth century. The inclination to use other than diatonic scales is so strong that when fretted and fixed-pitch instruments were available to black musicians, they were often played so as to simulate other scale structures. Guitarists often played with a slide (made from a knife, bottleneck, bone, or steel bar), and pianists alternated two adjacent notes in rapid succession, suggesting another, middle, tone. Modern musicians can similarly depart from conventional Western musical structure by using new and versatile instruments such as electric and pedal steel guitars and electronic music synthesizers.

When the blues combined voice and instrumentation in the mid-1800s it became a social dance and entertainment music. As it developed styles, conventions, and notable performance genres it also gained an audience, at first in the South, among both blacks and whites.

A national "race" record market developed in the 1920s, featuring mostly blues vocalists, and had the effect of both establishing certain musical conventions among performers and recording companies, and popularizing the music. The conventions included a "blues scale," a note series jury-rigged from African and European pentatonic scales to fit the piano's diatonic system; a basic song length of twelve (or eight, or sixteen) bars; a four-chord progression (I-IV-V-I); and a lyric/melodic scheme of three divisions (A-A-B). This lyric structure is illustrated in "Good Morning Blues," as performed by Jimmy Rushing with the Count Basie Orchestra in 1938:

> Good morning blues, blues how do you do?
> Good morning blues, blues how do you do?
> I feel all right. I've come to worry you.

Several of the first recorded blues vocalists of the twenties—Ma Rainey, Bessie Smith, Mamie Smith, and Ida Cox—achieved a stunning elegance and beauty within these conventions. At the same time, more rural performers—Blind Lemon Jefferson, Sleepy John Estes, Mississippi John Hurt,

Skip James, Henry Thomas, and others—made equally stunning and freer, less constrained recordings. Their influence, however, was restricted to a rural audience and didn't resurface until the fifties in the Chicago urban blues sound, and the mid-sixties in English rock. The high-style, usually female blues shouters, touring widely in vaudeville shows, had a profound influence on jazz and other American music of the twenties. Their blues have a life of their own, distinct from jazz, but like two members of the same family, are more alike than different.

Traveling Shows—Minstrels, Carnivals, and Circuses

A profusion of entertainments—vaudeville companies; medicine, wild west, and minstrel shows; circuses; carnivals; and movies traveled through America between 1900 and 1930. Traveling shows were a powerful magnet for ambitious and inquisitive musicians. The spectacles were exotic and wonderful events, the performers in them worldly-wise troubadours. For many young musicians beginning to explore their new talent, traveling shows offered the perfect opportunity for adventure and musical training. As a consequence these shows also were a powerful force in the musical development of America, absorbing musicians of widely different backgrounds and styles, then spreading developing new styles widely.

EDDIE DURHAM. *Born 8/19/1906, San Marcos, Texas. Guitar, trombone, arranger, and composer. Performed and arranged for many jazz orchestras, including the Walter Page Blue Devils, the Bennie Moten Orchestra, the Count Basie Orchestra, Jimmie Lunceford, Glenn Miller, Jan Savitt, and Artie Shaw. Pioneer electric guitarist.*

My father was a fiddler . . . born in Mexico. He used to play for square dances and I used to play with him. He would play his fiddle and take some of us kids along and get two hatpins, and he would play his fiddle. We're standing there, playing rhythm on it [the fiddle neck, with] those hatpins. . . . That fiddle would sound like a drum . . . and what a rhythm it was. . . . He'd kill two or three rattlesnakes and he'd get the rattles and dry them out and put them in the fiddle . . . and the rattles would amplify the fiddle. . . . This was about seventy-five miles south of San Antonio, place they call San Marcos. . . .

I could read [music] because my brother studied music. . . . He joined the army, which was the Twenty-fourth Infantry Division, the Rough Riders. So I used to go out to Mexico where he was stationed, on the border. . . . He'd get me a place in town and he would teach me some music. He started teaching me trombone and guitar . . . and I could read. . . .

You had to have a gun when I was living out there . . . for rattlesnakes
and wild animals. . . . They used to wear them to town when I was a
little boy. I used to go to the theater, and the guy would have movies
once a week, silent movies, and a guy would be choking a woman. . . . A
guy would say, "Charlie, you ain't gonna let that polecat choke that
woman," . . . and he'd shoot up the man's screen. . . . The cops would
come in, [but] . . . every week he'd shoot up the man's screen. . . .

I got a guitar from some guy in Greensville, Texas, . . . and I went
away for a show called Doug Martin's Dramatics. . . . That's where I
learned guitar. . . . It was a tent show, a regular stage show. They had
classics and everything. It was a white show, [but] they had a minstrel
show with them too. . . . All the circuses had a sideshow called the minstrel show. . . .

The minstrel show would always consist of about a nine-piece band
that could play jazz or swing or whatever you call it, and they'd use
tunes like "Alabama Bound." . . . When the curtain would rise they'd
have all them big striped hats [on], and the guys would be sittin' there,
about six or seven guys. There would be a dancing team [and] a comedian way over in the corner sitting down. . . . One of them would start
laughing . . . and the crowd would just break up. . . . I know one guy was
called "Pork Chop" and one was named "Lasses Brown." Boy, they
cracked some of the funniest jokes. . . . They had the white gloves and
one had big red lips and the other would have big white lips. . . .

If they ever put me off a show it would be for laughing at those comedians. . . . Those guys were good in those days. . . . I was [later] with
the Georgia Minstrel and Alabama Minstrel and some shows like
that. . . .

I got started in arranging [when] I decided to go with the [Miller
Brothers] 101 Wild West Circus. . . . I was the youngest guy on the show.
It was larger than Ringling Brothers, because it had three or four tribes
of Indians, just like the movies. [In] one scene four or five covered wagons [would] come out with a lot of people. Fifteen Indians would come
out on horses, you know, shoot them, burn up the wagons. . . . Those Indians would fall off the horses . . . but they had hay around all out
there. . . .

They had two bands, a big white band and the black band. The black
band was the jazz band, because they had a minstrel show over there.
. . . The black band was a small band but they still had three trombones
and trumpets, and all that. . . . The shows closed early, around ten
o'clock at night, and we'd give a dance from ten to one, something like
that. . . . Yeah, fifty cents to come in, or a quarter, the town would come
down. . . .

I'd get the guys to rehearse, [and] those old guys could play. . . . That's how I started writing, but it was all for me to learn harmony, because if I made any bad notes they could break away until I straightened up. . . . That's how I learned to voice, so much vocal and five-part harmony, because I had to play around [and] . . . to experiment with those horns. . . .

I stayed with the 101 maybe a year. . . . We played all over, Oklahoma, Kansas, Texas, all out West. . . . I wrote some numbers, like they had slide trombones, a whole family of trombone songs, . . . Parson Trombone, Sally Trombone. . . . The band stopped when you're marching and the trombones would play all that stuff. . . .

I was a fancy guy. I'd make a jazz break, one of those Johnny Dunn breaks,[3] and those guys framed up on me. . . . When we're marching . . . to the park where everybody cuts out, all the trombones were going to take out, they had it framed up with the leader, to see whether I was going to play the part, you know. . . . Finally I learned it, I waited for them to take down on it . . . and I made a jazz break. Man, it was a jazz break, and the public [was] all over the street. That's how I got them [the band] with me. They thought I knew something. . . .

We played Yankee Stadium, and they left, . . . went to Europe. I was afraid of boats and everything else, that's when I left. But I had my degree anyway. I graduated from Street University.

LAWRENCE DENTON. *Born 2/11/1893, Heartville, Missouri. Clarinet, arranger, bandleader. Active in Kansas City jazz in 1920s, toured widely. Co-founder of Kansas City's black musicians' union, Local 627 of the American Federation of Musicians.*

I had a brother and before I ever took up notes we played guitar and mandolin. I played guitar and he played mandolin, but he could play anything he'd hear, and then I would second behind him. . . . [We played] just ragtime and popular music, . . . there wasn't so many blues out then. . . . I was only eight years old. . . .

I didn't hear much music way back early unless a minstrel show come to town. . . . Minstrel shows come there and then we'd hear the band. And then we'd go to Ringling Brothers Circus, the first time I guess was about 1903. I heard music there, playing the show. . . .

They had a little town band—colored—and a white band. . . . That's where I started the clarinet at. We played there and when the carnival would come there about in August, rodeo I guess you'd call it, we played for it. . . . The band started there in 1905 but I was a little young then so I didn't start until 1908, [when] . . . I was about fifteen years old. . . . I started in the second band, just a town band, Professor Levi Payne's band. . . . The band was seventeen or eighteen pieces, all of them worked at the cement plant. . . . They didn't play for any dances, they just played for marches and in the street, and the different lodges[4] would have a little state convention here and they'd play for it. . . . They had parades quite a bit, the fourth of July, holidays like that. . . .

In 1916 I traveled with the circus, the Coleman Brothers circus. It had two rings and a stage. We played smaller towns. . . . They had everything that the big show had, only they played smaller towns. Our biggest town we played that summer was Superior, Wisconsin. They didn't pay much in them days, it was about twelve dollars a week. . . . We traveled in our own train cars. Our little show had twenty-five cars.

[When we played] the blacks was mixed in with the whites; it wasn't segregated in the circus. It might have been down South, but I didn't play the circuses there. . . . The audience wasn't segregated at the circuses, and of course we played all up North and West, you know. After that I played with the minstrel shows in the South where it was segregated. . . . We played one night white and one night colored. The show was the same for both audiences. . . . It was just a comedy and minstrel shows was comedy, had the black faces. All minstrel shows that I ever saw had blackface, especially the colored. Of course there used to be a [mostly] white minstrel too, Algie Fields, and they blacked up too, just a few of them, sitting on the stage. . . . I was with them six months. . . .

I first traveled with minstrel shows and circuses before I ever traveled in vaudeville. Of course, the sooner you could play classics the sooner you worked. . . . Minstrel shows, they played in theaters in towns. . . . We'd make a parade and then we'd circle in front of the theater and play a concert. . . .

We'd play an overture and some marches and a trombone smear and a couple, three rags. The concert would run from twenty to thirty minutes. We played all of them rags, Down Home Rags, Squirrel Rags, Temptation Rags. A lot of them rags [were] out in those days [1912-21]. . . . At the theater we played everything. We featured pictures there, . . . played all the classics. . . . [At] some of the pictures like *King of Kings*, they'd send the books [musical scores]. . . .

The highest level was the other kind of shows, like Earl Carroll Vanities. . . . His chorus girls was beautiful. . . . That was high class. That was a little more higher class than the burlesque.

DRUIE BESS. *Born 7/24/1906, Montgomery City, Missouri. Trombone. Played with minstrel shows, including Harvey Minstrels and Herbert's Minstrels, and jazz bands, including Jesse Stone's Blues Serenaders, Chauncey Downs's Rinkey Dinks, and Walter Page's Blue Devils. Among the most proficient trombonists of the era.*

[My father] was on the carnival just one year, from my remembering, . . . played that summer [1914]. It was about five, six months. [The carnival] would go right up here in Missouri, they didn't get no further. They was up here as you go into Kansas City, Sedalia, Missouri, around up in there, they was goin' toward Kansas City. They had acts. The carnival wasn't that big, but it had merry-go-rounds, and ferris wheels, and everything like that. . . . [The band] played just them marches. Just like "White Tops" and all them old standards. . . . See, I started off playing standard tunes. I remember "St. Louis Blues" and "Memphis Blues," we had those in stock. . . . But ragtime was the first. They had all these old ragtime numbers.

Eddie Barefield: [In 1923] we went out with the carnival, and as we were traveling around with this carnival we were making about ten dollars a week. So another carnival came through and offered me and the trumpet player, Leroy White,[5] fifteen dollars a week, and so we joined this carnival. That's when we took our trip down through Texas, Missouri, and Kansas and all that, and that's what brought me on the road. . . .

It was a black and white carnival. The minstrel show was black. And when you had a carnival you had concessions, you got a minstrel show, you got an athletic show, you got all these different shows. . . . It usually takes place in what you call a fairground, or some empty spot, and you have a circle of tents with concessions. . . . Like you have popcorn and you have things where you throw balls and they have African Dodger, a guy's got his head stuck through a hole and you throw. If you hit him you can get a prize, and then they have an athletic show where they meet all comers. . . .

On the athletic show they'd bring out wrasslers or the boxers and [they'd call], "Ladies and Gentlemen! Whoever can take on one of these guys can get ten dollars a round!" Then they'd find some guy in the audience who accepted, and everybody'd go in and watch it. . . .

Sometimes there's a "Hey, Rube" when somebody gets in a fight or something . . . and all the people in the carnival would come to the rescue. . . . Like when you say, "Hey, Rube," that means that one of the rubes in town, like a farmer, has started trouble, and everybody comes. . . . The actual performers in the show weren't so tough, because they were all show-business people. . . . But the roustabouts and the people working on the show were hiding from the law and escaped convicts, at that time. . . . In those days you had a lot of really bad people on the carnival. . . .

Then they [would] have the minstrel show, and when they put on the show they always have a ballyhoo. Before the show the band would come out in front, and the girls would come out, and you'd play a couple of numbers, and the hawker would spiel, and everybody would go in, pay the prices, and see that little show. . . .

We didn't have uniforms then, because you're setting in front of the stage and playing. We wore mostly just what we was wearing. . . . In those days everybody tried to dress up when they did something they thought was important. . . . After you got off the carnival (we'd usually close around 11:30 at night) we had a chance to go around, but most of the towns we played didn't have nothing happening at that time. We played all those little one-horse towns. . . . We slept on the train. We had [our own] cars on the train.

I had promised my mother that I would come back and go back to school if she would let me go with this carnival. So when September came, and Labor Day, [and] it was time to come back to school, this is when I went to Kansas City. We slipped off the carnival and went to Kansas City. . . . I sold my horn to get to Kansas City, so I was there without an instrument, so I couldn't work anyplace. I was just wandering around; but I couldn't let my mother know where I was because she would make me come home.

So I met these different people . . . and I learned this from the bums that I was staying with out in the park . . . there was a pool hall on Eighteenth and Vine[6] in the basement . . . and they let you come in and sleep on the pool table. . . . One day I was there and a band was rehearsing. . . . They were on their way to California, so we got acquainted and they asked me if I wanted to go to California. I told them I didn't have a horn. They said, "We'll get you a horn." But my mother sent a detective around and took me back to Des Moines.

Jesse Stone: My father was in Brown's Tennessee Minstrel, which was an uncle of mine's show. The show was a majority of family members, aunts, uncles, cousins, even a couple of grandmothers—I had two singing grandmothers. Everybody was on the show except my grandfather on my father's side. . . .

I was on the show when I was four [1905]. We had a dog act. They were all cocker spaniels. Of course they had been trained to do the routine without me, but it looked as though I was a trainer with short pants. . . . I had a whip like the guys do in circuses and they would get up on these little boxes and they would roll over and do flips and all that kind of stuff, but they knew the routine. . . .

I did comedy. The last thing was all the boys, all the males on the show were supposed to be working the farm or something like that, we'd all be layin' down asleep. The man comes in and finds us asleep, and one at a time he beats us over the behind, and it would just be a slapstick,[7] a loud sound. Each one has a different line, like a gag he says as he runs off the stage. That was the closing scene and everybody came in after that. . . .

My father was the first one to do a chorus line in a minstrel. . . . They had photographs and on the bills these girls . . . wore hats with big plumed feathers, . . . and of course their skirts weren't too short. They were around their knees, more like a tutu that ballet people wear, that flared all out, and I can remember some of the old pictures . . . all of them would pose and had their fingers under their chins and all that sort of stuff. . . .

My father played drums in the street band, a marching band, and he played in the pit when they would do the overture, before the curtain. They had a thing called "Drummer Boy" back there in those days and they had another thing called "Sliding Sam," it was a trombone solo. . . . There were two violins, trumpet, trombone, piano, bass horn, drums. That was it. . . . One night they would feature my uncle [on trombone] in the pit, the next night they would feature my father on drums. . . . They could read music at that time, but they didn't know the definition of an arrangement. They knew it was handwritten music and even when I came up in school they called it "homemade music." . . .

They'd have a parade in town and they would get to like a street corner and then my uncle would make an announcement about the show and what to expect and the prices and the time the doors would open and all that sort of stuff, and then we would parade back to the theater or the hotel or wherever we were staying. In the summertime we'd always wear a cap. Places that didn't have theaters, they'd have what they'd call opera houses back there in those days, and we'd play some towns in Wisconsin and northern Illinois, North and South Dakota. . . .

[We got around] by every means. There were times when we would hire farmers with hayracks and we'd load up on wagons that they used to haul corn and wheat. If there was no train to the next town, we would hire them and they would take us to the town. . . .

We'd stay in hotels and sometimes we'd stay in private homes, and it seemed as though the people were honored to have us stay in their homes, because a lot of times people would coax us . . . to stay. So we divided up and stayed in various homes, three or four in each home. . . .

We didn't run into any black people in Wisconsin, Minnesota, North and South Dakota. In fact the people didn't know what we were when we came up there and some of them thought we were Indians. They would even ask us what tribe we were from. . . . One woman in Canada when I was a little boy, she tried to buy me from my mother because she knew about slavery and she thought that it was still possible to buy me. She offered my mother five thousand dollars cash money for me at that time. . . . I stayed at her house. We were there for the Canadian fair or something. I lived with her that whole week. The first time I ever was in a bathtub was in her house. She had a bathtub. Most of the white people I knew didn't have bathtubs. They didn't have running water. . . .

There was no prejudice at that time in that part of the country. . . . My social life was mixed with white, my first girlfriend in school was a white girl. And my sister, . . . her boyfriend was a white boy, a little Jewish boy. . . . The white boys and girls came to our parties and we went to their parties. . . .

[We called what we played in the minstrel show] ragtime. . . . We played very simple things, simple chord changes. . . . They didn't have the blues flavor. The blues flavor really comes from down . . . in the South. This was Kansas, and our contribution to music from Kansas didn't start until later when jazz became popular. We really came up with a lot of jazz musicians out of there.

For these and many other musicians of the era minstrel shows were both an opportunity and an inspiration, a school and a profession. The aspects of minstrels that now often seem racist were then more often seen as legitimate forms of showmanship, and a good, versatile showman was always in demand.

Traveling Shows — Vaudeville and the TOBA

The goal of most traveling musicians in the period from 1900 to 1925 was to attain the exalted level of vaudeville. This was the most elaborate and, typically, best-paying entertainment of the era.

The white vaudeville circuit played in elegant theaters before well-dressed patrons and featured the best-known performers of the day. A large, white band was often employed for main performances and a smaller, black band played "hot" for dancing and general excitement. Vaudeville and movie houses (often the same thing in the twenties) would employ anything from a pianist or organist to a full twenty-piece band, and a featured "get-off" soloist would usually have an opportunity to play a hot jazz number or two. As jazz bands began to develop in the twenties they often played in a show environment, providing backup for dancers, comedians, and acrobats as well as playing their own music.

The Theatre Owners Booking Association was the most important black vaudeville circuit. Commonly referred to as the TOBA (or "Tough on Black Asses/Artists"), it featured large shows similar to those in white vaudeville, but played for black audiences in smaller theaters. The TOBA was the major arena for blues performers such as Ma Rainey, Mamie Smith, and Bessie Smith, and did much to popularize stylized blues songs with black audiences nationally. It was still vaudeville, however, and a wide variety of other artists like Louis Armstrong, Buck and Bubbles, Bill "Bojangles" Robinson, and Eddie "Rochester" Anderson would also be found in TOBA houses. This was the highest form of black theater in the first part of the twentieth century and became the training ground for many musicians who filled dance hall and nightclub orchestras in later years.

The TOBA was particularly important to the development of Kansas City as a jazz center, and provided an early reason for musicians to be "goin' to Kansas City." K.C. was the westernmost stop on the circuit, and tours frequently disbanded there, stranding musicians who often stayed. One of them was Bill "Count" Basie.

Lawrence Denton: TOBA was a circuit of colored shows, of musical shows and comedies. Most of them was comedy shows . . . The headquarters of the circuit was, I believe, in Washington [D.C.]. . . . Oh, they had them all over, they had them in Indianapolis, they had one in Pittsburgh, they had [one] in Philadelphia, they had two houses in New York . . . and all over the South. You know, Jackson, Mississippi; Atlanta, Georgia. . . . It was a lower income [circuit].

CLARENCE LOVE. *Born 1/26/1908, Muskogee, Oklahoma. Violin, piano, saxophone, bandleader. Led successful bands in Kansas City, Oklahoma, and Texas for many years. Still performs occasionally.*

They called them road shows. There was Drake and Walker, the Whitman Sisters, those were great shows that came through [Kansas City]. Basie came in there with Gonzelle White and they were just stranded, you know. We called it [the] chili route. . . . But they played a circuit.

SAM PRICE. *Born 10/6/1908, Honey Grove, Texas. Piano and vocal. Played with many bands, including Alphonso Trent, then performed widely as a single and as a bandleader. Many recordings. Currently active in New York and Europe.*

In 1925 I was dancing with Alphonso Trent's[8] band and I was learning to play a few little tunes. And [with] guys like Buddy Tate and Budd Johnson[9] that were around Dallas, we wanted to organize a little band. I had my mother fix potato salad and all that and invited the guys up and tried to organize a band. They refused to do so, and I chased them out of the house . . . and I just became sort of a drifter. In 1927 I went on the road with the TOBA.

There was a guy named Goldberg, was our manager. I think he

wanted me to dance. I told him I'd dance with him if they would allow me to sit behind and listen to the band play. . . . In the white places a [black] musician couldn't just roam all over the place or go in the bar or go outside or go in the dining room, because they had a specific place that was designated for you to go. . . . You went directly to that point and stayed there, and the point that I went to was behind the piano.

So I went on the show and I played . . . the piano. But as we went along we . . . added some musicians. They was always picking up musicians, guys quitting shows, guys in town wanting to get with a show. Guy may live in Atlanta and he wouldn't have the train fare home, so if he was in Houston he'd know that if he played four dates with a show he'd get home. He'd be in Mobile, Birmingham, Shreveport, and then Atlanta. . . . When he'd get home he'd quit. . . .

I didn't make no money on the TOBA. You went into a town and the owner of the show would make a deal with some woman that was to cook you meals and you got three meals a day. You had to come a certain time to eat and he would make some arrangements to pay your room rent [in] boarding houses.

During those days when Ma Rainey and Ida Cox and those people went out, if they had a band, the band was secondary. It was the singer who was the principal.

TORRENCE "T." HOLDER. *Born c. 1898, Muskogee, Oklahoma. Died 1979, Muskogee. Trumpet. Performed with several bands, notably Alphonso Trent. Reputed to play the "sweetest horn in Texas." Organized and led the Twelve Clouds of Joy until 1928 when the band deposed him for mismanagement. Continued to lead and perform actively through the 1970s.*

I started out with Ida Cox, the blues singer. I was in Muskogee, and Ida Cox was there, and Fletcher Henderson had to get a band for her, so they was around in town trying to find musicians.[10] Somebody told him I could play so he went down there and got me. I didn't know one note from another, I didn't know B-flat from C, but nevertheless I went down there and I started playing with Fletcher Henderson. 'Course, Fletcher could play, man, he was a musician. I didn't know nothing but playing loud and wrong. . . .

They had a theater down there [in Muskogee], the Dreamland. . . . That was TOBA, they called it "Tough on Black Asses." . . . I played one or two nights. . . . I didn't do nothing but mess up his show anyway.

CLAUDE "FIDDLER" WILLIAMS. *Born 2/22/1908, Muskogee, Oklahoma. Violin and guitar. Performed with many bands, including Alphonso*

Trent, T. Holder and Andy Kirk's Twelve Clouds of Joy, George E. Lee, Count Basie, and Jay McShann.

I left [home] with this show and never did make payday. So I had to be pretty easy going for him [the show director and star] to tell me a funny story [about the money] every week. . . .

He would have at least four girls and one or two comedians, and he was a comedian himself. . . . The girls would just dance, like come out and do routine dances and then maybe one of them would do some tap dancing and then one would probably sing a song. . . . They had one comedian was almost as light as you, and he'd darken his face and leave his lips white. . . . Then if he's black he'd still whiten his lips and put a ring around his eyes with makeup.

ERNIE WILLIAMS. *Born 6/8/1904, Winston, North Carolina. Died 1/27/86, Kansas City, Missouri. Drums and vocals. Performed widely, including three years with a show in Shanghai, China; directed and sang with the Blue Devils and Harlan Leonard's Rockets. Featured in the 1980 film "The Last of the Blue Devils."*

Toby, TOBA, we [called it] "Tough on Black Asses." I played every Toby[11] house in the United States. . . . You go on Toby clean down to Florida, clean to Louisiana and Texas.

[In the TOBA] you had rough times and you had good times. When you're doing one nighters [it's] bad, . . . hard [on the] soul, too. . . . But when you stay weeks you have a good time.

We had cars [and an] instrument truck. Some of the guys would ride in five Fleetwood Cadillacs. I'd tie the instruments on the back of the truck and you get from job to job . . . [and] that's how it [was] done. . . .

[I was] playing the drums, . . . dancing, everything. . . . You see the Toby show would go like [to] Dallas, maybe the Dallas [theater] had a house band, to play the pictures. If you say your show's going on Toby time, when they get the band and all, you know, [you play] the whole show. . . . Some houses would have their own house band and . . . they play their own stuff. When the pictures [movies] come on this house band would sit down and play [accompaniment for] the pictures, and the show band [TOBA band] would play the show [afterward]. . . .

[In a typical evening] we'd have whatever the action was. . . . It's like a vaudeville show. . . . You got the skits, have to do so much in so many acts, girls dance, [then] you'd have jugglers . . . and then they'd have a scene from a comedy, have a whole lot of comedy. . . . They used to have a boxcar scene where guys would ride a freight train, got the electricity fixed up so . . . it would fire up and do all this stuff. . . . Then after the other acts, [you] go on with the show, change the clothes [with] the girls, like a burlesque show.

BOOKER WASHINGTON. *Born 4/9/1909, St. Charles, Missouri. Trumpet. Featured with the Bennie Moten Orchestra and Thamon Hayes's Kansas City Rockets. Remained active in Kansas City through 1983 with Art Smith's Kansas City Jazz Band.*

The TOBA would be performed in the evenings. There would be different acts or different people in every week. Now maybe Bessie Smith, they'd come in with a group of people, or they may be a star of a group, but you got to hear a variety of people that you never thought you would hear. . . . You had comedians, you had star blues singers, you had dance acts, just name it. . . . It was the only thing like that in Kansas City.

Brass Bands

Village brass bands (also called marching, military, and silver cornet bands) provided another important training ground for jazz musicians. In a primarily rural America, brass band concerts, Sunday concerts on the village green, and parades were commonplace. Most towns of moderate size had at least one brass band, and where there was a substantial black population there was usually a black band. These were disciplined, drilled, performing units that took pride in their marching precision as well as in their musicianship. Many performers, such as Booker Washington from rural eastern Missouri and Orville Minor from Kansas City, Kansas, speak eloquently of the important role that this regimented music had in their own development as professional musicians.

Brass bands continued to play a significant part in many musicians' lives even after the formative period of 1900-25. Early band sponsors (usually local civic organizations, organized for pleasure and charity and financed by local lodges) were supplanted by other associations (ranging from the WPA in the 1930s to city arts councils and the national musician's union from the 1940s to the present) and brass band-like music continues to be widely performed.

Booker Washington: My father . . . was a leader of . . . a marching band . . . at home. He used a cornet, too. It was my duty every Saturday to go in his parade to polish his horns. I'd polish the horn, then I'd start fooling around with a horn, and I started learning how to do it. I was blowing, then he started me out on a horn. . . .

[It was] a black band. . . . They made all the parades from home, clean to Forest Hill, all around St. Charles County. Which is a pretty big county. . . . 'Round my country they have picnics every summer. This place, everyone this week, this place next week, and so forth. His band always plays for them, white or black. They just made enough to keep them in uniforms. . . .

It was more or less a free-lance deal, a bunch of fellas got together. They decided when to rehearse, decided everyone [would] make music and they'd put in an association, what they call the Relief Association, that would qualify [for support] people that weren't able to work or poorer than we were, to furnish them coal in the wintertime . . . [and] food. . . .

We played what they call, at that time, pop music. But old fashioned. That was in 3/4 [meter], dance, just mixful dance music, "Turkey in the Straw," all that kind of stuff. People had a good time. The brass band was the main thing in my home town. . . .

[When I moved to Kansas City to go to college] I went to the band-master [at Western University, Kansas City, Kansas], Guiou Taylor, and asked him could I have a horn. He said, "Can you play a horn?" I said, "I can." . . . So he went to the band room and gave me a trumpet. . . .

[With different teachers] one would take me for intonation, one would . . . write out the scales, . . . one would do this and one would do the other, and put it all together, I was a musician. . . . At first I blew "Reveille" and "Taps." . . . That's all I could play. . . . After a year's time I joined the band . . . as third trumpet player. Within a year I was playing solo trumpet . . . and I played in the band until I graduated. . . .

When I come out of school I just did this [playing in a brass band] on the side. . . . We had about twenty pieces. It was popular, as far as we were concerned, 'cause people looked for you every weekend, to be playing somewhere. . . . We played all over Kansas City. . . .

See, it really started [in Kansas City] under Daniel Blackburn, he's the bandleader, bandmaster. Oh, he was an oldtimer, but this band was playing when I was in school. . . . [Now, in the 1970s] it's just seasonal work. . . . The municipal band, brass band here . . . [which followed] after the WPA band,[12] . . . they're more modern and harder [than my father's brass band]. You take Sousa marches and all those type marches, . . . just strictly marches, [and] sometimes we'd play a little waltz, like out at the rest homes, or maybe some other kind of thing, just [to] break the monotony. . . . All they wanted was musicians that could do it. As long as you were unionized, you could play.

Lawrence Denton: I was the first clarinet player for [the Daniel Blackburn] band for a year. We played concerts. That was before the war [World War I]. I played ten concerts there in the park. They had seats out there, benches and everything. Sometimes we played for three or four thousand, five thousand people would come out there to hear the band. A lot of white [people] would come [too]. . . . We played a mixture:

ragtime and marches, and classics, waltzes. Yeah, Daniel Blackburn. He had the concerts from 1917 to 1945. . . .

[The Second Regiment Band] was the band that I joined on the Missouri side [of Kansas City]. That was the second year I was up here [1915]. That was William Melford's [band]. The lodges in them days, they had a drill team, they used to drill like soldiers, the band. Yeah, the Knights of Pythias. They would go to conventions, the drill team would be in a contest for a prize. . . . A lot of them [had] . . . drillmasters . . . [that] had been in the Ninth and Tenth Cavalry in the Spanish-American War. There was a drillmaster in our band that was an old army man. . . . They was very experienced in drilling. That's where they got the name, Second Regiment. . . .

When a [lodge] member died we'd have what they called an annual sermon. Once a year they'd have a sermon at the church, and the band would play a street [parade]. . . . Then they'd play for the funeral. Oh, we used to be on the street pretty near every Sunday . . . all through June, July, and August. . . . We played marches, funeral marches, dirges. . . .

They had a lot of bands way back there. We had a band in Kansas, and Blackburn and Melford over here, and another, Chisholm I think was his name. . . . Had a couple in Kansas City, Kansas, and had a ladies band over here, [Josie William's] band. . . .

I played with an orchestra [the Dave Lewis Jazz Boys] after 1917. Then in 1918 [I] was drafted from there into the army. That was in July 1918. In September 1918 we went to France. . . . We formed a band which had band members from all over, Louisiana, Mississippi, Los Angeles. . . . We had thirty-two pieces. . . . It was a marching band and we played overture selections, we played [pieces like] "Morning, Noon, and Night" [and] "Poet and Peasant."

I made assistant bandleader and the bandleader was a white fella, lieutenant. . . . We only saw him about once a month. He left everything to us. . . . In April we went to Paris and entertained for the officers. Now Jim Europe's band[13] was there all winter. When they came back to the states in March 1919 we went there [to Paris] and took their place. Stayed there till August. . . . They [the French] were great. There wasn't no difference in the color [of your skin] with the French.

ORVILLE "PIGGY" MINOR. *Born 4/23/1912, Kansas City, Missouri. Trumpet. Active in many Kansas City bands, including Jay McShann, Oliver Todd, and Dee Stewart. Currently active in K.C.*

I just went along with the custom [playing in a marching band]. I was raised on that kind of music, first learning to play the horn. That fella that was teaching me [Mr. Hatcher] had a marching band. . . . It was a lodge band, a march band. . . . My basic knowledge was playing marches and the like. . . . I was thinking about learning whatever they were playing, you know, just [to] go along with the deal. . . . My brother had been doing it, and his friends did the same thing, so I just decided I'd go and jump in there with 'em rather than play basketball and chase girls.

Going to School—Formal Music Training

The pursuit of formal intellectual training and artistic accomplishment was a major theme in post-Reconstruction black American life. The writings and examples of figures such as George Washington Carver, Booker T. Washington, and W. E. B. Dubois provided inspiration in this pursuit, and the "Harlem Renaissance" of 1900-30 became a symbol of intellectual and artistic success. Among the important effects of this movement on blacks nationally was the proliferation of music professors, who, in high schools, local parlors, or informal "academies," brought rigorous musicianship and considerable sophistication to beginning musicians. The aim of their teaching was usually to uplift fellow blacks and impart the skills of European high culture. The practice often included attempts to blend aspects of the black heritage with European art music, thus further ennobling and lending respectability to the "race." Among the many "professors" who played important formative roles in the careers of prominent jazz musicians were Major N. Clark Smith, Charles Watts, and William L. Dawson in Kansas City, and Zelia M. Breaux in Oklahoma City. They taught and inspired generations of musicians and in so doing helped to create the jazz style of Kansas City.

PARRIS "DUDE" LANKFORD. *Born c. 1894, Kansas City, Missouri. Drums. Played in local parade and school bands until joining Bennie Moten's first band, B. B. and D., in 1917. Performed with Moten until 1922 when he went on the road with various vaudeville, circus, and carnival troupes.*

Charlie Watts. . . . I played with him in the theater at Nineteenth and Highland and in dances with him and his brother, Frank Watts, [who] played trumpet. Charlie [also] taught piano and violin, right up there at Twelfth and Woodland.

Charlie Watts was a learned piano player; he had been learned and he could teach it. He was a musician. . . . I was a drum carrier for awhile, but then I got so I could read. Charlie Watts taught me. . . . They had a valve trombone, and that's what I started on with Charlie Watts, but I changed from there and started playing piccolo in the Pickaninny . . . Band.[14]

Clarence Love: I went to Charles T. Watts Conservatory of Music to be
a fiddler. . . . It was in a private home. . . . Most every kid from my age
on down that played took private lessons. My mother paid a dollar a
lesson. . . . I studied violin and I had to learn the piano. . . . He had the
job as supervisor of music of the public schools (we weren't integrated
back then), all the black schools. . . . At the last of the year he'd combine
all the schools together and we'd have a big concert, [with] marches. No
popular tunes at all. Concert music. . . .

I played with Charles T. Watts until I went to high school, and each
high school had its own music teacher. Of course we [black students]
didn't have but one high school, Lincoln High. William L. Dawson
came there. . . . I played mellophone in the band. He stayed the four
years that I was there, . . . from '22 to '26. One of the toughest music
teachers in the country. A lot of boys came out under him. . . .

When I went to school we had to take ROTC . . . [and] William L.
Dawson was just as bad as a sarge [in the ROTC]. He'd stand over you
and you'd be reading [music]. If you didn't do it, he'd hit you on the
hand. In fact . . . about two or three times he got in a fight with the
students about music. I know one time he and a boy like to fell down
the whole flight of stairs. (The music room was upstairs.) . . . He was a
fiery son-of-a-gun but he knew music. He was the only man I ever
heard play a duet on the trombone.

HERMAN WALDER. *Born 4/2/1905, Dallas, Texas. Alto saxophone. Prominent performer and arranger in Kansas City with many bands, including
George E. Lee, LaForest Dent, Thamon Hayes, and Harlan Leonard. Widely
regarded as an important early influence on Charlie Parker.*

[At Lincoln High School in Kansas City, Missouri,] I got into a band
with some of the greatest musicians I've ever known. . . . I was under
Major [N. Clark] Smith. . . . Oh, that cat was a masterpiece. Man, I remember, he come by me and I made the wrong note. Man, he took that
baton and hit me right on the top of the head . . . till I got it right. . . .
He was a masterpiece, but after he left, we had a helluva band.

WILLIAM SAUNDERS. *Born 1909, Arkansas. Saxophones and flute. Played
extensively around Kansas City, notably with Bennie Moten and Bus
Moten, and as one of the Four Tons of Rhythm.*

One day Major Smith told the class that music was melody, harmony,
and rhythm. Being a kid, I paid no attention. The next week the first
thing he said [was], "Saunders, stand up here and tell me what music
is. . . . You don't know, do you?" He had a ruler and he said, "Put your
head on the table. Music is melody." BOOM! "Harmony." BOOM!

"Rhythm." BOOM! "Now go home and tell you Mammy I hit you." But I know what music is.[15]

Orville Minor: I first got to play jazz in junior high school. It was a little different thing [than what I had been doing before]. . . . kind of like stepping up a little faster. You begin to find out where the rhythm was. . . . That's when I played my first solo on trumpet, trying to improvise. I didn't know the exact notes I wanted to make, but I made 'em and I got cheers, you know. From then on it was straight ahead.

BERNARD "STEP-BUDDY" ANDERSON. *Born 10/14/1919, Oklahoma City, Oklahoma. Trumpet and piano. Performed with Leslie Sheffield, Jay McShann, Benny Carter, Billy Eckstine, and Roy Eldridge and led own group. Early be-bop trumpeter and musical companion of Charlie Parker. Currently active in Kansas City as pianist and bandleader. Author of "Sufferin' Cats," an unpublished history of modern jazz.*
There was a wonderful music teacher [in Oklahoma City] by the name of Miss Zelia M. Breaux. She was really something else; she was a giant, man. . . . She played trumpet in her younger days . . . and the violin in the orchestra, [and] piano . . . accompaniments. Went down a different operetta every year, . . . school things. . . . She, more than anyone I think, turned the whole town on, musically, in the black community.

Instructors like Watts, Dawson, Smith, and Breaux could be found in established black communities throughout the country. Their skill and dedication played a major part in nurturing a generation of Midwestern musicians that belied the common stereotype of early jazzmen as naive, inspired artists. Many of the innovators of Kansas City jazz thus possessed significant fundamental skills that underlay their artistry.

NOTES

1. Another category of performer well known in this rural context was the "musicianer," who was typically not a singer or entertainer but was noted for his instrumental abilities.
2. A melismatic syllable in music is one which is sung or played elaborately, with many notes.
3. Johnny Dunn was a popular black trumpeter of the day. He was well educated in music (at Fisk University), and had been a featured attraction with Mamie Smith's Jazz Hounds, one of the more popular bands of the early and mid-twenties. Dunn was noted for his bravura solos that were unusual for the time.
4. Lodges, clubs, and benevolent societies were an important part of black

American social life through the 1960s. They provided a community and lent formalism and respectability to an often bleakly racist environment.

5. Trumpeter Leroy "Snake" White was a very active performer in the Midwest before World War II. Following the carnival job, he and Barefield and saxophonist Lester Young worked at the Nest Club in Minneapolis (c. 1930). Later White joined Walter Page's Blue Devils in Oklahoma City, where he remained until their breakup, which is described in chapter 5.

6. Eighteenth and Vine was the crossroads at the heart of Kansas City's black downtown in the thirties. Many of the city's best-known jazz clubs were at this intersection.

7. The term "slapstick," used to describe a genre of broad comedy, derives from a sound-effect device of the same name used in carnival and vaudeville shows and described here by Jesse Stone.

8. For many years the Alphonso Trent Orchestra enjoyed the best-paying job of any black jazz orchestra in the Midwest at Dallas's swank Adolphus Hotel.

9. Both Tate and Johnson later became prominent as jazz saxophonists. Buddy Tate performed for many years with Count Basie and is still very active. Budd Johnson has had very broad experience, playing with such orchestras as Earl Hines, Boyd Raeburn, Billy Eckstine, Woody Herman, and Dizzy Gillespie. Also noted as an arranger, Johnson is among the great swing-era musicians who successfully made the transition to be-bop and modern jazz.

10. Fletcher Henderson was a noted pianist, arranger, and bandleader. His orchestra was among the finest of the twenties and thirties and featured at various times such instrumental stars as Louis Armstrong and Coleman Hawkins. After disbanding his orchestra Henderson was very active as an arranger, notably for Benny Goodman. Before becoming a bandleader, however, Henderson worked with several organizations, including as the musical director for the Black Swan Troubadours, a revue sponsored by the Black Swan record company. Henderson toured with this ensemble from November 1921 to July 1922, and was in Arkansas, Oklahoma, and Texas in February and March 1922. This could have been the tour that T. Holder recalls. During this period, however, Ida Cox was regularly performing on the TOBA circuit with White and Clark's Minstrels, while the Troubadours were not on the circuit, despite frequent performances in TOBA theaters. T.'s memory in this instance could therefore be confused, or he could be recounting an event that has not previously surfaced in jazz research.

11. "Toby" was a common slang term for the TOBA circuit.

12. One of the many projects of the Works Progress Administration (WPA) in the 1930s was to provide work for musicians. WPA bands were sponsored throughout the country, including Kansas City.

13. James Reese Europe led a huge (over 100-piece) black military band that pioneered the use of ragtime in orchestras. Europe achieved his greatest prominence playing in France and England during and immediately after World War I, and provided many Europeans with their introduction to jazz. Europe was murdered soon after his triumphal return to New York in 1919, and so was kept from fulfilling his musical promise and gaining a more prominent place in jazz history.

14. Charles Watts's Pickaninny Band was an orchestra made up of some of

Kansas City's black youth. It played widely around the city, was an important training ground for musicians like Dude Lankford and Lawrence Denton, and helped establish music as an attractive career for local black young people. Soon after Dude quit the Pickaninny Band, they left K.C. for a successful tour of Australia.

15. Litwak and Pearson, *Goin' to Kansas City*, 21; used with permission.

2

Sources of the Early
Kansas City Jazz Style:
Ragtime and New Orleans Jazz

Jazz is an American music that has both African and European roots. According to legend, jazz was born in New Orleans at the turn of the century, moved up the Mississippi to St. Louis and Chicago, and then spread throughout the land. Like most legends, this one contains a core of truth. By the 1890s the mingling of New Orleans's numerous traditions, particularly the black, Creole (mixed-blood French, Spanish-American, and Negro), French, and Spanish, resulted in a unique, hybrid music. It coexisted with and resembled several other genres of music, including brass band, ragtime, popular, and "novelty" music, but eventually became greater and more fruitful than its contemporary or antecedent musics.

New Orleans jazz was the starting point for jazz. The first great jazz composer, pianist Jelly Roll Morton, and the first great recorded jazz soloists, trumpeters Louis Armstrong and Freddie Keppard, cornetist Joe "King" Oliver, and multi-reed man Sidney Bechet, came from New Orleans. Most of the influential early jazz recordings before 1926, including the first jazz recordings (made in 1917 by the Original Dixieland Jass Band, a white ensemble), "Livery Stable Blues" and "Dixieland Jass Band One-Step," featured New Orleans musicians and the supple beat and rich polyphonic textures of their style.[1]

Controversy certainly exists over New Orleans's claim to be the birthplace of jazz. Many musicians, including Wilbur DeParis (Indiana-born trombonist and bandleader), Eubie Blake (Baltimore ragtime pianist and composer), W. C. Handy (Memphis pianist and composer), Walter Gould (Philadelphia ragtime pianist), and Lawrence Denton (Missouri clarinetist), assert that they heard or played jazz years before hearing anything of New Orleans music. Even so, the preponderance of evidence is so strong, the music so distinctive, and the influence so dramatic, that New Orleans can be reliably recognized as the birthplace of jazz.

Jazz's development can be seen as part of the larger continuum of American popular music, especially dance music. In the twenties, jazz became the hottest new thing in dance music, much as ragtime had at the turn of the century, and as would rhythm and blues in the forties, rock in the fifties, and disco in the seventies.

But two characteristics distinguish jazz from other dance music. The first is improvisation, the changing of a musical phrase according to the player's inspiration. Like all artists, jazz musicians strive for an individual style, and the improvised or paraphrased solo is a jazz musician's main opportunity to display his individuality. In early jazz, musicians often improvised melodies collectively (thus creating a kind of polyphony). There was little soloing as such, although some New Orleans players, particularly cornetist Buddy Bolden, achieved local fame for their ability to improvise a solo. Later the idea of the chorus-long or multi-chorus solo took hold. Louis Armstrong's instrumental brilliance, demonstrated through extended solos, was a major influence in this development.

Even in the early twenties, however, some jazz bands had featured soloists, and show orchestras and carnival/minstrel bands often included one or two "get-off" men. Unimprovised, completely structured jazz does exist, but the ability of the best jazz musicians to create music of great cohesion and beauty during a performance has been a hallmark of the music and its major source of inspiration and change.

The second distinguishing characteristic of jazz is a rhythmic drive that was initially called "hot" and later "swing." In playing hot, a musician consciously departs from strict meter to create a relaxed sense of phrasing that also emphasizes the underlying rhythms. ("Rough" tone and use of moderate vibrato also contributed to a hot sound.) Not all jazz is hot, however. Many early bands played unadorned stock arrangements of popular songs.[2] Still, the proclivity to play hot distinguished the jazz musician from other instrumentalists.

Kansas City jazz was characterized by the fundamental elements of jazz described above, but it was also noted for its own distinctive style. Many of the important sources of that style described in chapter 1 — rural music-making, the blues, traveling shows, brass bands, and formal musical training— formed much of the musical and cultural context for K.C.'s musicians. But ragtime and New Orleans-style jazz were also directly influential. Formal ragtime began in Missouri near Kansas City. Many early K.C. musicians began their careers as ragtime players, and ragtime songs were central to every musician's repertoire. New Orleans jazz revolutionized most musicians' concepts of music-making, and the songs of that city and its major composers, particularly Jelly Roll Morton, were similarly indispensable

elements of the standard repertoire. Together, ragtime and New Orleans
jazz were among the key building blocks of Kansas City jazz, and remained
important parts of that style.

Ragtime

Ragtime combines the rhythmic complexity of African music with the
harmonies and forms of European music. Around 1900, several American
composers from Missouri and elsewhere began to write formal piano rags.
Later, small ragtime ensembles played for dances, picnics, and other festive
occasions. Ragtime soon became a national craze, providing ideas and
rhythms for much of early jazz.

Folk Rags

"Ragging the beat" is a very old practice in American folk music. It consists
of enlivening the rhythms of a song, usually through syncopation — over-
laying differing rhythmic patterns and varying rhythmic stress. By this
technique almost any tune can be crudely syncopated. Rural Afro-Amer-
icans, often slaves, seeking to spice up rhythmically trite European-derived
songs, probably were the first to use this playing style. Folk ragtime became
a fixture of country dances for both whites and blacks.

Scott Joplin used this rhythmic tradition to create a more formal, "clas-
sical," ragtime. He adapted ragtime to the complex harmonies of European
art music, making the syncopated rhythms more regular (and usually slower)
and combining them with original melodies, themes, and phrases from
black folk tunes. In doing so he was among the first, and certainly among
the most successful, of many black composers who sought to "elevate" their
racial heritage by formalizing and orchestrating what was originally folk
music. Joplin's success can be heard in the remarkable body of music he
created between 1898 and 1920. Such notable composers as Stravinsky,
Ives, Debussy, and Milhaud borrowed from Joplin's ragtime airs and from
those of other ragtime songwriters. But the greatest testament to ragtime
lies in the unaltered work of Joplin and the other great ragtime composers,
including James Scott and Arthur Marshall.

Jazz Rags

Following Joplin's creation of a formal ragtime style in the brothels and
honky-tonks of Sedalia and St. Louis, Missouri, skilled pianists in other
parts of the country embraced ragtime. Jelly Roll Morton, the first great
jazz composer, included rags in his vast repertoire, and many of the earliest

jazz bands made use of rag forms in building their style. Many groups played whole ragtime compositions, although often speeded up to display their virtuosity. One example of these popular ragtime songs, Euday Boman's "Twelfth Street Rag," was recorded dozens of times in the twenties and thirties.

In Kansas City, brass bands and dance orchestras used rags in their performances. Charles T. Watts, a prominent local music teacher, reflected a national trend by instructing his students in ragtime technique. One of them, Bennie Moten, became noted initially as a ragtime pianist and later as the leader of Kansas City's first and possibly greatest jazz band. James Scott, a piano prodigy and ragtime composer whose songs included "Climax Rag," "The Fascinator," and "Quality Rag," was best known in Kansas City as a piano virtuoso and band leader in K.C.'s major black theaters. Charles L. Johnson, composer of tunes such as "Dill Pickles," and "Doc Brown's Cakewalk," was also prominent locally.

Much of early jazz styling came from the overlay of bluesy soloists on a theater orchestra, which brought out a "jazz" feeling by syncopating, or ragging, the melody of popular songs. In this way the rhythmic devices of Scott Joplin and his peers were adapted to the repertoire of orchestras of the twenties and thirties, particularly in Kansas City where ragtime was part of every musician's basic vocabulary.

Druie Bess: Yeah, ragtime was the first [jazz] music there was. They had all these old ragtime numbers. I remember the first time I ever heard ragtime, it [was] that old Scott Joplin. Yeah, that was the first.

Lawrence Denton: We had a jazz clarinet player with us [in the minstrel show]. . . . Jazz was kinda like jazz is now, it was just more of a ragtime. They ragtimed the pieces, see, . . . they just jazzed up the popular music. . . .

I played with Jim Scott . . . back in the twenties. . . . He was a great piano player, great classics. [I played with him] at the Lincoln Theater, Eighteenth and Lydia [in Kansas City]. At the theater we played everything. We featured pictures there . . . [and] played pretty near all the classics. . . . We played his [ragtime] pieces, one . . . called "Frogs." We had a book with some of his pieces in it.

Jesse Stone: In the minstrel show . . . we played . . . ragtime . . . [but] Scott Joplin was a more accomplished musician than existed among [most of] the black people in those days. We played very simple things, simple chord changes.

Booker Washington: In my home town . . . all that there was was ragtime at this moment, see [c. 1919]. What they called ragtime then, is what we were playing down there [in K.C. jazz bands]. Just ragtime, just good old stomping ragtime music.

SAM GRIEVIOUS. *Born c. 1905. Reeds and booking agent. Performed in many Omaha bands, including Ted Adams and Dan Desdunes.*
The only orchestras working around here [Omaha, Nebraska, c. 1920] was Ted Adams and Dan Desdunes; both had four or five pieces. . . . Back in the teens and that time [we played] ragtime. You buy orchestrations. . . . It was called ragtime, syncopation. [We played songs like] "Clarinet Marmalade," "Sensation Rag," "Kitten on the Keys." Then after that ragtime came the blues era. The two most popular blues singers in the country at that time was Bessie Smith and Ma Rainey. That didn't last too long before then came in jazz, and that came in from out of New Orleans.

New Orleans Jazz

It is likely that the first place to enjoy the blend of black folk music (blues), brass band ensemble style, and European popular and folk music that we call jazz was New Orleans. Rural blacks and urban Creoles met in the social clubs, theaters, cabarets, bars, brothels, and parks of this multicultural Southern city and together created a new music that featured group improvisations and transformed American music.

Among the areas where jazz was played was Storyville, the city's redlight district. Its many brothels often provided work for pianists and, occasionally, bands, although more band work was found in street parades, funerals, and social club functions. Later, river boats and dance halls employed jazz ensembles, led by figures such as Freddie Keppard and Joe "King" Oliver. After 1917, when Storyville was closed down as part of a nationwide crackdown on prostitution, many of the city's finest musicians left, some for Chicago and New York. Among them was Louis Armstrong, soon to become the first giant figure of jazz.

For musicians in Kansas City, as in much of the rest of the country, New Orleans jazz had a profound and liberating effect. Riverboat excursions and traveling bands preceded the Original Dixieland Jass Band's first recordings of jazz in 1917, so that some Midwestern musicians were listening to and experimenting with the new sound as early as 1912.

DON ALBERT (Albert Dominique). *Born 8/5/1908, New Orleans, Louisiana. Died January 1980, San Antonio, Texas. Trumpet, bandleader. Performed in New Orleans and then with Alphonso Trent and Troy Floyd in Texas. Led his own bands through the 1940s, continued to be active as a trumpeter in San Antonio through the late 1970s.*

I played [in parades and funeral bands]. Before I played I carried the horns for the trumpet player Manny Perez. We always had bands, like the Tuxedo Brass Band, the Excelsior Brass Band. [For the funeral marches] a lot of them had relatives in the bands, and it was easy for them to say we're going to play for . . . the dead. . . .

From the time it went to get the body at the funeral parlor to the church, from the church to the grave site . . . they played the old hymns like "Closer Walk with Thee," . . . while they were marching [with] a slow step. . . . From the grave site they would leave and go back. That's when the jazz was playing. . . . "Didn't He Ramble" was the main one they would play when they would be comin' back. . . . There were always at least ten or twelve [musicians in the band]. . . .

New Orleans bands [other than parade bands] were small, like the basic five or six pieces, and that was what they now call Dixieland jazz, and they weren't finished [formally trained] musicians. They played beautiful music [but] the difference [between a New Orleans band] and [Alphonso] Trent's [big band in Texas in the 1920s] was that it [Trent's] was a band of at least twelve men. Twelve members which required arrangements. A six-piece band didn't have to have any arrangements. The sounds were made to sound different and the tempos were different and so was the music.

The rhythm [in the Texas bands] was especially the thing that was different from New Orleans. The drums used a silent beat . . . and the sustained beat which was different with the big bands in Texas. The drummers would read in parts and consequently they got off of the rhythm a little bit and came back to it, which the New Orleans drummers didn't do. Different feeling on the drums, . . . and the playing of the cymbals, . . . altogether. . . .

[The Creoles of New Orleans] were finished musicians, they could play any type of music. But when we go down to the jazz, then we go back to the era of King Oliver and Buddy Bolden and fellows that were black.

Sam Grievous: The way I look at it, New Orleans is the home of jazz. . . . That's where it spread from. [We] would try to copy after them.

Ragtime was more syncopated. Jazz is syncopated, mixed with blues. It's kind of two in one, but not as much syncopation as ragtime. . . . There wasn't improvising in ragtime. . . . During jazz, Louis Armstrong came in the limelight and made it very popular. . . . The blues never did fade out, but ragtime did. . . .

It [jazz] was then [in the teens] being played in the South, because I'd traveled south on Minstrel shows and I'd heard it. In Birmingham, Alabama, Memphis, and New Orleans.

Lawrence Denton: [I heard] New Orleans music . . . before then [the first jazz recording in 1917]. They used to send excursions from Shreveport. That was in 1914, '15, '16, '17, ran about four years. Whole trainload, fifteen, sixteen coaches, then they'd give a dance, and they brought their own band, called it [the] Caddo band.[3] . . .

[The Caddo band] played the same kind of stuff [that Kansas City bands played in the 1920s]. It was a band from down there, New Orleans, King Oliver, you know. They brought jazz to Chicago. . . . They didn't call it jazz, not in 1915, but it was jazz. Yeah, it was all improvising, even the trumpet player, their trombone player, they improvised all through the pieces. They was great, . . . and a lot of those musicians ended up in Chicago [with] Erskine Tate's Orchestra. . . . You see, the jazz comes from down there [in] Louisiana. That's the old stand. New Orleans was the home of jazz. . . .

The band was about . . . eight [pieces], . . . had a couple of saxophones, a trombone, a trumpet, and a violin and a drum. . . . They would parade on the street. . . . They'd [advertise] that parade with banners, saying where they was going to have the dance at. . . . So they'd give a dance one night at this place and the next night the other. They wasn't far apart, six or seven blocks. Next night, they'd make a parade, playing all this rag music on the street. . . . They was playing jazz then but we didn't know it. . . .

[In] about 1915 I asked one of the fellas, . . . the tenor sax player, . . . "What kind of music is that?" So he says, "That's ragtime." See, they was making all them runs, they was improvising to the piece. . . . Way back then, all we know was just to play it like it was on the paper, note for note. . . . They was all making them variations. . . . So they was jazzin' then. Oh, that band was hot.

In 1917 they had cut the excursions out, because half of the colored people would come up here, would stay, wouldn't go back. . . . I enticed a girl to stay up here and she stayed. She was one of the excursion people. . . .

I didn't hear the word "jazz" until after that, about 1918, when the Dixieland Jass Band had a record out named "Tiger Rag." . . . I bought that record.

CHARLES GOODWIN. *Born 10/26/1903, St. Joseph, Missouri. Died 1/3/ 1983, Kansas City, Missouri. Guitar and vocals. Active in many Kansas City bands, including George E. Lee, Thamon Hayes's Rockets, and, most recently, the Art Smith K.C. Jazz Band.*

There was a time when they would give excursions, the blacks would give excursions from Shreveport, Louisiana, to Kansas City, . . . [and] I think this kind of ties in with the two different types of jazz between New Orleans and Kansas City. . . .

This band would come up and do a ballyhoo thing out on the corner, right in the black belt . . . and I think this is how the two jazz things got . . . together. There's sort of a resemblance, even though the part down South was Dixieland and Kansas City's was called jazz. . . .

The first time I saw Baby Lovett[4] he come up on one of those excursions. . . . Then he come to Kansas City to live, brought his wife and his son. . . .

[In] Dixieland they had a pattern. The drummer always started the band off, like a march. . . . Now, by Kansas City, I think it sort of fades from Dixieland and starts a whole [new] thing, what we would call the Kansas City beat, . . . a two-beat thing.

Jesse Stone: I'd say [jazz] came from New Orleans. I think they were playing jazz right after World War I. I think that's when it started being formed there and it creeped northward years later. . . . We developed an independent style [in Kansas City], but they were way ahead of us, . . . they had more feeling. . . . We played collectively, cleaner, and in rhythm, but they played with freedom and with their own expression. They had their own individual expression [that] we just couldn't match. . . .

Just like, they played jazz for funerals, and different things like that that we wouldn't have thought of doing. They would march and the people would march with them. People would dance in the streets. In Kansas City they wouldn't do anything like that. They had parades that were very dignified. They marched in rhythm, . . . but they wouldn't think of getting out there and shaking themselves and turning circles and all that sort of stuff. The people in New Orleans, they were more uninhibited, they would do whatever they felt. . . . We were too dignified. . . .

[The parades and funeral marches] had a lot of influence on me being a bandleader, because I had to do a lot of things that came into my mind after I became a bandleader. Even before Cab Calloway started doing it, I was dancing and doing splits and everything in front of my band because I became uninhibited. Before then I felt sort of foolish.

Eddie Barefield: I first went to New Orleans in 1926, [or] the year before, and Louis [Armstrong] had left there. I think it's a little bit exaggerated about New Orleans, because jazz was being played everywhere [then], like Kansas City and Minneapolis and Chicago and New York. In fact the real home of jazz is New York, because everybody that could play anything left New Orleans and all of these little towns and came to New York.[5] . . . When I went to New Orleans all the good players had left there to come to New York.[6]

NOTES

1. Polyphonic music is made up of harmonizing but melodically independent parts or voices, as distinct from homophony, in which a primary melody is embellished with a chordal accompaniment. Most European "art" music is homophonic. Major Western polyphonic forms are the motet, the round, many canons, and some eighteenth-century fugues. Many important forms of folk polyphony also exist, including much of Pygmy music, Russian choral music, and many New Orleans jazz pieces.

2. Stock, or commercial, arrangements are scores to popular tunes marketed by music publishing companies.

3. The Caddo Jazz Band worked out of Shreveport, Louisiana, between approximately 1914 and 1921. As Lawrence Denton observes, it traveled widely and often, usually as part of a riverboat excursion. Several musicians later prominent in New Orleans performed with the Caddo Band, including clarinetist Charlie Love.

4. Samuel "Baby" Lovett was for many years K.C.'s most prominent and respected jazz drummer, and was a significant influence on the development of Jo Jones, Count Basie's drummer for that band's greatest recordings.

5. A common migratory path from New Orleans was that followed by Louis Armstrong, who first traveled to Chicago, then New York. Armstrong left New Orleans for a job in Chicago with Joe "King" Oliver's band (which had already left New Orleans) in the summer of 1922. He first played in New York in September 1924 with Fletcher Henderson's orchestra. By 1932 he had established New York as a home base for his frequent travels.

6. Barefield is correct for the period he describes, but probably misleading overall. By the mid-1920s New Orleans had indeed faded as an important musical center. The civic crackdown on vice, particularly prostitution, in 1917/18 caused many of the most lucrative jobs to evaporate, and it hurt the city's cash flow for entertainment. By the time Barefield arrived, most of the better musicians had already left town.

Band Contest near Sedalia, Missouri, c. 1900. Brass bands were enormously popular in the early twentieth century. This photo shows a gathering of several white bands for a contest/picnic around the turn of the century. Among band sponsors discernible from drum paintings are the MK&T ("Katy") railroad and several local fraternal organizations. (Courtesy of the Kansas City Museum, Kansas City, Missouri, and the Maple Leaf Club, Sedalia, Missouri)

Dan Desdunes Band, c. 1921. Dan Desdunes led orchestras and brass bands in Omaha, Nebraska, from 1916 to the early 1950s. This is his early, fraternally sponsored brass band that played for parades, picnics, concerts, club gatherings, and other large social functions. (Courtesy of the Kansas City Museum, Kansas City, Missouri, and Walter Harrold)

Black Elks Club Band, c. 1939. Fraternally sponsored marching bands were common in Kansas City's black community through the 1950s. This band parades down Eighteenth Street, the main thoroughfare of Kansas City's black downtown. On the left is Street's Hotel, then the city's best hotel for blacks and the home of Street's Blue Room, a popular nightclub. (Courtesy of the Kansas City Museum, Kansas City, Missouri, and the Black Economic Union)

Lincoln High School Orchestra, c. 1922. School bands were an important training ground for jazz musicians. Lincoln High, the city's most prominent secondary school for blacks, was blessed with a series of excellent music teachers, including Major N. Clark Smith (back row, center) and William L. Dawson, who imparted a musical foundation to a generation of jazz musicians. (Courtesy of Corrine Walder)

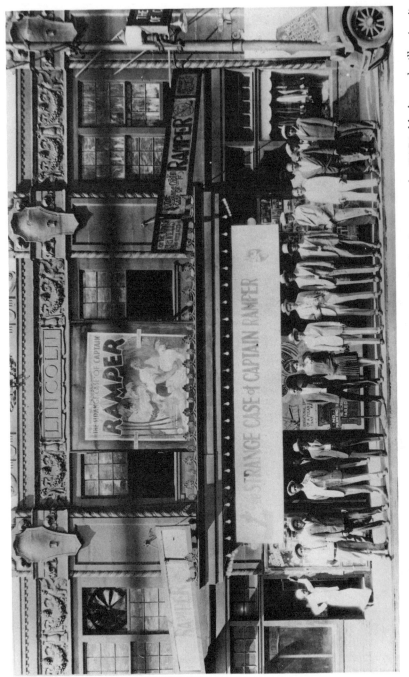

Lincoln Theater Staff, c. 1935. The centrally located Lincoln Theater was the local stop on the TOBA black vaudeville circuit, making it the entertainment center of Kansas City's black downtown. (Courtesy of the Kansas City Museum, Kansas City, Missouri, and Lawrence Denton)

Picadilly Circus Show Troupe, c. 1936. This show band and performing ensemble was typical of the kind of acts that appeared at the Lincoln Theater. A wide array of talent was featured, including singers, dancers, musicians, and comedians. "Speedy" Huggins, a well-known dancer and later a prominent Kansas City jazz pianist, is sixth from the left in the first row. (Courtesy of the Kansas City Museum, Kansas City, Missouri, and Lawrence Denton)

Beck and Walker Show Orchestra, c. 1930. The Beck and Walker group was a traveling orchestra (based in rural Missouri east of Kansas City) that played mainly in TOBA theaters like the Lincoln. (Courtesy of the Kansas City Museum, Kansas City, Missouri, and Adventure Sales, Dover, Missouri)

"CREST" TAMBOURINES
THE STANDARD MAKE

We Carry a Select Line Only

Finest Workmanship

Best Quality of Heads
The Best in the Market for the Money

PRICE LIST

No. 1. 10 inch Calfskin, 2 sets Jingles, Maple Rim, Fancy Painted .... $1.00 each

No. 2. 8 inch Calfskin, 2 sets Jingles, Nickel Plated Rim (Boys' or Ladies' Size)...... 1.50 "

No. 3. 10 inch Calfskin, 6 sets German Silver Jingles, Nickel Plated Rim, Professional. A fine article................. 2.50 "

No. 4. 10 inch Calfskin, 12 sets Jingles, Maple Rim, Painted Red .... 1.25 "
THIS IS OUR BIG SELLER.

No. 5. 8 inch Calfskin, 12 sets Jingles .... 1.40 "

No. 6. 10 inch Calfskin, 14 sets Jingles, Skeleton Model..... 1.75 "

THE CREST
BURNT CORK

There is Cork and there is what some call "Cork." Good Cork is healthful for the skin, while the other is very injurious. We make only the best that is used by the most prominent professionals. The difference in price is trivial, but the satisfaction obtained is worth three times the money.

The Crest brand is especially prepared from the best possible ingredients and we stand ready to guarantee every box purchased.

Price per box. 60 cents

Postpaid.

BONES

Of various well-seasoned woods, and weights, as used by well-known professional end men.

PRICE LIST

No. 1. Black walnut, boys' size, 5½ in., in sets of 4 pieces. $0.15 per set

No. 2. Rosewood, boys' size, 5½ in., in sets of 4 pieces.. .30 "

No. 3. Rosewood, men's size, 7 in., in sets of 4 pieces...... .35 "

No. 4. Cocoawood, boys' size, 5½ in., in sets of 4 pieces...... .40 "

No. 5. Cocoawood, men's size, 7 in., in sets of 4 pieces.... .45 "

No. 6. Ebony, boys' size, 5½ in., in sets of 4 pieces......... .45 "

No. 7. Ebony, men's size, 7 in., in sets of 4 pieces......... .75 "

Add 6 Cents per Set for Postage

CLAPPERS

Patent, Flat Walnut, with 2 Flappers. Especially recommended for boys and ladies. Price per set of 2 ... 20 cents, postpaid.

Some excellent effects can be made by End Men with Bones and Tambos, but as it takes a little while for some to master the manipulation of these instruments, we suggest they are ordered as soon as a minstrel show is contemplated.

Crest Tambourines are not Postpaid

Advertisements from *The Burnt Cork Encyclopedia*, c. 1899. This page from a performers' supply catalog and primer shows some of the tools of the minstrel trade. Both black and white minstrel performers would blacken their faces, often using a burnt cork. This practice had largely died by 1930, although vaudeville and minstrel shows remained popular through the thirties. (Courtesy of the Kansas City Museum, Kansas City, Missouri, and the University of Missouri at Kansas City)

Maple Leaf Club Calling Card, 1899. Scott Joplin, the giant among ragtime composers, was featured as the "entertainer" at the Maple Leaf Club, Sedalia, Missouri, from 1897 to 1900. Joplin and other members of this men's social club in the small southwestern Missouri town are jokingly described on the back of the card. Joplin's first published composition, "Maple Leaf Rag," was written at the club. It was published late in 1899 and became the first million-selling piece of sheet music, starting a national craze for ragtime music. (Courtesy of the Kansas City Museum, Kansas City, Missouri, and the Maple Leaf Club)

Louis Armstrong, c. 1922. Louis Armstrong led the exodus of New Orleans musicians after 1920, and was jazz's first great soloist. Both the ragtime music of Joplin and the New Orleans jazz style exemplified by Armstrong's early playing provided important wellsprings for the Kansas City jazz style. (Courtesy of the Kansas City Museum, Kansas City, Missouri, and Don Lampman)

3

The Territories: Jazz Emerges in the Midwest

The 1920s were the jazz age, a turbulent, exuberant time throughout America that followed the "war to end all wars" and marked the beginning of America's long dominance of the world economy. Times were lively, jobs were plentiful, and opportunities to earn quick fortunes seemed abundant. Hollywood, sports, and aviation were creating heroic figures, and social and moral barriers appeared to be falling. The atmosphere was ideal for the rise to popularity of an exotic new style of music that was often portrayed as risque, even dangerous.[1] Not only did the popular culture seek a new, less refined, more physical dance music, but new communications technologies—broadcast radio[2] and the phonograph record[3]—helped spread jazz quickly and broadly, allowing many styles to develop. During this period jazz was a national phenomenon with strong regional flavors. This chapter will focus on some of the most popular and musically significant jazz bands of the large Midwestern region that spawned Kansas City jazz and was popularly referred to as the "Territories."[4]

By the early twenties, recordings, radio broadcasts, and band performances throughout the country established the national popularity of jazz for both white and black audiences, and created a craze of proportions only previously approached by ragtime in the early 1900s. Not all bands of the twenties had performers skilled in the two most prominent characteristics of jazz, improvisation off a melody and "hot" rhythms, but nearly all could approximate them, and did so to satisfy their dancing patrons.

Jazz was then mainly dance music (and remained so until be-bop, or modern jazz, emerged in the mid-1940s) and was played in nearly every dance hall—and they were nearly everywhere. Although New York and Chicago were the most important jazz centers (New Orleans faded as a major center after 1919), every major city and most smaller ones had their own jazz bands along with other ensembles that also played for social dancing.

The need to supply entertaining dance music to a diverse public (as well as to play "hot" jazz and achieve personal and professional goals) dominated the artistic life of the 1920s jazz performer. Every band member knew that this was his bread and butter, and was careful to recognize the tastes of his audiences. Older dancers generally preferred waltzes, polkas, and fox-trots. Younger crowds wanted the latest steps.[5] By being skilled in such a wide variety of dance styles, Midwestern jazz bands could appear to be rural or urban, old-time or contemporary, depending on their audience. Versatility was highly prized.

Early jazz bands made most of their income from playing to live au-diences, following regional touring patterns that had been established by vaudeville, minstrel, and carnival shows. In this way groups of moderately well-defined touring "territories" developed. The most important of these, and the one pertinent to the development of Kansas City's jazz style, was in the Midwest, where bands traveled from Minnesota to Texas, from western Pennsylvania to Colorado. Reputations were made and lost on the road as bands rivaled each other for the best engagements and tested each other's skills in mock-serious "battles of bands."

This vast central region actually encompassed several territories. Tours were arranged to allow a manageable series of one-night stands, but the touring circuits in the Midwest overlapped so extensively that musicians often saw them as one booking region. I shall refer to the entire area as the Territories, as did most musicians of the era.

These Territories enjoyed a rich and diverse musical heritage, and were fertile ground for the development of a distinctive jazz style. Classic ragtime composers such as Scott Joplin, James Scott, and Charles L. Johnson worked in Sedalia, St. Louis, and Kansas City, Missouri. Ragtime ensembles, brass bands, and dance orchestras entertained listeners and dancers throughout the region from the turn of the century. Songsters and blues musicians traveled widely, most often in rural areas, playing roadhouses, juke joints,[6] and Saturday night suppers. Minstrel, carnival, medicine, Wild West, and vaudeville shows, many including bands with featured "get-off" soloists, were popular attractions. Religious music also played a prominent role in many communities. Generally, though, Midwestern musicians played what the people wanted—dance music, be it sweet or hot,[7] old-fashioned nos-talgic or gutbucket stomping.[8]

The earliest jazz ensembles in the Territories were dance bands of three to six pieces. A rhythm section of piano and drums was always the core of the group and often included a tuba as the bass instrument. Vocalists were also ubiquitous; they usually required a megaphone to be heard in a large hall. Many bands added "horn" players (trumpet or cornet, clarinet, trombone, and saxophone were the most common), a banjo, and possibly a violin. They performed not only at dance halls, dine-and-dance cabarets, taxi dances,[9] and speakeasies, but also at family celebrations, riverboat rides, group outings, lodge conventions, private parties—anywhere large groups congregated. Depending on their audience, they played a mixture of the hits of the day (available either as piano scores or full arrangements), blues, jazz compositions, and head arrangements.[10] Winning with the audience was not tricky—a strong-voiced, attractive singer was helpful, and musicians usually tried to stress a song's melody so that the audience could follow the tune. Even the most brilliant improvisers usually "swung the melody," until styles changed radically in the mid-forties.

By the mid-twenties big bands of ten to fifteen pieces supplanted smaller groups as the most common type of jazz ensemble and the one most appealing to musicians. The increased size of a big band provided a fuller sound with a greater variety of textures and colors. Some big bands, like Walter Page's Blue Devils, evolved directly from vaudeville bands. Others, like Bennie Moten's Kansas City Orchestra, slowly increased in size (in Moten's case, from a trio in 1918 to a ten-piece band by 1926). Still others, like T. Holder's Twelve Clouds of Joy, were assembled as big bands from the beginning and featured musicians from a variety of backgrounds.

Big bands had three sections: brass, reeds, and rhythm. The brass section included from three to five trumpet and trombone players, while the reed section had three or four saxophone players (most doubling on other reed instruments). The rhythm section began as piano, drums, tuba, and banjo and underwent a significant transformation in the twenties. In the early twenties even the best bands had an "oom-pah" quality to the music, given by the ponderous sound of most tubists and the staccato chop of the tenor banjo. By the thirties most bands replaced these with string bass and guitar. The bass could usually be played faster and cleaner than the tuba, and the guitar's more sustained tone blended better with more sophisticated orchestrations. (The string bass and guitar were not unknown in earlier jazz, however. As early as 1908 New Orleans bands sometimes included them. Even so, tuba and banjo were much more popular.) In the course of this instrumental evolution the two-beat "stomp" gave way to a more supple 4/4 swing rhythm.

Unfortunately, our understanding of the sound of these Territory bands is sketchy. The best resources are actual recordings, but even these have serious limitations. First, few big bands in the Midwest recorded with any regularity, and some well-regarded groups (including Thamon Hayes's Kansas City Rockets and the Nat Towles Orchestra) never recorded at all. Second, then as now, not all musicians responded well to the demands of the recording studio, nor did they always play their best in that atmosphere.

Third, a ten-inch, 78 rpm record plays for a maximum of only about three minutes and twenty seconds, and most recordings were considerably shorter than that. Yet many of the best tunes of the era could be extended in live performance for as long as forty minutes, creating substantially different works from those on record. Fourth, recording companies had definite ideas of what songs should be recorded and how they should sound, and these ideas did not necessarily agree with those of the band.[11] Finally, the recording equipment had severe technical limitations, resulting in recordings that often distorted a band's real sound, particularly that of the rhythm section.

Still, we can make some judgments from the recordings that are available. The music did become increasingly sophisticated during the twenties. Several prominent composer/arrangers, such as Jesse Stone (leader of the Blues Serenaders), Mary Lou Williams (Andy Kirk's Twelve Clouds of Joy), Walter Page (bassist/leader of the Blue Devils, later with Bennie Moten and Count Basie), Eddie Durham (guitar/trombone with the Blue Devils, Bennie Moten, and many others), and Buster Smith (alto saxophonist with the Blue Devils and Bennie Moten), were able to substantially improve musicianship in their bands. They had developed advanced concepts of harmony and rhythm, and in order to play more complex music were forced to train their fellow musicians in intonation and tune. As Eddie Durham recalls, the process was not easy: "In those days we only used . . . three-part harmony. When I went into Bennie Moten's band I was the fourth man [in the horn section, playing trombone]. . . . So I put in the sixth, that's the fourth part [of the chord]. . . . But you'd give a guy [that note], he'd stop. 'Man, I couldn't make that note. Sounds bad.' They didn't know how to tone it. . . . A little later on they got a little used to the sixth, but I had to play the note [for them]. Nobody could get it in tune."

Also during the twenties a number of outstanding soloists developed in the Midwest who stretched the aesthetic boundaries of the music. Among them were trumpeters Hot Lips Page and Bix Beiderbecke; trombonists Snub Mosley, Jack Teagarden, Druie Bess, and Eddie Durham; violinist Stuff Smith; pianists Mary Lou Williams, Pete Johnson, and Bill "Count" Basie; bassist Walter Page; guitarists Eddie Durham, Efferge Ware, and Floyd Smith; and saxophonists Buster Smith, Budd Johnson, Coleman Hawkins, Dick Wilson, and Lester Young.

Bennie Moten and Alphonso Trent had the most prominent black orchestras in the Midwest in the twenties; the Coon-Sanders Nighthawks were the most prominent white orchestra. Of these three only Trent failed to be recorded frequently. At least two other black orchestras, however, were the equal of Moten and Trent according to the few recordings available — Walter Page's Blue Devils and Jesse Stone's Blues Serenaders. In sum, the recordings confirm what those who remember the era claim — that jazz was everywhere, and that Territory jazz was some of the best played anywhere.

The 1920s were self-defined as the jazz age, and while that's a romantic generalization, it's largely accurate. Jazz—new, exciting, and disreputable—served well as a symbol for the times. But the era was built on an economic house of cards that tumbled in late 1929 with the start of the Depression.[12]

This was the time of jazz's youthful exuberance, and was the formative period for all jazz styles except Dixieland until avant-garde jazz of the sixties. During the Depression, Kansas City became the focal point for scores of out-of-work musicians and bands, but during the twenties K.C. was only one lively town among many. All the states of the Territories jumped with the sweet thunder of jazz.

Eddie Barefield: This whole thing [jazz] developed in the dances. In those days, everybody danced [in] every little town and little place, even places that weren't towns. We played places where it's forty miles out of town, and you wondered where the crowd was coming from, and that night it would be packed.

This happened all through these states and those places. They had plenty of dance halls, and it was a big promotion. Everybody had local bands, even Minneapolis . . . had about ten bands in there . . . one winter . . . because it snowed and they were stranded there. . . .

It was a ball. Everybody in those days . . . had good musicians. . . . I played in Milwaukee, Wisconsin, with Bernie Young's Band and they had a lot of famous players that came out, like Ed Inge, C. T. Randolph, [and] Mort McKenzie. . . . These guys all went from one place to another, and all of these schools[13] were just like a stepping stone, from grade school or kindergarten to college. You got a lot of experience.

GEORGE "BUDDY" TATE. *Born 2/22/1914, Sherman, Texas. Tenor saxophone, clarinet. Performed with many bands, including Gene Coy's Black Aces, T. Holder and Andy Kirk's Twelve Clouds of Joy, Nat Towles, Count Basie, Lucky Millinder, and Hot Lips Page. Extensive recordings. Continues to be very active international performer and recording artist.*

The T. Holder band . . . was a Texas and Oklahoma band, and we would come as far as Kansas City, then we'd go back there as Territory bands [would] to Texas and Louisiana and all places like that down South. . . . There was another band by the name of the Blue Devils and [Count] Basie was playing with it at that time. They were an Oklahoma band and Texas band also, and they also came up to Kansas City.

BUSTER SMITH. *Born 8/26/1904, Ellis County (near Dallas), Texas. Sax-*

ophones, clarinet, guitar, electric bass, piano, arranger. Prominent band member, bandleader, and arranger. Performed with many bands, including the Blue Devils, Bennie Moten, and Count Basie (co-leader of the Buster Smith-Count Basie Barons of Rhythm). The most influential Midwestern alto saxophonist of the era and a major influence on Charlie Parker.

[The Blue Devils] got to going down [to Arkansas], playing all summer, and we'd leave there and come back to Kansas City and play all winter. We had about eight days off out of the whole year [c. 1927]. We wasn't making much money, about thirty-five or forty dollars a week.

Buddy Tate: They had ballrooms in those days, . . . two big ballrooms in Oklahoma City, and maybe we'd go in and play six weeks . . . [and] we'd go from one ballroom to another. . . . The Blue Devils would [also] play six weeks. Well, when they close [one of us] you had to battle the band that was coming in. They always booked it like that, so on the closing night of an outgoing band, the incoming band always had to play a battle with them. . . . You had to be prepared so you didn't embarrass [yourself]. . . .

These were from Tulsa to Oklahoma City and maybe to Dallas, Ft. Worth, where they had some big ballrooms. . . . We're playing five or six nights a week. When a younger crowd come in you could really open up. Then when the older people come, you had to stick to that melody and turn it down. . . . But on some of the nights, man, you could open up and swing all night. Playing with the black crowds you could swing all the time. They want to hear you play jazz.

[On the road] we used to stay in private homes, mostly. [When] we used to play through South Dakota and Minnesota we stayed at white homes. We didn't do that down South. . . . With [T.] Holder [in the South] we used to stay in colored homes.

Don Albert: [Finding rooms] was a big problem. . . . [You'd] sleep in the bus — wasn't any accommodation. If we came to a town . . . we had to find out where the railroad track was, because on the other side of the track is where the Negroes lived, and sometimes they'd put us up in their homes. That was one means of getting lodging for the night, but not in any hotels or motels. That was out.

Clarence Love: [In 1929] we left [Kansas City] and went on this deal [touring the West]. We played places way out in the country. You'd think nobody is going to be here today. But here they come up in horse and buggies, wagons, and that night you'd have a *big* crowd. I betcha we played, in the state of Washington, every little town up in there. . . . We did that for nearly a year.

GENE RAMEY. *Born 4/4/1913, Austin, Texas. Died 1984, Austin. String bass. Active in many bands, including Oliver Todd, Jay McShann, Ben Webster, Coleman Hawkins, Charlie Parker, Dizzy Gillespie, Miles Davis, Lester Young, Count Basie. Featured on many recordings.*

In those days, everywhere you looked there was bands. There must've been eight or ten bands in San Antonio, and we knew four or five in Houston. There must've been twenty bands in Dallas and Ft. Worth. . . . At one time there must've been fifteen or twenty bands . . . in Omaha. . . . So, the bands, they spread out all over. That tour from Kansas City usually would take you down through Arkansas and Louisiana, over to Texas, back up through Oklahoma. They had almost a regular circuit. Almost every week you could find a different band in Austin [Texas].

[We played] in these old ballrooms. . . . In those days bands were really loud. The amazing thing about it is, the bands were so loud, yet still the singers didn't have . . . microphones. They had to sing through that megaphone. . . .

The [booking agents] would start in January to find themselves an ensemble that'd go to some of the resorts, either in the Ozarks or up in Saskatchewan and up in other parts of Canada, British Columbia, you know. So there was usually plenty of work in the summertime. . . . But Kansas City was year round. There was always plenty of music.

WALTER HARROLD. *Born c. 1908, Omaha, Nebraska. Drummer. Active in Omaha and on the road. Performed with many bands, including Lloyd Hunter and Nat Towles.*

[Our circuit was] North Platte, and Grand Island [Nebraska], and Sterling, Colorado, and Kansas, all around through there, South Dakota. . . . We played right close around, even Wyoming. The first time I rode a horse was up in South Dakota with Lloyd's [Hunter] band. . . . We played for polkas, anything they'd want. We played for square dances, too. They had that type of dance during intermission, and they'd ask four or five of us to stay on the bandstand to play the music for 'em. There'd be a caller out there to call the dances.

Buster Smith: We [the Blue Devils] played waltzes and sweet music up in Saginaw [Michigan], [for] people up there. Had some tunes that sounded like Guy Lombardo. Even in South Dakota they liked sweet music and we had to play a lot of that. I had to write a whole repertoire of sweet music to go along with it.

We used to play a lot of jitney dances where they'd charge a quarter to dance, and you have to play four hours and never stop. Just steady playing because they had a rope up around the dance floor, and the men had to pay a quarter to go in there and dance with the ladies. He'd tell us cut 'em [the tunes] short so he'd get the most quarters he could in there. You found a lot of that down there in Oklahoma, down in Shawnee, Seminole, in them oil fields.

Sam Grievious: I had a booking license, and if I wanted to break into a territory, I had a book with all booking agents all over the nation. When spring comes I would contact a booking agent in Wisconsin and I'd tell him about what kind of attraction I got here and I'd like to sell it, and I'd like for you to introduce it in your territory. We'd furnish the advertising, and he would accept it, for maybe four weeks. . . . Then we'd contact a white fella in Spring Grove, Minnesota, he broke us in a lot of places. . . . Play as far as upper Michigan, and then once you got in the territory, that's all you'd need. . . . There was a white guy whose father had a hardware store, and we sold him the band outright for a cut price for a whole week. He would book the band all through western Nebraska, go up in the Black Hills. . . . When he did that, why, we had the contacts for the future. This was back with the Omaha Night Owls.

Cities in the Territories

Most cities of that era had tales of jazz and exotic behavior. Several of these accounts paint images of the home turf that put Kansas City's legendary wild abandon into a regional perspective.

Oklahoma City

RALPH ELLISON. *Oklahoma City, Oklahoma. Author and critic. Also a musician and resident of Oklahoma City during the twenties.*
   In . . . Hallie Richardson's shoeshine parlor in Oklahoma City . . . I first heard Lester Young jamming in a shine chair, his head thrown back, his horn even then outthrust, his feet working on the footrests, as he played with and against Lem Johnson, Ben Webster [this was 1929] and other members of the old Blue Devils orchestra.[14]

Buddy Anderson: On Sundays, my church, CME Church, [was] just one block from *the* street, . . . Northeast Second Street, about three hundred block. They called that Deep Deuce and that was the main spot for the black community. . . . [There were] cafes and things. . . . They had kind of a little headquarters there where the cats would gang up and get ready to go to the gig and play. Everybody would just meet there and they get in their cars and go hit it. But on Sunday mornings going to church [I'd] see those cats with those instruments practicing early in the morning, . . . they was goin' out to play a gig, . . . [and] I'd give anything to be crawlin' in there. . . .

Sometimes there would be three or four bands in town, staying there for weeks at a time . . . [and] they'd have dances. . . . I couldn't help but see posters and things like that. . . .

[The] cats that had come into town and run into each other [would] just go and get their stuff [instruments] and go into some joint . . . and get to makin' it. There wouldn't be any charge for people to go in there, some gambling joint. . . . Like Count Basie and the Blue Devils and all that stuff like that, they all knew each other, and everything [was] family-like. . . . Mary Lou Williams and Dick Wilson, cats like that, just [have fun] when they get . . . home.[15] . . .

Those black musicians [even] played [Western swing music, popularized by white "cowboy" bands but having strong similarities to jazz]. They had to play it, because the people would kill 'em [if they didn't]. That's the thing they wanted to hear. [White bands like Bob Wills and the Texas Playboys] was over there [in the black clubs] jamming every night. . . . If they had a gig they'd come on over and sit down.

San Antonio

Don Albert: [We] had a few white bands [in San Antonio]. Ben Blue and Jimmy Joyce and bands like that would come in here [in the early twenties]. . . . Later on, after Troy [Floyd] got his band and a few other Negro bands [got] together . . . there were stationary bands [in town]. Lloyd Garden was one of them, Wardell and his Black Diamonds [was another], and later on we had Boots and His Buddies after we got my band together . . . in 1929. . . .

[We played] the Shadowland Ballroom every night, every night. It was a gambling casino, just like Las Vegas, worse than Kansas City! Slot machines, every card game you can name, every dice game you could name. . . . Prohibition knocked us out for a little while, but they straightened that out after a week or two. Didn't have to worry, [the] money was there. [The gambling room] was a great big room, five or six card [tables], five or six dice tables. The gamblers are dressed in tuxedos and the women in full dress clothes . . . [plus] waiters, and they started using dancers out of Hollywood, teams, a man and a lady. Fantastic dancers, doing the waltzes and adagios, and maybe some great singer.

Omaha

Sam Grievous: Back in the early days most of the clubs in this city had black musicians. . . . They was all run by underworld people and they all had colored musicians in 'em. . . . Some of them joints would run 'till four, five, six o'clock the next morning. You'd be going to work . . . and people [would be] just pouring out of the club.

You'd walk in, across this wall would be a bar, during Prohibition. Stand[ing] right there . . . would be a policeman in his uniform. They're selling whiskey, wine. Then you'd go in this door here, there'd be the ballroom, tables sitting around. On the far end was the stage with the band and entertainers. . . . Only whites [could go], but they all had colored bands. . . . They had a kitty, a box up there on the piano, . . . but the joint paid 'em a salary on top of the kitty. . . .

We used to have jam sessions every night. The main place was the Blue Room, Twenty-fourth and Lincoln. Then the union made a law against it [jam sessions]. . . . The establishments was getting music free.

We'd use Jimmy Jewell's dance hall, and white places also. . . . Had a band on this side, one on this end of the hall, one on that end of the hall. You'd play so many numbers and they'd play so many numbers. [When] we had a battle of the bands between the Omaha Night Owls and the Dixie Ramblers, you couldn't get in the hall. It was the two most popular bands at that time [in Omaha]. . . .

We had between one hundred and two hundred numbers [in the repertoire] at that time. You'd have to keep up with the public, in what they want, and mix it in, you know, some of the ragtime numbers, or jazz numbers or blues numbers. But you still have to give the public what is popular.

Walter Harrold: We had seven or eight bands of ten or twelve pieces around Omaha. Every year these guys all went on the road, was road bands really. Then they'd have a certain time, around the holidays maybe, around Christmas, . . . when all of the bands would come back home, and they'd all have a battle of music. You'd play about thirty minutes and . . . you'd get down and another band [would play]. We'd try to outdo each other all along. That used to be the best highlights of the year, when those bands would get together and battle each other.

[If we did well] in our town that would help us out. People would say, "Those guys are getting better every day, more people was on the floor when they played," so we'd get all the club dances and everything in town. [The major band leaders were] Red Perkins and Lloyd Hunter and Ted Adams. Nat Towles wasn't around then.

Major Territory Bands

Among the many jazz orchestras that toured the Midwest in the twenties and thirties, several stand out, both in the accounts found here and in the musical record. Bands such as Alphonso Trent, Troy Floyd, T. Holder's (and later, Andy Kirk's) Twelve Clouds of Joy, Lawrence Welk, Nat Towles, Jesse Stone's Blues Serenaders, and most notably the Blue Devils all enjoyed immense popularity in their day. The Blue Devils have come to occupy a nearly legendary status in jazz history as both the greatest source of talent of the era and the wildest, most freewheeling and recklessly enthusiastic band of all.

The Territory bands included for discussion here were chosen both because of their importance in the development of Midwestern jazz and because they are most frequently described in the oral histories. As a result, several fine bands—the Alphonso Trent, Troy Floyd, Jesse Stone, Nat Towles, and Lawrence Welk orchestras—receive relatively brief mention, while the two most important and most memorable Territory bands, the Twelve Clouds of Joy and the Blue Devils, occupy their own chapters. Also, several other well-known bands of the period—such as Boots and His Buddies, the Jeter-Pillars Orchestra, Gene Coy's Happy Black Aces, the Don Albert Orchestra, the Blues Syncopaters, the Milt Larkins Orchestra, the George Morrison Orchestra, the Omaha Night Owls/Dixie Ramblers, and Lloyd Hunter's Serenaders—are not included.

Alphonso Trent

Trent organized his first band, the Synchro Six, in Helena, Arkansas, in the late teens. In the early twenties he expanded to a ten-piece ensemble and moved to Dallas, earning an eighteen-month engagement at the Adolphus Hotel, one of the most prestigious in the city, and establishing his orchestra as unquestionably the best-paid black band in the Mid- and Southwest. At one time his sidemen earned $150 a week and drove Cadillacs. Nightly radio broadcasts made them also the most widely heard black band. In the Territories only the enormously successful Coon-Sanders Nighthawks, a white Kansas City band, was better known.

At various times Trent's orchestra included many of the finest musicians of the day: T. Holder, Harry "Sweets" Edison, Tatti Smith, George Hudson, and Peanuts Holland, trumpets; Snub Mosley, trombone; James Jeter, Charles Pillars, Hayes Pillars, Eppie Jackson, and Henry Bridges, reeds; Eugene Crook, banjo and guitar; Leroy "Stuff" Smith, violin; and A. G. Godley, percussion. Trent recorded eight sides in 1929, 1930, and 1933 that demonstrate the band's skill; but they also show that, while strikingly accomplished, he lacked the "swing" that made other groups such as the Blue Devils, Bennie Moten, Count Basie, and Jay McShann so distinctive. Trent disbanded his orchestra in 1934 to return to Ft. Smith, Arkansas, and family affairs.

T. Holder: I first started out [with Alphonso] Trent [c. 1917]. Trent came over from Ft. Smith to get me [when] . . . I was about twelve or thirteen.[16] He knew about me 'cause he didn't have much of a band and he kept running around 'till he run across me. . . . Trent was about the same age [as me]. He was a young man. . . .

We had a pretty nice little group there. We'd play all around. Do a dance, go on into Ft. Smith. Ft. Smith was kind of a headquarters for us. [Then] we'd come up here [Muskogee] and play a dance. Then we'd go to Tulsa, play a dance. Then we'd play in Oklahoma City. Then we'd go back home and count our money. There'd be five of us and we'd make ourselves two, three hundred dollars a piece and we'd go back home. That's all we did. Enjoy life. 'Cause we didn't know no better, and we didn't do no better, and we had a lot of fun doing it. . . . I was only home two weeks in the year. I'd look in on my mother, give her some money, and I'd be gone.

There was five of us originally. Then it got bigger and bigger, it got hard to cooperate, hard to keep the band in line 'cause we had so many men. I was kind of a manager. They'd all do what I said do. . . . It wasn't like I was the big boss, they'd just ask me about things. . . . I was louder than the rest of the boys. We'd go in, talk about some job, they'd all push me up in front. It was a commonwealth band,[17] one man wasn't no more than another man, 'cause I can play just as well as you can, and you can play just as well as me. We liked that, 'cause after we got started . . . we got so close together.

[Later] the manager of the Adolphus Hotel [in Dallas] heard the band, and he took us in, he hired us. We was about seven, eight of us then. We played in the hotel and then in this bar that was a cafe, and then we'd play a dance at night in the hotel. . . . When we went to the Adolphus Hotel we had to buy uniforms because we had to look like it, you know. . . .

Brent Forest . . . was an old-time bandleader, you know. He was the oldest man in the band, he was about twenty-two or twenty-three years old, he was a bass player, had one of them great big old tubas. See we had three saxophones, two trumpet[s], two trombones, piano and drums and violin. . . . [We played] every kind of song. We played classics, overtures, like "Poet and Peasant." We played a lot of classics because we had that boy [Leroy "Stuff" Smith] playing violin, and he could play a bit. [We also had a singer] named John Beatty. . . .

We played a lot of jazz music [too]. We had to play jazz music to do what we was doing. . . . That band wasn't no slouch. That band could blow you away.

In the Adolphus we'd go to work at nine o'clock at night and play till one, and that was mostly dance music. At noon we played kind of more classic form of music. Sometimes we'd do sweet music and some cat would come in and say, "Come on man, let's blow." Sometimes we'd do that, but that didn't happen often. . . . [The crowd] was strictly white. [We played] on the radio every night, station WFA in Dallas. We played there a long, long time. . . .

We played a lot of music that was arranged by different big arrangers. Like Bob Sylvester; he's a white man, though. . . . A lot of the boys couldn't read, so we'd stop and teach them the notes, and go on, finally we got the band so everybody was reading just about on the level. Then they began to get smooth. That's what made the band good. We had kind of a smooth band anyway, with that combination (of instruments). . . . We had two sax, then we had three sax, then we had four sax. We was getting up in the world. We had to arrange for that fourth saxophone, and we had to learn that, you know. . . .

Everybody shared alike, share and share alike. We'd go someplace and play, we'd cut that money right down the middle. We got around eighty dollars or ninety dollars a week a man [at the Adolphus]. . . . We got our room and board . . . out in town, you know, with the deal. . . . We didn't want to stay there [at the Adolphus], with as many fine-looking chicks as there was running around. . . . You know what happens, musicians usually find the nice-looking women, and usually have 'em too. You wouldn't have no trouble finding no woman, white or black. . . .

Then we made a whole lot of extra jobs too. We'd build up to two hundred dollars a week, and wasn't any of us used to making that kind of money. . . . We went on [later] to the Baghdad Club, between Fort Worth and Dallas. They had everything out there, races, gambling, everything. . . .

We played down in Ft. Smith, and there was a lot of places that wouldn't allow colored people around. So we'd get together and talk about it, and decide what to do. We'd call ahead, call somebody to find out what was happening, get the word. . . . There was a lot of places you couldn't play. They would take a white band but wouldn't take no colored band. Our band got so good that everybody wanted us. So that's what happened to that. We went from one job to another. . . .

I didn't leave Trent; we'd play a while and quit. That's how that happened.

Troy Floyd

The Troy Floyd Orchestra was the house band at San Antonio's Shadowland Ballroom in the late twenties, and occasionally toured in Texas, Oklahoma, and Arkansas. It played a version of New Orleans-style music, trying to reconcile small band interplay and polyphonic swing with big band orchestrations. Among the musicians featured were Benno Kennedy and Don Albert, trumpets; Herschel Evans and Buddy Tate, reeds. The Floyd group recorded twice, in 1928 and 1929, and broke up in 1932. Floyd himself moved to San Diego to operate a pool hall. The remnants of the band were taken over by Don Albert and continued to perform for many years.

Don Albert: Troy [Floyd] had lost a great trumpet player he had, Benno Kennedy, and I happened to go to a party where [Alphonso] Trent and [his] whole band was. Chester Clark said, "Why don't you get in Troy's band, he needs a good trumpet player and you'd fit in the seat." . . . So I wired Troy, he told me to wait in Dallas for him. . . .

The first job with Troy was out at the old place out here on Fredericksburg Road, the Shadowland Ballroom. . . . We went there and then . . . went to a couple of dates in Galveston and came back to the Shadowland in 1927. . . . Troy was getting all the work he wanted and I was getting more money than I ever dreamed I would ever make, fifty dollars a week. . . .

Troy [was playing] stock arrangements of popular tunes of that day. They were very much more advanced [than New Orleans bands]. It was a different type of music, more entertaining and more of a variety. And there were special singers. They had one singer, Eddie Sanders. He was an operatic singer but he fit into this band with these popular songs. . . .

Troy held back most of his soloists, he wanted his band to play everything right together. I used to feature a lot of Louis's [Armstrong] numbers in those days and he'd hold these things back. . . . We had Herschel Evans in the band, the greatest tenor player played. He held Herschel back. Maybe it's a blessing he did because Herschel would have outshone everything that we had in the band.[18] . . .

[In 1929 we had a recording session] over here at the Blue Bonnet Hotel [and] we had trouble collecting the money. Troy had gotten the money and had never given it to us. I ramrodded the investigation and I found the mailman putting it in the mailbox and I confiscated it, which I did wrong but we got the money that way.

[Troy] was a likable fellow . . . even though he just kicked you coming and going, you had to like the fellow. He had beautiful ways about him at times, it was only his vice that ruined everything—his love for gambling, dice, cards.

Jesse Stone's Blues Serenaders

Jesse Stone was among the most important arrangers in Midwestern jazz. He organized the Blues Serenaders in 1920 and they played primarily in

St. Joseph and Kansas City, Missouri. The band was noted for its powerful swing and creative arrangements, and included Eddie Tompkins and Albert Hinton, trumpets; Druie Bess, trombone; and Stone, piano. Probably only Alphonso Trent and the Blue Devils had comparable skills in the Territories during the late twenties, as demonstrated by the two recordings the Serenaders made in 1927.

Subsequently, Stone worked for many Territory bands, including the Twelve Clouds of Joy, George E. Lee, and notably Thamon Hayes's Rockets in Kansas City. He left K.C. in the mid-thirties, first for Chicago, and then New York, where he became a successful songwriter and arranger and led several seminal rock and roll recording sessions with Joe Turner in the late 1940s.

Druie Bess: I was playing with a band in Chicago they called Brown's Orchestra . . . [and] Jess Stone had a band over there, . . . right out from St. Joe in Kansas [actually St. Joseph, Missouri]. . . . He heard me play over there and he didn't have no trombone. Then he come and got me. . . . I expect it was about [in] '25. . . . I played with Jess 'bout two years, playing in little old joints around St. Joe. That's where I married my first wife. . . .

I was wild about Jess, . . . he was my buddy. . . . Jess wouldn't go nowhere unless he had me to play the trombone, . . . [but] then Jess went on down into Texas . . . [and] I wasn't with Jess [long before] . . . the Oklahoma Blue Devils came on in.

Eddie Durham: I went to Kansas City . . . around about '25. . . . I must have got stranded there with somebody. . . . When I went there I joined a band. We formed a brass section which was Eddie Compton and Paul Webster [and me]. . . . He [Eddie Compton] was a crazy guy, too. He was working on the side for a mortician, but the guy would always say, "I leave him here to close up and when I come back the next day, he picks the highest priced casket I've got, and when I come back he's laying in there asleep." . . .

[We also had] Budd Johnson's brother, Keg Johnson, then Budd Johnson . . . and Booker Pittman. . . . We had five. . . . I think Herschel [Evans] was with us at that time. So Jess Stone organized a band, and we went with Jess. . . . We didn't stay very long [but] we went over with Jess, the entire group.

Jesse Stone: I had one of the greatest bands I've seen, out that way [in Kansas]. Coleman Hawkins[19] . . . actually started with me; . . . we were playing together when we had four pieces. . . . I met Coleman through my violin player, George Bell, [who] told me about this cello player. . . .

So we tried to get him to join the group but he thought it was not a good idea to try to play dance music with a cello . . . so he got a saxophone and he was playing that sax in four or five months. Yeah, he could play it.

My cousin [played saxophone] too. . . . They both used to have the same style, . . . they used to "slap tongue," . . . popped a note, make it have a hard attack, . . . and they used to have a feature thing . . . where they would be doing this at each other like they were shooting pistols. . . . It was a novelty . . . [Coleman] left me to go with Mamie Smith. . . . She offered him more money than I could ever give him. . . . Then she came back and tried to get me. . . .

I didn't want to work with anybody else's band. I wanted to have my own band, . . . to play the things where you used arrangements. . . .

The Blues Serenaders really evolved from a school band . . . from St. Joseph. . . . I just kept a band going every summer and changing musicians. . . . My cousin lasted longer than anyone. Druie Bess was sort of a late-comer. . . . By the time Druie got to the band everybody was playing solos. The early bands, there's no record of what we were doing then because we sounded horrible and we used to practice in a pool hall. . . . A guy let us practice there because we attracted a crowd. That's the place where I taught most of the guys how to take off solos by writing them out for them. . . .

[On our first tour] we got stranded in . . . a resort that was down in Missouri. . . . [The manager] didn't pay us and we ended up [without] any money. . . . So we moved down near the railroad yards in a real dumpy hotel, all of us stayed in one room. . . .

Eddie Durham was one of the trombone players . . . and this woman who ran this hotel, oh, she was ugly. . . . But she liked Eddie Durham and she told us that we could stay there. Eddie didn't want to be bothered with that woman, you know, so we . . . dressed him all up, . . . a necktie from one guy, a shirt from somebody else, . . . carried him downstairs to her room and knocked on the door, pushed him in. Eddie did more to save the band than anybody else in the group. . . .

There was a guy named Frank J. Rock, an undertaker; he took over the management of the band. [We got involved with him] when we were in St. Joseph. We were starving and there was a guy who was building a broadcasting station in a little store. . . . I happened to be walking around there looking for something to do, . . . and I saw this guy in there and all I saw was wires. . . . I decided to go in, I said, "What are you making?" Because there were no radios then. He said, "It's an invention that plays music on the air. You send it out and people who have radios at home . . . can sit and listen to the music." I said, "You should want a band . . . I got a band." He said he could pay about five dollars a day. I thought it was pretty good. Five dollars for the whole band. I had eighteen pieces.

We started broadcasting in that place and the first day we broadcast, he started getting wires. . . . The third day we broadcast, Frank J. Rock walked into the place and said, "How would you guys like to work for me?". . . I didn't even have cab fare to go up to his house. . . . He said, "What do you need?" I said we need clothes, we need instruments, and he brought out a package of money. . . . It said "$2000," and that's the first money he gave me. . . . I couldn't believe it. No contract, nothing. We worked for Mr. Rock the whole time that he stayed with us, which was three years.

He bought us all new instruments and he sent us down to have these costumes. We decided to get tuxedos, but nobody thought of getting shoes. He said . . . report at such and such a place to have photos made. So we went to this photographer with these hobnail shoes on, wing collars with bow ties. . . . As a novelty thing everybody kept a shot of that because it was funny. . . .

[With] the Blues Serenaders . . . I had two trumpets and a trombone, four saxophones, and three rhythms. . . . Everybody doubled [played two or more instruments] in the band. There would be guys bringing clarinets, flute. . . . We packed them in. We played against some of the biggest MCA [a major booking agency] bands in the business and we played them down, because we had such a versatile band. We could entertain. We had a dance team in the band. We had a quartet in the band. A glee club. We had three comedians. We could do any kind of skits. The guys used to put on old women's clothes. . . . We could do at least ten or twelve weeks of shows without doing the same thing over. . . . We had four arrangers in the band besides myself. . . .

I'd enlarged the band from the time Mr. Rock first got the band. We've got, I think, seven or eight brass, four saxophones, guitar, rhythm, . . . and I'm standing up in front of the band directing, acting, singing. . . . I would sit down and play [piano] and sing, but I would do a lot of Cab Calloway-style jumping and dancing. I did the splits. . . .

We had the strongest band out in the West. . . . We had the territory sewed up. Nobody could play within two hundred miles of us, . . . nobody would try . . . because the people would just wait for us. They wouldn't go to the other dances. . . . Mr. Rock was sort of a mastermind. . . . We'd play all kinds of things. We played theaters. We did stage presentations. We did concerts, fairs, and colleges. We played proms. . . . We liked the dances the best. There was closer contact with the people. We saw their reaction and we'd get fired up when they'd get fired up and we'd get along with them. . . .

We made more money then . . . until Mr. Rock lost his father and turned the management of the band over to me, and I didn't know what to do with it. We just took a nose dive because I didn't know anything about the business end. . . .

I could never say that band broke up. It just kept evolving. Members would leave and we'd get somebody else. There was never a place where we said, "Okay, this is it." . . .

[In Oklahoma] we took a vote. T. Holder was making us this offer and members of the group . . . were adventurous and felt that they had the ability to join this great band. The band wasn't that great but we thought we were improving our status by going and working with T. Holder, because he had been working at the Adolphus Hotel in Dallas, and they broadcast from there. . . .

He wasn't honest. The funny thing about it, I didn't even notice. I wasn't paying it any attention. I was so wrapped up in writing and arranging . . . it didn't really make me much difference. Money back in those days wasn't too important to me. I was just amazed that I had this band that could play all this stuff.

Nat Towles

Towles, originally from New Orleans, organized a band in Austin, Texas, in the early 1930s that included several excellent musicians: Buddy Tate, tenor saxophone; Fred Beckett and Henry Coker, trombones; and C. Q. Price, alto saxophone. In 1936 Towles moved the band to Omaha, changing some personnel in the process, notably adding Sir Charles Thompson on piano. The Towles band was widely regarded as among the hottest of the late 1930s, but it never recorded. A portion of the band recorded four sides with Horace Henderson in 1940.

Buddy Tate: I joined on the Dallas end of Nat Towles's Band, me and Buster Smith. Buster Smith was with Basie's band, but when the band started going back . . . to Kansas City [from Little Rock], Buster and Joe Keith, the three of us went to Dallas and joined Nat Towles. . . . He had some good bookings up in the South Dakotas and places like that. So we settled in Omaha, Nebraska. . . .

We had a few novelty things and had a few singers, maybe four or five tunes that we used to sing at. We had more of that in Nat Towles's band, singing groups, like [in] Jimmie Lunceford [than in other bands].[20] Then I used to come to Kansas City with Nat Towles's band after I was in Omaha. . . .

We'd go find someplace to go every night. We could play all night long. We'd play a dance and then we'd go find where we could sit up and jam all night long, see what this cat's doing, you know.

Walter Harrold: Nat Towles didn't come around Omaha until 1935 or
'36 . . . and Nat had a good band. He had Buddy [Tate] on the tenor
saxophone . . . [and] a terrific band, but he never treated his men like
they were musicians; he just used them to make money. He didn't half
pay the guys any decent salary. He was a big shot himself; he'd go in
the restaurant and order a big steak, the guys couldn't afford a steak,
they'd go in there and get a ham sandwich. . . . If you asked him to loan
you five dollars he wouldn't do it, and I've heard many musicians tell
that experience. . . . That's why he didn't have too much luck with his
bands. He tried to hold 'em but they started spreading out, and they left
him all by hisself.

Lawrence Welk

Lawrence Welk was a virtuoso accordion player and led a smooth, highly
professional dance band. The presence of his orchestra in these accounts
highlights the wide range of styles that were popular in the Territories and
that fell under the broad category of big band music. As these musicians
recall, Welk's polka-flavored music was very popular in the heavily Ger-
manic and Scandinavian northern Midwest, and often won greater crowds
than the most prominent jazz orchestras of the day. William Saunders, for
example, recalls that when he played with the Tommy Douglas band they
would often suffer because they followed Welk on their circuit. Dancers
and clubowners would tell them that they drew only sparse crowds because
Welk had been in town the previous week and, with money for entertainment scarce in the Depression, they chose to dance to Welk. Saunders
attributes much of Welk's success to hard work; he rehearsed his band
constantly, always striving for a better, smoother sound.

Buddy Tate: Nat Towles took over that band that was already organized . . . in Omaha, Nebraska . . . but we had one booking agent. . . . We
played the jazz and Lawrence Welk played the polkas. Those were the
two bands. . . . He had his champagne thing. . . . He was very popular.

Walter Harrold: We [the Lloyd Hunter band] battled Lawrence Welk so
many times. A lot of times we met his band in North Fork, Nebraska.
Every time we played North Fork, we had to battle his band, and by
gosh, we'd get up there, play all our special arrangements, really puttin'
it on, blowing the roof off the place, when here he comes, plays his
little tunes, and the floor is packed and jammed. . . . Lawrence Welk, he
had that beat, he had that music, and they came there to hear him,
that's what they wanted. . . . They wouldn't dance [to us] until we played

a nice waltz or something slow. If we played some of them fast tunes
they wouldn't dance at all. . . .

Jesse Stone: Lawrence Welk had a band out at that time [c. 1935] and
he only had seven pieces. He was having it tough out there and he
wasn't playing [only] polkas and things then. He was trying to play jazz.
We would meet, because we had a favorite diner at night [where] we'd
always stop. He'd be going one way and I'd be going another. While we
were sitting there we would trade arrangements. Eating there and writing the parts out.

NOTES

1. Protests against jazz were plentiful. The town of Zion, Illinois, for example,
banned jazz in January 1921, ranking it with tobacco and alcohol as a sin their
citizens could do without. The term "jazz" itself was felt by many to have a sexual
connotation. Worse, its rhythms and the "wild" dancing it elicited were feared to
be leading young people to sexual abandon and degeneracy. Given the times, such
fearful expressions probably heightened interest in the music and its social setting.

2. Although experimental radio broadcasts of music had occurred as early as
1906, the first commercial radio stations didn't appear until 1920 with KDKA in
Pittsburgh and WWJ in Detroit. Almost from the start they broadcast music, at
first mostly "safe" music such as light classics, but soon including popular music
and jazz. By 1930 there were over thirteen million radios in American homes.

3. Commercial phonograph records preceded commercial radio broadcasts by
more than thirty years. Edison made the first wax cylinder recording in 1877, and
recorded the voices of many notable figures in the following year. His recordings
were sold commercially, but were fragile and expensive. The disc record, patented
by Emile Berliner in 1887, was far more commercially viable. Popular music and
comedy were staples of even the earliest recordings, and jazz was added in 1917.
Most important, recording technology was sufficiently simple that many small,
local record companies were formed. These companies often served "specialty"
markets, whether regional, ethnic, or stylistic, and by the mid-1920s many were
recording jazz.

The early decentralization of the recording industry gave a powerful boost to
the development of regional styles in all forms of music, including jazz. An artist
did not need to appeal to broad tastes to find a profitable record market. The
result was a proliferation of regionally popular artists who featured many different
styles of music.

4. The term "Territory" used in this context is probably an unintentionally
romantic allusion to the pre-statehood territorial status of many Midwestern states,
particularly Oklahoma, which attained statehood in 1907 after many years as
"Indian Territory."

5. A rough time-line shows that square dances and polkas were popular before
1890; schottisches, waltzes, and the two-step in the 1890s; the turkey trot—1900s;

the one-step, tango, hesitation and Boston waltz, and fox trot—1910s; the Charleston—1920s; and the lindy hop and jitterbug—1930s. Most Midwestern jazz musicians could and did play all these dances, as well as the popular jazz hits of the day and their own compositions.

6. Juke joints are rural nightclubs. The entertainment was usually informal, and gambling, drinking, and dancing would often go on through dawn.

7. "Sweet" was the common term for more sedate dance and concert music. Bands were often distinguished as being either "sweet" or "hot." The former would be likely to feature a mellow-voiced singer and play slower tunes, while the latter would be known for up-tempo, more strongly rhythmic songs.

8. "Gutbucket" is a slang term for a rough-toned, somewhat raucous, as opposed to smooth, performance style; it is also referred to as "low down," "funky," or "growling."

9. Taxi dances offered men the opportunity to dance with women by buying a cheap ticket (usually a nickel or dime a dance). Floor directors dictated the dance to be played and the tempo, and made sure to keep the tunes short, so the men would buy more tickets.

10. Head arrangements are derived from group or solo invention during a performance. The ability to create heads often distinguished the great bands from the merely good.

11. Jay McShann's first recording date (described in chapter 15) was an example of artistic manipulation by a record company.

12. Much of the farm belt suffered an earlier depression in 1921 when prices of farm products collapsed, and few had even partially recovered when the 1929 market crash occurred.

13. Barefield is referring to various bands as "schools" of music. These schools, or bands, cross-pollinated one another in the Midwest during the 1920s as musicians listened to their peers in concerts and clubs and as they shuttled among orchestras, always seeking a more promising or better paying job. This fluidity allowed ample opportunities for the transmission of new musical ideas and helped create an environment conducive to the development of new performance styles.

14. Quoted in *Esquire's World of Jazz*, 55.

15. Mary Lou Williams and Dick Wilson were both featured performers in Andy Kirk's Twelve Clouds of Joy, which was often based out of Oklahoma City.

16. Holder was actually closer to nineteen years old in 1917.

17. In a commonwealth band the income is split evenly among the members and, typically, the members vote on major band decisions, including where to play. Many bands of the era were commonwealth bands.

18. Herschel Evans became a featured soloist with the Count Basie Orchestra before his untimely death in 1939.

19. Originally from St. Joseph, Missouri, Coleman Hawkins was the first great saxophone player in jazz. He started playing with Jesse Stone, was featured with the Fletcher Henderson Orchestra in the mid-to-late twenties, and became a key figure in both swing and modern jazz.

20. Lunceford had one of the best known and hottest bands in the country during the thirties. Many of his best arrangements were by K.C. musicians, particularly Eddie Durham.

4

Tales from the Territories: The Twelve Clouds of Joy

The Territory bands that most occupy the memories and imaginations of Kansas City-era musicians are the Twelve Clouds of Joy and the Blue Devils. However while Andy Kirk was a disciplined, well-organized manager and leader of the Clouds, the Blue Devils were a commonwealth band whose lack of consistent leadership eventually destroyed the group. Their stories are, respectively, of perseverance and success, and exuberance and failure. In many ways their experiences exemplify the joys and sadnesses of road life in the twenties and thirties.

T. Holder's Twelve Clouds of Joy

T. Holder formed the first edition of the Twelve Clouds of Joy (a band that was not always twelve pieces) in Dallas, Texas, in 1925 and led it until he was dismissed by his fellow bandmembers in 1928. The band never recorded during Holder's tenure, but did establish its reputation as one of the most versatile and professional bands of the period. Among the outstanding performers in the first Clouds were Carl Smith, Harry Lawson, and T. Holder, trumpets; Buddy Tate, Earl Bostic, and Fats Wall, reeds; Lloyd Glenn, piano; and Andy Kirk, tuba. After being fired, T. Holder went on to lead many other bands through the 1970s, but never found as great an ensemble as the Clouds of Joy.

As the reminiscences of Holder himself and those of his bandmembers and colleagues make clear, T. was neither a skilled manager nor a very reliable bandleader. He was, however, a charismatic figure and an excellent musician who was typical of many of the first generation of jazzmen and bandleaders, relying on intuition rather than planning, and seeking good times above all.

In this book, he and Dude Lankford (who appears in chapters 1 and 11) are our links to the earliest days of Midwestern jazz. These men, and the history of the first edition of the Twelve Clouds of Joy, are colorful reminders of the funloving and reckless spirit that so often characterized jazz in the twenties. This spirit led to both the legendary qualities that Holder's Clouds of Joy and the Blue Devils enjoyed and, to a degree, their lack of success. In contrast, other ensembles, such as Andy Kirk's Twelve Clouds of Joy, Bennie Moten's Orchestra, and Count Basie's Orchestra, enjoyed lasting success, at least partly because they were able to temper their restless, free spirit with good band management.

T. Holder: [Forming the Clouds of Joy] was kind of a necessity. I had done gotten a little older and realized that I hadn't gotten much, wasn't going nowhere. I decided, I just told everybody, well, "I'm going to get up a band myself. We're just lettin' all this work go and we ain't doin' nothin'." I just decided, me and myself, I'd get me a little band, so I did. . . .

I was good at putting bands together and making it pay. I just gained the confidence of fellows, and then a bunch of musicians would get together. You got to see what you can maneuver. . . .

In Tulsa [after leaving the Alphonso Trent band] I had a twelve-piece band in the Louvre Ballroom called the Twelve Clouds of Joy. I organized the band myself. We stayed there about four years. . . . That was about 1925, '26. When the market crashed [in 1929] we was [still] making it at the Louvre.[1] Didn't have no money to lose in that. We threw our money away just as fast as we could get it. . . . I had nine pieces [first]. I think one of the guys in the [booking agent's] office named the band [the Twelve Clouds of Joy]. Mary Lou [Williams and] Andy Kirk came later. Jesse [Stone] came later. . . .

They got me fired [from the Clouds of Joy]. I was going with some little old girl in Dallas, Texas, and we was playing in Tulsa. I left the band and went down there and met my girl, you know. And they got the management together and fired me. . . . They kept on going. They hired a boy out of Kansas City, a trumpet player named Chester Clark, to take my place. [Andy Kirk] took over as leader, and put me out in them streets. I had a rich old lady in Dallas. My old lady's daddy had left her full of money; [so I] didn't care [about] nothin'. [Then I] didn't do nothing. Walk around, eat and sleep. . . . I didn't want no job. I had a good woman, didn't need to go noplace. . . .

Basie and them [the Blue Devils] knew me, and they was in Oklahoma City. They heard that I wasn't doing nothing, and they had that

job in Oklahoma City, so they sent over and got me, and I worked over
there with 'em for a while.

Claude Williams: I left [the Pettiford family band] to join the T. Holder
band in Tulsa. . . . T. was a good solo man and he [could] read pretty
nice [too]. . . . I might have been over in Tulsa jamming or something
and he heard me [and] hired me just to play fiddle. . . . I wasn't exactly
the first in there. They was going strong when I joined, I think this was
about '27. In fact, new personnel such as John Williams and Mary Lou
Williams came after me. . . . We got quite a few new members out of
Denver [including Andy Kirk]. . . .

[We would play] at the Louvre [Ballroom] for three months and then
go to Oklahoma City and play three months, . . . [just] jitney dances.
That's where you buy a bunch of tickets and there'd be a gang of girls
standing around and you just go and ask a girl for a dance and if she
accepts . . . you give them one of the tickets. The girl was just there to
dance, and the man had to pay for the dance. [In] those jitney dances
you'd get to play maybe two choruses, maybe two choruses and a half if
it's fast enough. The fella that was out there [the dancemaster], he
would call the different dances and you got to be ready to play whatever tempo he called. . . .

It was T. Holder's Twelve Clouds of Joy in the beginning, and they
had some kind of misunderstanding and all the boys, they sort of got
down [on] T. He wasn't handling things just right so we all just made up
our minds while we was in Tulsa to get another manager. . . . One night
. . . T. took a night off, like . . . and went down to Dallas. I think he went
down to get some money because he had drawed up too much of the
money. T. liked to gamble, you know. He went down to Dallas to get
the money but he didn't make it back Saturday night to pay the fellas,
and that was the bitter end. That did it. . . . So we all quit and we made
Andy Kirk [the leader] since he was just about the oldest, and he was
more settled than any of the rest of the fellas. . . .

T. liked a good time . . . and T. would lose a lot of rest. I mean, we
had trouble; . . . sometimes [he'd] go to sleep on the bandstand. Gambling all night and playing the dance all night didn't really leave him
too much noway. The rest of the fellas took care of business. . . . When
he did come back [from Dallas] he had money to pay [the band] but
they had all just [quit]. . . . So that's the way the band just worked over
into Andy Kirk's Twelve Clouds of Joy.

Ernie Williams: Man, why T. Poppa! Yeah, that man could get a band
together faster than any man in the country. . . . You see, one Christmas
day . . . T. left Oklahoma City and he . . . done taken all the . . . money

and gone to Dallas. . . . Chester Clark found out . . . and [he] want to
shoot old T. . . . See, T. liked to gamble all the time. Could play, too.

Buster Smith: T. Holder was a great man. He had Andy Kirk's band,
the Clouds of Joy. They got to fussing and going on and made T. Holder
mad. . . . He ran off with the band's whole week pay, come through
Oklahoma City and got him a car, talked with us [the Blue Devils], and
left, come on down here [to Dallas], was down here three weeks, and
come back through Oklahoma City with a band, blew down Andy Kirk.
Buddy Tate was in the band, had a whole big repertoire. . . .

The reason Andy Kirk's brass section, trumpet section was so good is
that T. Holder trained 'em.

Buddy Tate: [The Clouds of Joy were] the first big band I worked with
after I left the family band [and] . . . the St. Louis Merrymakers . . . in
Wichita Falls, Texas. . . .

[I] was playing around in Texas . . . and we'd go and listen to this
[Austin, Texas] band, T. Holder and I. It was organized, playing good
arrangements . . . but they didn't have any leader . . . with a reputation.
So old T. went over and talked to them and they said, "We'd like to
have you for the leader." He says, "I have to keep my tenor player
[Buddy Tate] with me." There was three brothers in that band. . . .

So he takes over the leadership of this band . . . and we go out West,
Midland, Texas, [to] an oil boom [town]. [There] was a lot of money out
there, . . . and we worked for about six weeks. Or maybe two months,
playing every night and the band was . . . by then . . . really on track.

We were making about eighty-five dollars for three days, . . . which
was a lot of money then. 'Course, it was an oil boom town. Then we'd
go to Oklahoma City, play on a Sunday night; . . . play a dance and
make twenty dollars a man. . . . We'd split the swag, is what we'd call
it. . . . With bands like the T. Holder band we used to get a dollar fifty
for a couple . . . if you're popular enough. . . .

We had a boy, Lloyd Glenn was the name, he was the writer [for the
band][2] . . . and we were doing heads [arrangements] too. . . . The band
was very successful. . . . We would come as far as Kansas City, then we'd
go back there as Territory bands [would] . . . to Texas and Louisiana and
all places like that down South. . . .

It was nice, we all had our own car(s), . . . maybe three or four cars in
the band. We did have a big Packard . . . and T. Holder had a Cadil-
lac. . . .

We had about two big ballrooms in Oklahoma City and whenever
we'd come in we'd play six weeks. . . . When they close [a band out] you

had to battle that band that was coming in. . . . We'd get together [too], we had a very good band.

Of course T. [Holder] . . . really missed the boat, because he was really an organizer. He could put a band together in a week. Man, it was fantastic. . . . I stayed with that band, oh, must've been seven, eight years.

Earl Bostic Joins the T. Holder Clouds of Joy

Buddy Tate: We had . . . a saxophone player that played . . . like . . . Frankie Trumbauer.[3] . . . But he wasn't too interested [in playing solos] so we had him playing first [saxophone].[4] In the middle of a passage sometimes he would put the saxophone down on the stand and polish his nails. So we said, "Man, we got to get a saxophone player."

So we were looking for somebody, a good man, because we had some hard styles to play. We used to play an arrangement by King Oliver called the "Mule-Face Blues" and "Louisiana Bo-Bo" and boy, it was hard. Those people that wrote in those days didn't know how to orchestrate right.[5] . . .

We were playing a dance one night in Tulsa. Dances would very seldom go any later than twelve o'clock in those days, but when you get in town you see all the guys on the street, the musicians, and they'd gather around and talk. . . . One of the fellas, by the name of Bill Lewis, says, "There's a kid up here, man, he's fantastic. He makes snakes. This kid does everything on the sax." . . . So I went up and listened to him, sure enough. He was all over that horn, boy. He was triple tonguing and doing everything. . . . I walked up and I introduced myself, says, "I like the way you sound." He says, "I know you, my name is Earl Bostic." I [asked him if] he was interested [in joining the band]. He said, "I never worked with a big band, I don't know if I could make it." I says, "You let us worry about that." . . .

So I asked him to come down [to hear us] and think about it. . . . We played this [number], this is the one that really gets the crowd; sure enough, this boy [the other sax player] went through his act, sits the saxophone down. So when we got off I got all the guys over to meet him [Bostic] and he says, "The band really sounds fine, fellas, but you do need a saxophone player." . . . So we told him about the money [he would make]. He says, "I'm ready." We carried him right in the car. He wouldn't even go home, got a toothbrush, maybe a little overnight bag and . . . so we carried him on down to Seminole [Oklahoma]. This was about 1930.

Now after we get him [Bostic] down there we . . . wonder, can he read [music]? We didn't know. . . . So he's just playing . . . [and] the band director called "Louisiana Bo-Bo," that hard one. We'd been rehearsing the reed section and the brass, the rhythm. Then we'd come together [and] think we can play it good enough. . . . He didn't even look at it. We said, "This cat must be crazy. . . . We gonna have fun here." . . .

So we says [to Bostic], "Just knock it off; what tempo you want." He says, "I'll try to stumble through it." You know we made our mistake. We let him stomp it off and we didn't get out of the introduction. He ran through it like it'd throw your pants off, that's the God's truth. . . . The joke was on us. Some of the guys that got out of the introduction just played eight bars. When they got through there was nobody [playing] but him and the drummer . . . [and] the drummer was tired. . . . We let him alone after that. . . .

Oh man, he could read. . . . He was a virtuoso. . . . He could play . . . way out, progressive,[6] but he made it big, just playing the melody. That's what people wanted to hear.

Howard Litwak and I encountered T. Holder in the early spring of 1977 in a nursing home in Muskogee, Oklahoma. He had entered the home only recently, as Jay McShann had been astounded to find T. performing in Joplin, Missouri, as late as 1973. By the time of our meeting T. had just lost a leg as a result of diabetes, but was in good spirits and eager to talk about his adventure-filled life. Recollections were occasionally cloudy but his spirit was indomitable. He looked forward with great anticipation to a visit by his ex-wife, the same woman who had sustained him after he was fired from the Clouds of Joy.

Andy Kirk and the Twelve Clouds of Joy

In contrast to many bands of the era (notably Walter Page's Blue Devils) who were continually fraught with bad luck and missed opportunities, much of what Andy Kirk touched when he took over leadership of the Clouds of Joy in 1929 turned to gold. After the Bennie Moten band, popular as national recording artists from 1926, and Count Basie, who reached national attention in 1936, Andy Kirk's Clouds of Joy was the Territory band to achieve greatest national recognition, enjoying a string of hit recordings from 1936 through 1945.

Although known as a "sweet" band rather than a hot band like the Blue Devils and Basie, Kirk had several strong soloists, including: Mary Lou Williams, piano; Dick Wilson and, later, Don Byas, saxophone; Ed "Crack" McNeil and, later, Ben Thigpen, drums; Floyd Smith, guitar; and Pha Terrell, vocals. Of these, Mary Lou Williams was the most important, despite her being an accidental addition to the band in 1929.[7] She quickly emerged as not only an outstanding pianist but also as an unusually creative composer and arranger. Among the keys to the band's later success was the presence of "the Lady Who Swings the Band." Mary Lou went on to a very successful career as a soloist and composer.

Claude Williams: I joined [the Clouds of Joy] . . . in about '27 . . . [and] Andy [Kirk] was there before me. . . . He was playing tuba, but he could also play sax, so . . . when he took over he hired an upright bass man and he started playing sax with the group. . . .

When we worked for T. [Holder, we] had a settled thing, steady work between those two places [Tulsa and Oklahoma City] and we didn't need to go nowhere else then. When Andy took over, that's when we first came up to Topeka . . . and then we got in touch with this booker, I believe it was the Serviss Corporation, and they're the ones that started booking us all out East and around. . . .

We did some recordings right after we left T. . . . We were in Chicago . . . and made a number called "Snag It." Oh boy, we must have messed up about two dozen [takes of the recording]. Every time Harry Lawson, the trumpet player, would get to his solo . . . he couldn't think of nothing to play. . . . It was real exciting. That was my, . . . and a lot of us, first time to do any recording. . . . We went to Chicago strictly to record. We wasn't working there. . . .

At different times . . . in Tulsa and Oklahoma City . . . we would switch off with other bands [playing ballroom engagements]. . . . I think George E. Lee did a switch, and between George and Bennie Moten they had the best bands up here [in Kansas City] then. We had some better musicians than either one of them did, but it took us a little while after we left T. to get our band situated for a regular dance. We had all our arrangements cut up into minute and a half, and not over two minutes, all for the jitney dance. So we had to get new arrangements. . . .

Mary Lou and [her husband] John Williams came in the band together . . . [and] they were there before we quit T. They was both on a . . . TOBA show, Gonzelle White.[8] . . . She was playing good piano but we just wanted a sax man. A fella named Marion Jackson was the piano player.

The way that Mary got started playing piano with the group was, we played . . . a week or two . . . in Topeka, and . . . me and Jack, that was the piano player, was riding together. I had a Packard sport roadster. . . . We stayed in Topeka, and we was drinking alcohol and orange juice, that was still Prohibition days. After we partied two or three hours we had in our minds to come on to Kansas City. . . . I drove practically all the way, within ten or fifteen miles of Kansas City and I'm getting sleepier by the minute. I looked over at Jackson and he was wide awake. . . .

Boy, that cat drove about five miles, went to sleep, and . . . we was just lucky going off the road we didn't hit nothing. . . . It just totaled the car . . . and Jack . . . shattered the bone in both legs, so he was laid up . . . and that's when Mary Lou started to playing in the band. I don't know what happened to Jack.

Buddy Tate: The Clouds of Joy . . . didn't change much [when Kirk took over]. . . . [It was] pretty much the same band [as T. Holder's]. . . . Only thing was, [when] Mary Lou [Williams] came in, she started doing . . . quite a bit of the writing . . . and Dick Wilson took my place. [Wilson was a] very good tenor player, stylist. They got Dick Wilson [from] Zack Whyte's band, that had broken up. He joined them and [soon afterward] they made "Until the Real Thing Comes Along" and they were in. . . .

The singer was Pha Terrell. Beautiful ballad singer. The band was very smooth, . . . light, and they recorded very, very good . . . [Pha Terrell] never hit anybody in the world [but] he'd knock out, I mean down — out. Little skinny cat, man. You know people used to jive with him and they say, must be a faggot, high voice, and the name, Pha. They soon found out, if they tackled him. . . .

[I did regret not joining Andy Kirk in 1935 when I had the chance] but not for long . . . because later I ended up with Basie. Then maybe if I had [joined] I wouldn't have ever gone with Basie. . . . But when they would come back out, through Omaha, they'd drive big cars and everything, really on the big time, I'd say, "I could've been in that."

BILL "COUNT" BASIE. *Born 8/21/1904, Red Bank, New Jersey. Died 4/ 26/1984, Hollywood, Florida. Originally a drummer. Toured with TOBA road shows from 1924 to 1927, when the Gonzelle White show disbanded in Kansas City. Played piano in local clubs and the Eblon movie theater until joining Walter Page's Blue Devils in 1928. Joined Bennie Moten's Orchestra in 1929 and formed his own band, with Buster Smith, upon Moten's death in 1935. Continued to lead his big band until his death in 1984, with a brief interruption to lead a nine-piece band between 1950 and 1952.*

There were two, three large bands in Kansas City at the time [early 1930s], George and Julia Lee and [the] Andy Kirk and Chauncey Downs Orchestras. . . . I'd be listening [to other piano players] to learn some ideas [and] . . . I think Mary Lou [Williams] was right on top of all of it. I don't think anybody was as great as Mary Lou at that time. I think Mary Lou was number one.

MARY LOU WILLIAMS. *Born 5/8/1910, Atlanta, Georgia. Died 5/28/81, Durham, North Carolina. Piano and arranger. Learned to play in Pitts-*

*burgh, Pennsylvania, and began performing professionally at age four.
Went on the road as a pianist in 1925. Married saxophonist John Williams
in 1927. Became pianist for the Twelve Clouds of Joy in 1929. Immediately
achieved prominence. Recognized as being among the outstanding pianists
and arrangers in jazz history, and among the pioneer modern jazz stylists.
Active as a performer and teacher until her death in 1981.*

My husband . . . John Williams, Andy Kirk hired him, they were in
Oklahoma then, playing all the Territory. They got a job in Kansas City
and they decided to make their headquarters there. I used to sit and
jam and travel with the band, but they had their own pianist. I did this
until we reached Philadelphia, and something happened to him [the regular pianist] on one of the shows, and I jumped on the Steinway and
played. The owner of the theater said to Andy Kirk, "You don't need
that man, just take the little girl." That's how I got the job. I guess I
was about sixteen or seventeen. . . .

Andy Kirk's band had the greatest readers. At one time most of the
musicians didn't read, and Andy Kirk had terrific readers in his band.
We'd pull out an arrangement and play it on the job without rehearsing
it. We never had any that couldn't really read. They spelled, which
means they were slower than the good readers. . . . [The musicians who
couldn't read] made better improvisational musicians. They had nothing
to stop them. . . . They could do it without thinking about reading
notes. . . .

I used to have crazy ideas and never write 'em down. Andy Kirk used
to come to the house at eleven o'clock in the morning, he'd stay until
twelve or one at night, and I had arranged two things for the band, to
come back that night, 'cause I was sick of sitting there twelve hours.
The only thing was wrong I think was the trombone and tenor. So he
showed me how to voice them and I started arranging from that day
on. . . .

During that period you had three saxophones. I needed a fourth because we were doing bigger parts. So I used a trumpet man blowing in
a hat so he would sound like a saxophone. . . .

Andy Kirk's band played [for] everything. They played for proms . . .
and dances. We played everything, and then we'd come back swinging
like Count Basie. . . . [We'd] play sweet music until twelve o'clock, then
everybody'd start playing. They were afraid of losing the dancers.

Buster Smith: There was only one band that we [the Blue Devils] was
kind of shy of, them cats were tough, and that was Andy Kirk. . . . We
had a better reed section than they did, but they had a better brass section than we did. We couldn't get our brass to hit and phrase like they
phrased.

NOTES

1. Actually, T. Holder had probably already been dismissed from the Clouds of Joy by the time of the stock market crash in the fall of 1929.

2. Lloyd Glenn became a prominent pianist and arranger in early rhythm and blues and rock recording sessions. He currently works out of Los Angeles.

3. Trumbauer was a very popular C-melody saxophone player, and longtime partner of the legendary Bix Beiderbecke. Before Coleman Hawkins burst upon the scene Trumbauer was the most influential saxophone player in jazz.

4. In jazz ensembles the "first" player in a section—either horns (trumpet, cornets, and trombones) or reeds (saxophones and clarinets)—led, but would rarely solo. The featured soloist usually played the second, third, or fourth part of the orchestration.

5. A skilled orchestrater would arrange a piece to fit the comfortable playing range of the instruments available. Early jazz bands often lacked skilled arrangers, and musicians were forced to undergo considerable instrumental gyrations to perform a piece as written.

6. "Progressive" jazz in this context refers to modern, post-swing forms of jazz, in which traditional melodies were less emphasized, and musicians had greater freedom to use dissonance, complex rhythms, and other practices that often resulted in music that was less readily accessible to the casual listener. Tate's point is that Earl Bostic possessed the skill to play progressive jazz, but preferred to concentrate on more popular and commercial performance styles.

7. Mary Lou Williams first recorded with the Clouds of Joy in 1929, but didn't join the band as a full-time member until 1931.

8. Count Basie was with the Gonzelle White show when it disbanded, stranding him in Kansas City in 1927.

5

Tales from the Territories: The Blue Devils

Of all the bands figuring in the Kansas City story, none excites the imagination more than the Blue Devils. Rough and ready, wild and reckless, supremely talented, undisciplined barnstormers, they were the stuff of legend. The band's major figures were: original leader Walter Page, bass and saxophone player, the brilliant foundation underpinning some of the hottest bands in swing, from the Blue Devils through Bennie Moten and Count Basie; Buster Smith, alto saxophone player, composer, arranger, force of stability, and true loyalist; and Ernie Williams, drummer, blues-shouting vocalist, director, and, through part-time tailoring and odd jobs during the many hard times, financial supporter of the band.

Other musicians who were privileged to be among the Blue Devils were: Lester Young, Reuben Roddy, and Theodore Ross, reeds; Oran "Hot Lips" Page (Walter Page's cousin), and James Simpson, trumpets; Eddie Durham, Druie Bess, and Dan Minor, trombones; Edward "Crack" McNeil, drums; Willie Lewis and Bill "Count" Basie, piano; and Jimmy Rushing, vocals. It was the strongest lineup of that era in the Midwest, partly because the band possessed such extraordinary spirit and enthusiasm. Unfortunately, that energy was matched only by the lack of management skill and bad luck that led to their breakup. Several from the Blue Devils alumni organization then went on to provide the seeds of Bennie Moten's final and greatest band, and of Count Basie's original orchestra.

The Blue Devils began in 1923 in Kansas City as Billy King's Road Show, a traveling vaudeville/carnival troupe. Trombonist Ermir "Bucket" Coleman was the titular head of the band, but Walter Page was its musical leader. Page, a big (over two hundred and fifty pounds), quiet man, was among the best-educated musicians in the region, having studied under both Major N. Clark Smith and Charles Watts, K.C.'s two great music teachers of the twenties. Page also attended the University of Kansas as a music student.[1]

The Billy King Road Show disbanded in 1925 in Oklahoma City, where Page kept the band and renamed it "Walter Page's Original Blue Devils." Buster Smith was one his first additions as Page began expanding from the original nine pieces to thirteen. Also in this early group were Harry Young-blood and James Simpson, trumpets; Reuben Roddy, saxophone; Willie Lewis, piano; Ermir Coleman, trombone; Edward McNeil, drums; and Jimmy Rushing and Ernie Williams, vocals. It is significant that most of this group stayed with the band until its demise in 1933. Important later additions included Dan Minor, who joined in 1927; Lips Page and Eddie Durham, early 1928; Bill Basie, July 1928 (Basie stayed for only about eight months); Druie Bess, 1929; and Lester Young, 1932.

Moten's raids of the Blue Devils began with Bill Basie in 1929, soon followed by Lips Page, Jimmy Rushing, and Eddie Durham. Finally Walter Page himself left for Moten in 1931 and turned the band over to Leroy "Snake" White. They continued on an increasingly difficult and unprofitable series of tours until their final disaster in Beckley, West Virginia, in 1933, a story told here by Buster Smith.

From 1925 until 1933, however, they were among the finest bands in the region and were certainly the most romantically appealing. They epitomized the spirit of the era in many ways. As you read their accounts try to envision the scene—dance halls packed with enthusiastic dancers, long drives between jobs on dusty Southwestern roads, and good friends enjoying their music and each other.

Ernie Williams: The original Blue Devils was Billy King's [Road Show in Kansas City]. . . . Willie Lewis was the [first] piano player with the Blue Devils. Originally he'd . . . do all the arrangements for the band, 'fore he left. . . . We broadcasted every day at Oklahoma City. . . .

Me and [Walter] Page went down the track and got Buster Smith. [He] was working upstairs over at Ella B. Moore's theater . . . in Dallas. . . . I used to play in there and Buster would play the clarinet. [Then we] brought Buster back to Oklahoma City.

Buster Smith: Oklahoma City is where it started at [for me], the Blue Devils. Then they came here [Dallas] in '25. Wasn't but eight of 'em, and they gigged for a little while around here. I was playing with a little house band, wasn't but three of us, piano player, and a drummer and myself. I had an old A-flat clarinet and we just played all night long for a dollar and a half. I got tired of that and old Ernie Williams came by to my house, begged me to go with him, said, "You can play the lead on whatever we play." Well, I knowed the tunes. . . .

The first man that had it [led the band] was a fellow named Coleman, we called him Bucket. He was kind of hard to get along with and the boys fired him and turned it over to Walter Page. But Walter Page, he didn't have much business about him, why he just got tired of rassling with it. . . .

Willie Lewis, Coleman, and Walter Page, they was the main ones and they were good musicians, all of 'em. And they played in tune. . . .

After I got up there the piano player, Willie Lewis is his name, great reader, sight reader . . . showed me a little bit about the notes, music and what-not. So I just sat right down and stayed on my clarinet, and got to reading a little bit. They put some music up before me, kind of caught on and the other boys was following me. After I learned to read a little bit I come to writing music for the saxophones. I didn't know anything about the trumpet section, brass, so I studied the book a little bit, found out the trumpets was all in the same key the tenor [saxophone] was and the trombone was in the same key, in the bass clef, the saxophone was, the alto. . . .

I started writing for all of them then, wasn't nobody arranging in the band except me; they didn't have no arranger except maybe some arranger would come through there. . . . We used to do a lot of that experimenting with sounds. Sometimes they wouldn't sound right . . . and we'd have to bring 'em together, have some of the men double. Some chords you couldn't make no five-part harmony. . . . [Walter Page] could have [arranged] but he wouldn't try. Walter Page was very smart, great reader, too. He was a good musician. All them old fellows were good musicians.

Sam Price: I remember hearing the Blue Devils [in the mid-twenties, in Dallas, Texas]. When the saxophones would be playing a riff,[2] Jimmy Rushing would be singing and Lips [Page] would . . . play anything he wanted to. . . . He didn't have to play with the [trumpet] section. He'd be up high, Rush'd be singing and the rhythm and the band'd be playing something else. It'd be fantastic.

Ernie Williams: [We] had them Blue Monday parties [in Oklahoma City], early in Monday morning, and . . . the girls would put their brown powder on, and the other girls would step out. . . . The kids going to school would . . . slip off [and dance] and [then] go on back to school. . . .

I know the time we played out in East Texas. . . . You have a bandstand out in the country. The guys would just drive their cars up, and the lights from the automobiles flooded the stage so the audience would dance. . . . Them guys would take the money out, just throwed it [at us] and [we'd] take the money and divide it up, . . . take the expenses out of what's left, get the gasoline and oil and be gone to another town. 'Way out in East Texas.

Buster Smith: We got some jobs in Arkansas. It [was] two years [that] we got to going down there, playing there all summer, [and then] we'd leave there and come back to Kansas City and play all the winter. We had about eight days off out of the whole year. Wasn't making much money, about thirty-five, forty dollars a week.

We got quite a few of them fairs in the summer time; they'd have fairs all around [like in] Huron, South Dakota, and we'd go up there and play them fairs . . . [for] white audiences. See, they had people all around them ferris wheels at night, and sometimes [even] in the daytime they'd come and want to dance, play a matinee there. We'd stay in some big private homes, some big boarding houses. Most of them fairs up in that part of the country, they run a week. Yeah, we loved those. We got good pay from them. . . .

We had about three repertoires, and that's to catch all the people, depending on the kind of music they like. That's what kept me busy writing music all the time. We had one repertoire that wasn't nothing but sweet music, and we had one that had a lot of waltzes in it and some of the country music — like "Turkey in the Straw" and all that stuff there. . . .

We had a little technique in order to get a crowd at a dance. We had five or six boys run around with prospective customers. . . . We had . . . half try to do it with the upper class. Make a play with them, hang around them, and them were the guys that went dressed up all the time. But we had some other boys that were liable to put on some overalls or anything, get into town, go over and shoot pool, around all the scallywags and things like that, [we'd say], "We'll meet you at the dance," and they'd all be there.

Jesse Stone: The biggest upset we ever had in our life . . . happened to be in Sioux City, Iowa, . . . and it was a battle of bands between Page and Jesse Stone. We got up on the stand first because we were considered like a house band there. We played there regularly. Well, we started out with some of our light things, little ballads. And these guys [the Blue Devils] hit right off the reel, *wham*, and they didn't let up all night long. They had a tough band.

They were just sharper, cleaner, more powerful, and they had more material, which was an upset to us because we had five arrangers, including myself. How could anybody have more material than we had? We had a book about that thick, you know, all arrangements. These guys came in with *three* books. Three books the same thickness. . . .

The vocalist . . . Ernie Williams . . . was very impressive. And they did group singing. That was the first time we ever heard any rhythm talk by a band . . . and the people went crazy about it. It was like a chant, like an African chant or something. They didn't do it with a loud voice. Everybody's voice seemed to be like the same level and it had a heck of an effect. . . . They would do riffs when they would sing. . . .

The reed section was very impressive [too]. But individually they weren't any better than our musicians. When it came to individual solos . . . we could blow them out. But collectively they had a sharp hitting band . . . and their arrangements were interesting. It looked as though they had spent a lot of time rehearsing.

One of the reasons [they beat us] is because we were complacent. We had enjoyed such a successful tour that we were just killing everybody . . . and these guys, they were actually ragged. Their uniforms were tattered and they came in an old beat-up . . . airport bus. It was about ready to cave in. We said, "It ain't no problem." And they gave us the biggest shock of our whole career. . . .

It didn't [hurt us, though]. . . . Even though they made a big impression they didn't follow it up because they were only here a week and [then] back to their own territory. . . .

No booking agent was handling them then. They were booking themselves. We were crying for a return engagement . . . and we were ready for them the second time around, but it never happened because the band disbanded.

Buster Smith: We played a whole bunch of battles. We used to play rings around Bennie [Moten], because he wanted to play all them old tunes he made, and he'd stick with them a lot. . . .

We had a better reed section than Bennie [Moten] had. He didn't have but one man to get off and that was Jack Washington [baritone saxophone player], and he didn't want to make no solo unless somebody made it [wrote it out] for him. We'd get off. We built the band around them solo things.[3] We had Lips [Page] on trumpet over there and we had Dee Stewart . . . second trumpet. In other words we tried to be a band that could just get off instead of just read the music.

The Moten Raids

Booker Washington: We [the Bennie Moten band] were down in Oklahoma City. The Blue Devils and our band would play a place named Forest Park. . . . They had big dance halls then, one band'd get on one side, the other band get on the other side. We played against each other. . . . Well naturally, I'm going to say we came out on top. But that don't make it so. The Blue Devils had a real band. 'Course, Bennie Moten was king around here at that time. . . .

Bennie couldn't pull . . . Basie . . . off [his job with the Blue Devils right away]. . . . Basie stayed down around there, did all the little shows, but when we [got] the big jobs [then] Basie [joined] and [he and] Bennie would play piano. . . . Then he added more pieces and we made a tour. He added Hot Lips Page [and] Jimmy Rushing. . . . This is when the Blue Devils broke up.

Buster Smith: Most of the time we lived out of a paper sack. You stayed out on the road all the time, and nobody never had enough money to amount to nothing. We just lived from hand to mouth, but the boys all were happy, we were glad just to be able to play music. Kept the band together. The band would be twelve, thirteen pieces, fourteen, and dropped down, sometimes wouldn't be even but three or four. Most all of 'em would leave after a while, especially Walter, Walter Page. . . .

Bennie Moten was after Walter Page, in fact, Bennie Moten was after a whole lot of us in there. He first got Joe Keyes [out of the band, in 1929]. I got him out of Houston. . . . He and his three brothers were all musicians down there, so he was a good trumpet player, a good reader, so we got him into the Blue Devils. Bennie needed a trumpet player so he stole him.

Then the next man he stole [was] Jimmy Rushing. The next man he got was Hot Lips Page. At the same time he was still after me but I didn't want to leave Ernie [Williams], . . . and then another thing. I knowed I was going to throw a man out of a job, and that was Harlan Leonard [Leonard was then Moten's alto saxophone player]. See, they was going to let Harlan Leonard go for me. That's what kept me from going there. If it made me rich I wouldn't do it. . . .

I stuck together with Ernie. He didn't do nothing but try to play a little drums, but we got some better drummers so we just put him in front of the band, directing the band. Everybody thought he was the leader but he wasn't the leader. [He would] sing a little bit you know.

Lester Young Joins the Blue Devils

Druie Bess: I went down there [to Oklahoma] with the Blue Devils and I stayed with them about four years, '29, '30, '31, '32. [In] '33 that band fell to pieces in Beckley, West Virginia. . . . That band was terrific [though]. . . . That was about the best band in the West at that time.

None of them was outshadowed in that band. And when Lester Young come in . . . it was just terrific. . . .

I never will forget it. It was upstairs in a joint. He was playing "After You've Gone" . . . and Page says, "Who's that fast saxophone? . . . I'm going to get him in my band." We had just drove up there . . . and this boy . . . ran upstairs . . . and got ahold of Lester. . . . They talked to him and talked to him, and we was working out of Minneapolis anyway, and Page got him into the band. He was in the band about two years, and every time he played, played something different.

Buster Smith: The band got all tore up there [after Moten began to raid the band] and he [Ernie Williams] and I kept on reorganizing it, and ended up in Minneapolis and that's where we got old Lester Young. We played a big dance up there and we got through that night, we went by the club where Lester Young and Frank Hines and Eddie Barefield was playing. We needed a good tenor player, we had a player but he wasn't a get-off man, he could just read, so Lester's such a good reader and a get-off man too, so we just finally stole him. In fact we tried to get him to go the next day, but he wouldn't go because he was working, "No, I ain't going nowhere."

So I went up there and sat in with them that night. They thought I was playing a little something, so we said we had to get that boy. . . . We [had] bought some new Fords, two of us, so we went back in town, we just passed through there, we was off a couple of days, and he looked and see us with brand-new cars, he thought we was raising sin, making big money, got some brand-new cars. We looked around and here he come with his bag, yeah, suitcase, and horn and got right on in the car. . . .

[Barefield] was great. [Alto saxophonist Eddie Barefield was also in the band with Lester Young.] We wanted him too, but we didn't have a place for him then. We had Theodore Ross on first alto. [Lester] could play baritone too and clarinet. Walter Page was playing baritone and bass fiddle and bass horn, he played all three of 'em. After Walter Page heard Lester playing baritone he said, "We sure need this boy to keep me from doubling on baritone." I had gotten to writing some parts for the baritone and he would have to keep blowing right along with the reed section.

[Then] we didn't have but three reeds, Lester Young, myself, and [Theodore] Ross. That was two alto and a tenor. In order to get that big sound . . . we got some C-melody reeds and put 'em in the altos, and went and got some baritone reeds and put it on the tenor and that made it loud. It gave us that big sound. . . .

After Walter Page left we made Leroy White, we called him Snake

White, [the leader]. We tried to give the leadership to Lester [Young], he said, "Buster you take it." Well, I didn't have time to hustle those jobs, 'cause I had to do all the arranging, 'cause I was writing music every day. So Ernie said he didn't want it, so we gave it to Snake White . . . and that's when it looked like bad luck hit us.

Ended up going to St. Louis and a fellow there carried us on down to Virginia in an old raggedy bus, got in the mountains there and all that snow, and broke down and were there two or three days before we could get out of there. We went down and played a few dates, and in Lynchburg, Virginia, the banjo player quit us. That was his home, Reuben Lynch.

A commonwealth band was what the trouble was. That's where I found out that anything commonwealth could never amount to nothing. . . . The thing is, there's thirteen of us, whenever we wanted to do something, accept a job, we have to sit down and have a discussion, and we'd always have voting on it and seven would vote for it and six would vote against it. Or vice versa. It looked like everywhere we'd get a chance to get a good job somewhere, that seven would vote against; they'd want a little more money.

Like when we got to Cincinnati, Fats Waller was playing at [radio station] WLW, and he had a little four- or five-piece band.[4] He liked us and wanted us to sit in with him out there and work regularly. He offered us, I think it was eight hundred dollars a week. We wasn't doing anything there. . . . So we got to talking on it, and seven of 'em said we ought to get a thousand dollars, . . . "That's Fats Waller, he's making plenty of money." We couldn't never get together on it so we ended up going on back down to Virginia. Went all the way to Newport News and that's where we got stranded there.

Ernie Williams: We had a commonwealth band. We split up all the [money]. We didn't care, 'cause food then [was cheap]. . . . Well you see, at that particular time, there wasn't but one or two guys had some money. I hate to say this, but I was the one that could get over the money a little bit. . . . I used to get money from the . . . oil rights. . . . It was on my property down there [in Oklahoma]. . . . My Grandma owned it. They would say, "You don't have to worry about nothing, man.". . .

See, the management's makin' money, we didn't get any, [so] I'd be out there hustlin' to do somethin' else. I could make me some money [and] I didn't care. I'd go out, play, fix up, sold [things], do anything you know. Shoot a little craps. At that time I was gambling. . . .

We'd take the money out, take all [the] expenses out and split the money up. Sometimes we'd [be] on the road, didn't have a quarter, we'd have sardines, but didn't have nothing.

The End of the Road

Buster Smith: We ended up back in Martinsville, Virginia, and that's all
the further that we could get. Some doctor there had a dance hall up
over a drug store. He couldn't afford to pay us except about once a
week. We got stranded there and wouldn't make enough money to pay
our rent hardly.

A boy came from Bluefield, West Virginia, and he said he had a job
for us back over in Bluefield. . . . He was a youngster, about twenty,
twenty-one years old, and he thought he could take the band and make
some money with it. But he told us a story. . . .

So we hired two cabs—we done lost our cars, broke down, had to
leave some of them—to take us over to Bluefield. We found the boy
had us playing in a little old place there that wouldn't hold fifty people,
and we was supposed to be getting a salary, and it ended up that we
was playing for the door.[5] . . . It was a little white place we was playing
at and we found that most of the people liked that country music. We
had a few tunes in there we had, we could play country music, . . .
waltzes, and sweet music and stuff like that, . . . but 90 percent of the
music was built around that jump stuff, you know.

We played there about three or four days and Zack Whyte heard
about us being there in Bluefield, had a big band in Cincinnati, so he
came down there in a big bus, great big Greyhound bus; he didn't want
all the men, he wanted nine. He wanted most of the reed section and a
couple of the trumpet players; he didn't want the rhythm section. Said,
"No, man, if you're not going to take us all we're not going to go."

The taxicab drivers is waiting for us to make that week so they could
get their money. We owed them seventy dollars. They got scared that
we was going to run off without paying them, so they went up there
and garnisheed the instruments, so we couldn't move. The law come
down there and let us play with the instruments, and when we'd get
through playing at night they'd get the instruments and carry them on
to jail. Drums and all, bass fiddle too.

So there we were. Well, all right. That made the man at the hotel get
scared; he put us out of the hotel. The law had the instruments, so he
didn't have any security, except some old raggedy clothes we had.

The funny thing is the trumpet players got smart, they got to sticking
their instruments out the window before the law would get there, let the
law be walking with [just] the case. George Hudson was one of 'em.

We ran into an old boy, heard about us having the trouble there, he
lived way out on the suburbs of town. He knew me. He said, "What
you all going to do?" I said, "We're going to hobo away from here."

I think six of the boys sent back home, sent for the people to get 'em some money to get tickets to get back home on, ride a train or bus or something. But the seven, we couldn't get along, and I was in the bunch. So this old boy gave us $2.80. He said, "That's all I got."

We knew a few people back there in St. Louis, 'cause this agent that carried us down there first, he lived in St. Louis, so we thought we'd get back there and get with him, and he'd do something for us. . . .

We had to leave the instruments. We found a colored lawyer who said it would cost us two hundred dollars to get those instruments out of there. He said, "I feel for you. I'm a colored man just like you, I'm going to go on there and get those instruments and let you all play, but I'll have to stay with you and keep the instruments until I get my money back." So he did that, bailed the instruments out.

[When] we left there, I don't even think the man [at the dance hall] gave us a quarter 'cause he was waiting until the week ended to pay us out of that, but we didn't stay there a week.

We went down in the mountains there and caught one of them great big old freight trains. They had all the boxcars locked, see, they had stuff in 'em. We went down there right in the mountains. . . . [It was] the first time I ever seen an engine that big, had thirty-two wheels on the engine, one of them great big Mountain Jacks.

We went down there and caught that and we was running. The trombone player, Jap Jones, he like to got hurt. He was running, and I was the last one to catch him, he was watching me, cause I had a dinner bag tied around my shoulder. Had a sack of Bull Durhams [tobacco], this boy said, "Now Buster, you keep the dinner and the lunch meat." I think we had eighty cents left when we got done buying the lunch meat, and one sack of Bull Durham tobacco.

The only thing we could catch was one of them coal cars. It was half full of coal, we got all down in that coal, we got up in them mountains where its cold at night. . . . I was kind of leery of catchin' it 'cause it was running kind of fast. I said, "Well, everybody is on it, I better grab something." I grabbed the thing, Jap passed by me, the train passed by. Said, "What are you doing?" He said, "I wanted to see if you was going to catch it!" Then he catch it a couple or two cars behind me and was looking at me and running all at the same time, trying to keep up with that step, and [he] run into one of them signs, with the lights on it, switch sign. [It] knocked him down, but he come to himself and finally caught it.

Just as we got on there, I betcha it wasn't half a mile, the train went through one of them tunnels. And man everybody was smoky and dirty. . . . See they ain't got no top on 'em, got them great big old chunks of coal in there. We stayed in there about fifty or sixty miles.

Got up there and the old train had a switch, and we found a boxcar that was open. It was empty and we got in there and put a big stick in the door so the thing wouldn't run up on there and lock you up. A man could starve to death in there. We got in there and there was nineteen white boys . . . and there was a big fire in there. So we rode that coach all the way into Cincinnati. It was in October [1933].

[Then] we hoboed on into St. Louis. . . . The white boys said, "We on our way to Seattle, Washington, . . . and we going to hobo city, y'all come and go down. Everything's all right now. . . . We've been traveling through here for years; we know what it's all about." We got down there . . . in a little draw up under some big trees, had a great big old twenty-foot by thirty-foot carpet laid down, and they had some utensils over there and an old cabinet sitting there and had a sign up under it, said, "Leave it like you find it."

We didn't have to hustle no food. Those white boys, every time the train stopped they'd go out in the neighborhood, about two or three blocks from the train, and come back with all kinds of food, loaf of bread and great big old pieces of ham and baloney and stuff like that. . . . We got in Cincinnati, they found some work and got some food to bring back and cook over there. Had spices there, salt and pepper and all that stuff. Even had some rocking chairs sitting there.

So meantime we got to St. Louis, the seven did. So the old boy that had the agency, he knew us and came down there, he had a great big old nine-room house, he told us to come up there and stay till we get our business straightened out. I thought that would be all right. I had a great big old suitcase with all the music in it. I went on up and went to sleep. And he stole our repertoire. He hid it. I'll never forget that music.

We stayed over there about three days and Bennie Moten heard about us being there and he sent some cars over there to pick us up, and put all of us in his band, that was left. [That was] Jap Jones, George Hudson, Lester Young, Snake White, Abe Bolar, Theodore Ross; there was seven of us.

That was in '33, and things got tough; Bennie wasn't doing nothing, but he kept his band together.

We had left our wives over there in Martinsville. Wasn't but two of us had our wives with us. I had my wife, and [so had] George Hudson the trumpet player. . . . We left 'em over there and we was supposed to go back over there. The wives, they heard about it from the taxicab drivers. . . . My wife, she had to work around there, scratch around there, got some money, and she beat me in Kansas City. When I got there she was already there. . . . She thought it was a bad deal. It wasn't long before we separated.

Druie Bess: What caused the Blue Devils to break up was a boy . . . had booked the band and it was our last resort for a booking. I don't know, it was just a bunch of bad luck. We wasn't making no money up in there. . . .

We was making one last stand there . . . and we figured we'd get our money because this boy's father was a doctor. [But] ain't nobody come [to the dance]. . . . It poured down snow that night. . . . That was one of the most pitiful sights I ever saw. . . .

I always kept a little money. I never was just dead broke. Never. I always made a point [of it]. So I wired home to my sister. . . . I told her to send me some money. The money just came flyin' . . . and I was ready to go. . . . Some of them was talking about bummin', grabbin' a freight train. I couldn't do nothing for 'em. I didn't want to do that for myself. So that's just the way it was. . . .

When the Blue Devils broke up in '33 . . . we all went back to Kansas City and tried to get the band back together. [But] I figured they'd never get the band back together no more.

RAYMOND F. HOWELL. *Born c. 1910, Kansas City, Missouri. Drums. Original member of Chauncey Downs's Rinkey Dinks in Kansas City in 1924; joined Jap Allen in 1929, and the Blue Devils in 1931. After their break-up he continued to play in and around Kansas City through the early seventies.*

I never will forget [the break-up of the Blue Devils]. [We] went to Bluefield, West Virginia, the Black Knight nightclub . . . and the fella had our instruments attached. . . . He thought we were going to slip from him without paying him. We owed him some money . . . and a majority of the fellas, they caught freight trains. I didn't. I stayed out there [at] a theater and went on up in New York. I don't like freight trains. I always did what my parents told me: . . . "Keep some money in my pocket. Don't catch no freight train.". . . So I was the only one there [left] from the band. . . .

I hated to see that band break up. I really did. Everybody in New York was talking about that band. . . . We had a nice time, man. I wish those days would . . . come [back] over here. I'm telling you. Everything was different.

NOTES

1. Walter Page was both an excellent musician, being a skilled sight reader on both string bass and bass saxophone, and an important innovator. He was among the first to feature string bass instead of tuba or bass saxophone as the rhythm

section's bass instrument. This structural change had a liberating effect on jazz rhythms, and made the supple drive of swing jazz possible. Page was also one of the outstanding performers of his generation and had an important personal impact by inspiring a generation of bass players. The strength and innovation of his playing can be heard in both the Blue Devils' recordings and his work with Moten and Basie. Page was a little-recognized giant of jazz who played a major role in creating the swing style that later became identified with Kansas City.

2. In a riff arrangement reed, horn, and rhythm sections create brief harmonized passages with strong, danceable rhythms. These then become the base for the soloist's more individual expression.

3. Buster Smith's sense of the Blue Devils' strength clearly differs from that of Jesse Stone. Stone's focus on their ensemble work and Smith's on their solos can be rationalized by noting that the Blue Devils were one of the greatest riffing bands. Despite their stress on the soloist and danceable rhythms, great riff bands had such strong ensemble riffing that the soloing was sometimes eclipsed. Still, the riff is a group improvisational and rhythmic device and can be thought of as the building block for the solos, even if the riff is so strong that it dominates the performance. Examples of strong riff-dominated tunes that were primarily created by ex-Blue Devils include Bennie Moten's "Moten's Swing" and "Toby," and Count Basie's original "One O'Clock Jump."

4. A noted pianist, songwriter, and entertainer, Waller was the author of "Honeysuckle Rose," "Ain't Misbehavin'," and many other songs.

5. The band's only income came from admission paid at the door. No salary was offered.

Alphonso Trent's Adolphus Hotel Orchestra, c. 1929. Trent's long engagement at this swank Dallas hotel (for whites only) was the best-paying continuing stint of any black jazz band in the Midwest before 1930. Trent's frequent radio broadcasts from the Adolphus further established his reputation as one of the top bandleaders in the region. (Courtesy of the Kansas City Museum, Kansas City, Missouri, and the Mutual Musician's Foundation)

Nat Towles Band at Krug Park, 1939. Towles led Omaha's best-known jazz band of the late 1930s. His orchestra featured Buddy Tate on tenor saxophone from 1935 to 1939, and provided Jay McShann with much of his core ensemble when he "raided" Towles in 1939. (Courtesy of the Kansas City Museum, Kansas City, Missouri, and the Western Historical Museum)

Tommy Douglas Orchestra, c. 1940. Douglas toured widely through the Midwest from bases in Topeka and Kansas City, Kansas. Among many fine musicians who performed with him, the most prominent was alto saxophonist Charlie Parker. (Courtesy of the Kansas City Museum, Kansas City, Missouri, and Duncan Schiedt)

Lloyd Hunter Orchestra, c. 1927. Hunter led a jazz band in Omaha through the early 1930s. With a slightly different group of players than the one shown, the Serenaders (as they were usually known) recorded once, with blues singer Victoria Spivey, in 1931. Jo Jones, later Count Basie's drummer, made his recording debut at that session. At other times Hunter employed such fine performers as Dan Minor (trombone), Sir Charles Thompson (piano), and Johnny Otis (vibraphone and piano). (Courtesy of the Kansas City Museum, Kansas City, Missouri, and Duncan Schiedt)

T. Holder's Twelve Clouds of Joy, c. 1927. This was Holder's final Clouds of Joy aggregation. During their heyday in the late 1920s this Oklahoma- and Texas-based band ranged throughout the Midwest, earning top pay and dressing to show it. *Left to right:* Claude Williams (violin and guitar), T. Holder (trumpet), Theodore Ross (reeds), Bill Haygood, Lawrence "Slim" Freeman (reeds), Harry Lawson (trumpet), Alvin "Fats" Wall (alto saxophone), Andy Kirk (tuba), Marion Jackson (piano), and Harry "Stumpy" Jones. (Courtesy of the Kansas City Museum, Kansas City, Missouri, and Claude Williams)

Andy Kirk's Twelve Clouds of Joy, c. 1930. After the Depression hit America, lower pay made extensive band travel more difficult to justify. Here Andy Kirk's band rests beside the road, en route to another gig. *Left to right:* Bill Durvin (banjo), Claude Williams, Alvin "Fats" Wall, Bill Massey (vocals), Harry Lawson, Theodore Ross, Flip Benson, Edward "Crack" McNeil (drums), Andy Kirk, Lawrence "Slim" Freeman, and Eddie ⸻ (trumpet). (Courtesy of the Kansas City Museum, Kansas City, Missouri, and Claude Williams)

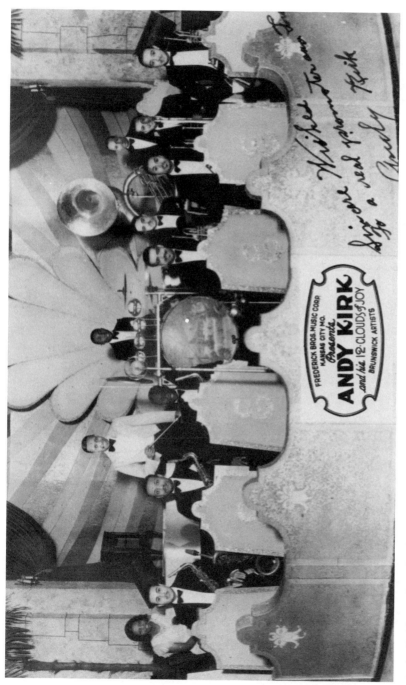

Andy Kirk's Twelve Clouds of Joy, c. 1934. This was the Kirk band that achieved fame through hit recordings and sell-out tours, and included two brilliant performers, pianist Mary Lou Williams and saxophonist Dick Wilson. This photo was inscribed to Omaha promoter Jimmy Jewell. (Courtesy of the Kansas City Museum, Kansas City, Missouri, and Jimmy Jewell)

Walter Page's Blue Devils, c. 1926. This earliest known photograph of the Blue Devils suggests the closeness of its members, many of whom stayed with the band until its demise in 1933. *Left to right*: Ermir "Bucket" Coleman (trombone), Harry Youngblood [?] (trumpet), Theodore Ross (reeds), Druie Bess [?] (trombone), ———— Benton (banjo), Walter Page (bass, reeds, and tuba), unknown, Oran "Hot Lips" Page (trumpet), Buster Smith (reeds), Reuben Roddy [?] (saxophone), Ernie Williams (drums and vocals), Edward "Crack" McNeil [?] (drums). (Courtesy of the Kansas City Museum, Kansas City, Missouri, and the Mutual Musician's Foundation)

Blue Devils Orchestra, c. 1927. Taken in a radio broadcast studio, this photo shows the band with its "Blue Devil" symbol painted on the bass drum. *Left to right:* Oran "Hot Lips" Page, Buster Smith, _____ Benton, Walter Page, Ermir "Bucket" Coleman, Willie Lewis (piano), James L. Grant (trumpet), Ernie Williams, Bill Owen (alto saxophone and clarinet). (Courtesy of the Kansas City Museum, Kansas City, Missouri, and Charles Goodwin)

The Thirteen Original Blue Devils, c. 1932. After Bennie Moten's raids on the Blue Devils, Ernie Williams (center) became the "conductor" of the band. Also in the band during this period was Lester Young (fifth from left). (Courtesy of the Kansas City Museum, Kansas City, Missouri, and Frank Driggs.)

6

The Road Leads to Kansas City

The traveling circuit through the Territories was often tortuous. Rough, dirty roads, poor playing conditions, crooked promoters and booking agents, and plain bad luck all were part of the life. Through the 1920s, however, the hardships were usually tolerable. Pay was generally good and work was plentiful. The Depression changed this rapidly. With massive unemployment and lower living standards for most Americans, few were comfortable paying twenty-five or fifty cents for an evening of dancing. Mid-America was then predominately rural, and farmers had been suffering their own depression since 1921 due to historically low farm product prices. The national economy just made things worse, and increasingly led many farmers to use destructive tilling practices.[1] These in turn set the stage for the dust storms of 1934-37 that made life for most rural Midwesterners—and those who entertained them—almost unbearable.

The work, and the soil, dried up, and bands found themselves on increasingly long and unprofitable tours. Musicians quickly realized that Kansas City was somehow immune from much of this, and the migration to the jumping town that began in 1929 with the Depression continued through the 1930s and the Dust Bowl days.

Sam Grievious: Back in [the teens] there wasn't no highways. They traveled only by train. . . . We used to go from Omaha . . . as far north as the edge of South Dakota on a train and we went to [different cities in] Nebraska and like that, and everything was on the train. . . .

[In the twenties] we [the Ted Adams Orchestra, a regional band based in Omaha] decided that if we would get us a car, we could make a little more money. . . . So we got a car. . . . There was no highway, nothing but wagon trails. . . . When it would rain, you'd be all night going two miles, 'cause that gumbo would get up between the wheels and fenders, and you'd have to get out and dig it out. . . . It wouldn't go a hundred feet hardly before you had to get out and do it again. Be all night before you could get anywhere. . . .

[During the Depression, promoters] would put the dance hall in partnership with you; . . . house take thirty [percent], give you seventy. You get maybe forty or fifty cents. Before you get home, have a flat tire, cost you fifty cents to get it fixed. . . . If you had to cross a bridge, had to pay a bridge toll. When you get through with it you haven't made a quarter. . . . That was day after day like that.

Walter Harrold: [With Lloyd Hunter's band[2]] we had a lot of bad breaks out on the road. . . . Maybe we'd go from here [Omaha] to Sidney, Nebraska; when we get there the doggone ballroom is three feet under water. They'd cancel us out. Then we'd go from there to North Platte, we'd have an engagement the next night. We'd have three or four blowouts and everything, be a hour late getting there, and they had hired another band, so we missed out on two engagements there. Then we had to go to Norton, Kansas, we had a four-day fair to play there. . . . We hadn't made a job, so our money was getting short and everything. We got down there late, so the guy docked us for that first night. . . . It's just things like that you run into on the road.

Goin' to Kansas City

From the 1880s Kansas City had a reputation as a loosely controlled, free-spirited city where those with cash could find most anything they wanted. In the early days, the big spenders were usually cattlemen and farmers, flush with the earnings of a season's work and ready for a good time.

This aspect of the city's life continued through the early twenties. Vice then became somewhat more organized, and control filtered to several Italian clans that became established in the city's North End. By the mid-twenties it is likely that K.C.'s vice, although colorful and fairly open, was not dramatically more active than in any other major, mob-influenced city, such as Chicago or New York.

Events changed significantly in 1926, however, when Tom Pendergast, Kansas City's "boss," formed an alliance with Johnny Lazia, leader of both the city's rackets and the important North End political machine. Their arrangement gave Lazia control over the city's police department and, correspondingly, nearly free reign over the city's rackets. Pendergast got

Lazia's vote block and, according to reliable accounts, a personal skim from every night's gambling receipts.

This agreement rapidly turned Kansas City into, in Westbrook Pegler's words, "The Timbuktu, . . . Sodom and Gomorrah, . . . of the Western world."[3] The political and social aspects of the Pendergast era in "Tom's Town" are treated in a later chapter. Of importance to musicians, and to the evolution of Kansas City's jazz style, was that money was rolling, flowing through K.C. In the thirties, when the rest of America was devastated by the Depression and musical jobs evaporated, Kansas City rocked, and a generation of Territory musicians came to mingle with the already lively native musical scene. Wonderful music and exciting times resulted.

WILBUR "BUCK" CLAYTON. *Born 11/12/1911, Parsons, Kansas. Trumpet and arranger. First worked professionally in California with several bands, then traveled with Teddy Weatherford's band to Shanghai, China, where they played from 1934 to 1936. After returning, Clayton stopped by K.C. on his way to New York, met Bill "Count" Basie, and joined his band, replacing Hot Lips Page who had already left for a solo career in New York. Clayton remained with Basie until 1943 when he was drafted. With this band he was noted for both his ensemble and solo work, particularly with Lester Young and Billie Holiday. He remained very active upon his return from military service until dental problems led him to retire. Clayton was inspired to return to music by hearing Orville Minor play trumpet (without teeth) in 1975, and continued to be active until his second (and presumably final) retirement from performing in the early 1980s. Still active as an arranger.*

I was always going to Kansas City. I went to school in Kansas, and we'd go up to Kansas City every weekend to go to a dance, listen to a band, go to theaters. . . . [There] was a big railroad called MKT, Missouri, Kansas, and Texas. So all of the people during that time [that] was coming from Texas through Oklahoma, up to Kansas City, just stopped. . . .

There must have been at one time about a dozen big bands in Kansas City. All big bands. Even down in Dallas, Texas, they had four or five big bands, and eventually they'd leave Texas and come up to Kansas City, like Budd Johnson, Lester Young. They'd come up from down South and they'd end up right in Kansas City all the time.

Sam Price: I went back down the circuit, all the way back to Dallas [in the late twenties]. Then that traveling feeling was in my blood, so then I got with . . . the TOBA going in a different direction. We went to Tulsa first, then Oklahoma City, . . . and then another show came and I went from Oklahoma City to Kansas City with that show. . . . Then after that I just stayed in Kansas City . . . [for] three or four years, to 1932.

I stayed there because of the mood and a lot of friendly people and a lot of fellows that I knew, that were developing into good musicians, [like] Booker Pittman, Budd Johnson, Buddy Tate.

Eddie Barefield: I'll tell you, Kansas City was really a choice bid at that time, because every band of that territory, that come out of Texas and Oklahoma, all came to Kansas City at one time or another. Eighteenth and Vine was the center. They had Street's Hotel, which was between Eighteenth and Nineteenth on Vine, and . . . across the street there was the Lincoln Theater, then right on Eighteenth and Vine in the basement was this pool hall, Piney Brown's, the Subway [Club].

We used to play around Kansas City . . . and jam every night. No matter what you were doing, if you were on the street at three or four in the morning and you got a . . . call that the Blue Devils were in town, and a bunch of guys [were] down in the Subway, jamming, well, you just picked up and put your clothes on and go down there and start blowing with everybody.

Eddie Durham: Times were hard, and all the guys got that far and they couldn't get no further. That's the real truth. There wasn't any bands sending for them so they just ended up in Kansas City because they could live. . . . If I go stay somewhere, I wasn't going to pay. Nobody ever bothered you about money in those days. . . . Everything was handy, generous.

I think that had a lot to do with it. . . . I know that's as far as I got. . . . Basie got stranded [in Kansas City too]. . . .

Kansas City [musicians] thought they was the greatest. They formed a clique there. . . . Anybody ever hit this town, we'd get right out there. . . . They used to jam at four o'clock in the morning, boy. That's the way the town was. The jam sessions went on all night and all day. I remember one night there was Ben Webster, Coleman Hawkins, and . . . it must have been Don Byas. They had a battle of tenors [saxophones]. I think they started it at eight o'clock and they finished at eight o'clock the next morning. They used about five or six piano players. One guy would go home and sleep, and they'd call up the next guy. . . . This guy would make it a half hour, hour. . . . That went on and on. It was going on at the Subway [Club]. . . . [That] was the main place.

JOHN TUMINO. *Promoter and booking agent. Managed and booked several bands, notably Jay McShann, Harlan Leonard's Rockets, and Julia Lee.*

I thought it was great. . . . I was young then. I was one punk kid and having one hell of a time. I thought it was all made for fun. Who needed any worries? All you worried about was having a good time, who you going to date tonight, and where you going to go. . . .

Kansas City was one of the few cities that didn't have a depression, they were booming. . . . But gambling, man, you've got a gold mine right under your little old joint. It only takes two or three of those little old slot machines to take in a hundred dollars a night, each. In those days a hundred dollars is like a thousand today. . . . This was a veritable Las Vegas, only it was illegal, but legal. Nobody touched them. . . . You had to have the right connection with T. J. Pendergast, that's where it was. You're fully covered, and if you payed your little old touch, whatever he wanted, and that was it. . . .

Gene Ramey: Everybody was trying to make it to Kansas City. . . . Kansas City then was . . . kind of a focal point for people to go to for an urban center in those days. . . . That was like the first stop. The next stop, if they made it, [was] to Chicago. Some of them wanted to go to St. Louis. But it was Kansas City, most of all, because this was it, and [it] became most famous, and mostly through musicians . . . traveling. Every time they would come into a town, they would say, "When you come to Kansas City. . . ." Just like an invitation, like they had a regular . . . goodwill ambassador going around.

William Saunders: I think Kansas City music is a potpourri of musicians being stranded or coming through here because they heard about all of these nightclub jobs here and they said, "Man, we're going to Kansas City."[4]

NOTES

1. Low farm product prices and heavy debt burdens brought on by farmers' efforts to increase productivity through expensive mechanization and ever larger fields led to farming practices that were terribly destructive of the soil. Relatively high-profit crops were constantly planted, rather than using soil-preserving crop rotation programs. Rows of trees that had lined fields and provided crucial windbreaks were cut down to gain the last increment of arable soil. When the Midwestern climate turned to an inevitable cycle of dry years the result was a "Dust Bowl" that destroyed the livelihoods of thousands of farmers.

2. Lloyd Hunter's Serenaders were one of Omaha's best-regarded jazz bands. They recorded once in 1931 as back-up for blues singer Victoria Spivey in a session notable mostly for featuring a young Jo Jones on his first recording. Jones later became the star drummer for the Count Basie Orchestra and was widely felt to be the greatest swing drummer of all. Hunter later unintentionally earned a place in K.C. jazz lovers' hearts by providing (along with fellow Omaha bandleaders

Red Perkins and Nat Towles) a significant portion of the talent for Jay McShann's big band. McShann came to town in 1938 to find musicians and did so by raiding the local bands.

3. Quoted from the *Kansas City Star.* Copyright 1948, *Kansas City Star.* All rights reserved.

4. Litwak and Pearson, *Goin' to Kansas City,* 17; used with permission.

7

Tom's Town: The Pendergast Years

The development of jazz in Kansas City and the character of the cultural scene that surrounded it are inseparable from the environment created by the corrupt but socially progressive political machine of Thomas J. Pendergast.

His machine dominated the politics of Kansas City from 1900 through the 1950s, and held nearly absolute power in both the city and the state of Missouri from 1926 through 1936. Although Pendergast had no personal interest in either music or black Kansas City, the economic vitality that his reign helped to stimulate and the flourishing vice that he permitted are critical elements that led to Kansas City's becoming an extraordinary musical center in the 1930s, instead of just another Depression-ridden Midwestern city.

Tom's brother Jim was the first Pendergast in Kansas City, arriving in 1876 at the age of twenty. Jim settled in the industrial West Bottoms, near the junction of the Missouri and Kaw (or Kansas) rivers, where packing houses, railroad yards, factories, and warehouses provided industry for the young city. In 1881 Jim opened the Climax Saloon (named for a racehorse whose winnings provided his seed money), and that tavern served as both his political base and the root of the Pendergast political machine.

The Climax Saloon offered two services in addition to liquor and inexpensive food: gambling (although illegal) and crude banking. Cards and dice were nearly always found, and working men could not only cash their pay, but could also hold part of it behind Jim's bar for safekeeping. It was a place where the indigent of the First Ward could go if they needed a loan or something to eat. When asked in later years to provide a definition of the word "boss," Tom Pendergast said, "It's just a man who has a lot of friends." The process of gaining friends for the Pendergasts began with Jim in this saloon.

Jim took an interest in the disorganized politics of the day, and in 1892 was elected alderman, a position he held until 1910. By 1900 Jim's influence extended into the Italian North End, site of Kansas City's largest red-light district. When Jim delivered the votes necessary to elect Democrat James Reed mayor in 1900, Reed responded by giving a large share of patronage to Pendergast, making Jim the strongest political leader in the city and a necessary ally for any local election victory.

As Jim's health failed he increasingly delegated political responsibility to his younger brother, Tom. In 1910 Jim gave up his alderman's seat and endorsed Tom for the position. Tom won easily, and upon Jim's death in 1911 Tom assumed control of a powerful political organization.

Tom's personality was different from Jim's in important ways. Jim was content to wield political power on behalf of his immediate constituency in what friends and foes agree was an even, honest, and frequently altruistic fashion. Tom was considerably more aggressive, willing to use illegal tactics in pursuit of greater power. His first move was to challenge his only strong Democratic rival, Joe Shannon of the Ninth Ward. Tom personally never sought a higher office than alderman—his power was behind the scenes— but when his candidate defeated Shannon's in a primary for county judge, the state Democratic hierarchy acknowledged Tom's power and began to shift patronage away from Shannon to Pendergast.

From this strengthened position Tom aided liquor interests, protected gambling, and favored certain contractors. He never lost sight, however, of the need to cement local support. When a person moved into a neighborhood, the local precinct captain would help get utilities installed and make sure that the resident was registered to vote. Poor people often received handouts of food, fuel, and clothing, as the Jackson Democratic Club, Tom's official organization, functioned as a local welfare system. The various political clubs under Pendergast's control served as social centers, holding dinners, dances, picnics, and parties. The machine remembered the importance of having friends.

Parallels to Roosevelt's later New Deal relief and welfare programs abounded in the Pendergast administration and, even though Tom eventually resorted to repugnant tactics to preserve his power, for the most part his administration provided necessary services for the disadvantaged. The base of his support always rested in the poor, the black, the Italian, the immigrant. These groups, disenfranchised by other major political groups, found a benefactor in Tom Pendergast and his ward lieutenants. Even in the blackest days of his administration, stories of murder and vote fraud were contrasted with innumerable accounts of anonymous gifts to needy families that could only have come from Tom. The dichotomy in his character was deep, and he kept a city alive until his greed drove him down.

The corrupt elements in Tom's administration grew increasingly blatant, and a citizens' reform movement developed in the early twenties. Recognizing that he could make reform work for him, Pendergast threw in with the reformers who wanted to bring him down, and endorsed their revisions in the city charter, which included nonpartisan city council elections and the appointment of a city manager by the council. The machine strategy was to elect a majority to the reconstructed council. This majority then elected Tom's candidate, Henry F. McElroy, as city manager in 1926.

Soon after this coup Johnny Lazia, a young North End racketeer, gained political supremacy in his wards by kidnapping key members of his opposition's organization on election day. Pendergast realized the need to absorb this new power into his fold, and struck a deal. Lazia gave Pendergast his five thousand- to seven thousand-vote block in return for control of the city police department and subsequent free reign over the rackets. Tom (according to accounts from reliable sources) also received a straight daily skim off gambling revenues. In return, Lazia promised to keep the rackets "controlled" by restricting them to certain parts of the city and to keep "white-collar" crime out of the town.

It is from this point that Kansas City was transformed from an historically open but not extreme city into a truly wide-open town. There had always been red-light districts, but they expanded. Prohibition enforcement ceased altogether. (There were no felony convictions for Prohibition violations in Kansas City during the entire period of that law—this in a city famed for its bars, nightclubs, and speakeasies.) Slot machines were everywhere, and most nightclubs featured many forms of gambling—cards, dice, roulette. With Lazia in control of the police force, Kansas City became a safe zone for gangsters in need of a hide-out, and the likes of the Barker Gang, Alvin Karpis, and Pretty Boy Floyd were often seen in swank nightclubs.[1]

The great social and economic achievement of Pendergast was to shield Kansas City from the worst of the Depression. City Manager McElroy, in direct violation of the city charter, used every manner of budgetary ruse to pad the city and county payrolls with employees who were friends of the machine. A New Deal-style public works program developed in the late twenties with a ten-year plan for ambitious public construction projects (with important contracts always going to Pendergast's own ReadyMix Cement Company). Whenever possible, human labor was substituted for machines to increase the jobs available.

Thus Kansas City enjoyed relative affluence which, combined with the permissive atmosphere that allowed hundreds of clubs to flourish, served as a magnet for musicians from the Territories.

Pendergast's personal power, and the dominance of his machine, ended through a combination of factors. Tom was addicted to gambling, especially on the horses. Friends knew that he had private teletypes in the basement of his mansion to get quick information on race results around the country. He also was part-owner of a local racetrack, the Riverside, and employed a fleet of cars and drivers to deliver his winnings and (mostly) losings to and from bookies nationally. It has been estimated that Tom was losing more than $2 million annually by the mid-1930s, and had become known among bookies as the biggest sucker in the country. Even his substantial income from rackets and city contracts to his cement company couldn't cover losses of this magnitude, and he began dipping directly into the public till. Pendergast's fraud culminated in embezzlement of state insurance funds. When this was discovered the stage was set for his conviction of tax evasion.

The wide-open rackets, for years relatively well controlled in the public eye, also became grotesque. On June 17, 1933, FBI agents carrying an escaped convict back to Leavenworth prison were met at Kansas City's Union Train Station by Pretty Boy Floyd and two accomplices. The agents, accompanying policemen, and the prisoner were killed. Lazia, who had set up the assassination, was soon afterward machine-gunned to death in front of his apartment in the heart of Kansas City's most fashionable shopping district.

Similar tactics spilled into politics. In March 1934, K.C.'s "Bloody Election" was held, in which three poll workers, rivals to Pendergast, were murdered, and several others were badly beaten.

All this became too much for the public to stand. Even the Roosevelt administration, for whom Pendergast was a valuable ally and the political "godfather" of Harry Truman, joined local investigations of K.C.'s political situation. The state prosecutor assigned to Pendergast was Maurice Milligan, whose brother had been defeated in a U.S. Senate race by Truman, and who thus bore a personal grudge against Pendergast.

Pendergast entered prison in 1939. His organization, however, hung on for many years after, led first by Tom's nephew Jim and then by Judge Bernard Gnefkow, but it never again held so dominant a sway over the city.

Unrestricted racketeering began to quiet down during the Pendergast investigations in 1938, stifling some of the spirit in the jumping town. World War II finished the job. Post-war Kansas City retained many traces of its former glory, but was no longer a musical center. In the mid-sixties, racial strife, urban redevelopment projects, and accelerating integration destroyed any remaining vitality in the old black downtown. Now K.C. enjoys a small, lively core of old masters and young students, in many ways reminiscent of the early days of apprenticeship and jam sessions, but in miniature and in relative isolation.

Boss Tom

A remarkable aspect of Tom Pendergast and his administration is the extreme degree of loyalty for the Boss felt by his cronies thirty-five years after his death. No one who worked for or with Tom will say a disparaging or even mildly critical word about the man or his actions. The following accounts include those of Henry McKissick and Bernard Gnefkow, who were both key members of Pendergast's later machine. (Gnefkow became its leader in the late fifties.) In these roles they held considerable power in Kansas City, in Missouri, and even nationally, despite the waning influence of the machine. The inevitable taint today of a link with Pendergast then would lead many to deny their role or even association with such a figure, but not these men. They typify Boss Tom's colleagues who, years after any opportunities for prosecution have passed, are steadfast in their loyalty to his integrity and memory.

HENRY McKISSICK. *Born 3/18/1900, Kansas City, Missouri. Died 10/14/ 1984, Hot Springs, Arkansas. Ward boss in the Second (predominantly black) Ward, first under Cas Welch and then the Pendergast machine.*

I don't know how to describe [Tom Pendergast]. He was a wonderful man, I know that. He did a lot for the poor people. . . . They'd come up in his office day after day; he'd give them a five or get 'em some help and get 'em in the hospital or something. Wonderful man.

BERNARD GNEFKOW. *Born c. 1900, Kansas City, Missouri. Became a judge of election in 1924, kept the honorific title of "Judge" the rest of his career. Political worker and recipient of patronage jobs until 1932 when he became Tom Pendergast's personal secretary, where he remained until Pendergast's conviction. Became a justice of the peace in 1943, and chairman of the Jackson Democratic Club (the rubric for the Pendergast machine) after the death of Jim Pendergast, Tom's nephew.*

I fell into being [Pendergast's secretary] after the first one got sick. Kind of fell into it. He must have been very friendly or he wouldn't have had all the friends that he had. Mr. Pendergast was like a father to me, and I admired him regardless of what happened later on. Everybody has their faults and I'm not going to criticize anything that he said even if it's worth criticizing. . . . I don't think there's any better man, far as I'm concerned, and as far as the poor people in Kansas City was concerned in those days.

I know he was a very kindhearted man and I think the city was much better off with him as a political leader. . . . You must remember that in those days people were hungry, people were cold, people were starving, and the political organization set up and they gave them coal.

We got to the place where we bought coal by the carload and delivered 'em to people. The Jackson Democratic Club did it. . . .

We had a crowd [to see Mr. Pendergast] at the Democratic Club from six o'clock in the morning to twelve noon every day. . . . I imagine the majority of them would want jobs or would want favors or something, poor people. Everybody came down to see Mr. Pendergast, senators and governors and aldermen and everybody else. . . .

[No one had preferential treatment to see him] except women. We had orders . . . that I would not make the ladies wait out there with the rest of 'em, and if they came down to put 'em in as quickly as possible. He was of the old school that believed that ladies came first. . . .

Anybody that had over ten minutes must have had something very important to take up. He had a quick decision. He had a "yes," "no," or "I'll see about it, come back and see me." He'd make a note about it and he would tend to it. He didn't put 'em off; he wasn't the kind of politician who'd say "come and see me next Tuesday" and then not have an answer. He would have an answer. If he could do it he'd tell 'em. If he couldn't, he'd tell 'em no. That's all. . . . [Only] toward the last he'd make notes of what people wanted him to do, [before he kept notes in his head]. . . .

[Felix Payne, prominent black political leader, gambler, and nightclub owner] was a friend of Mr. Pendergast. . . . Tootie Clarkin [nightclub owner and gambler] used to come around [the Jackson Club] once in a while. Eddie Spitz [nightclub owner] belonged to the North Side faction, . . . [Johnny] Lazia's district. . . .

I don't think we ever talked about [the gambling going on in Kansas City]. It was taken for granted. I knew that [Felix Payne] was a gambler. There was a lot of gamblers. When you'd go out to Las Vegas ten years ago you'd see a lot of Kansas City people there. . . .

A lot of us called him the Boss. . . . [It was] definitely a friendly town.

Raymond F. Howell: Pendergast run this town. When Pendergast say "Oop," you'd better "Oop." That's right. But he was, in some ways, a good man. . . . You can't say nothing against him.

The Political Process

Kansas City's local ward system was the means by which patronage was obtained and dispensed, people were directly served, and the wheels of the town were greased.

Bernard Gnefkow: The black people in those days, . . . the late twenties and the early thirties, . . . were Republicans. . . . It was the party of Abe Lincoln. . . . I think black people are more loyal to people who are good to them than white people are. . . . Roosevelt converted 'em, just like Abe Lincoln made Republicans out of all of 'em up until the time of Roosevelt. . . .

Back in the early thirties, McElroy, who was the city manager, instituted a public works program and called it the CWA. I think that the WPA that Roosevelt instituted later on was more or less modeled after it. They created jobs through a bond issue. . . . We had projects digging sewer lines, paying men sixteen dollars a week and they'd flock for the jobs. . . . Projects were all done by hand. . . . If a police job or a fireman job came open and you could get it for one of your friends, you tried it. You sent [people] to your ward leader . . . and he had his connections with Mr. McElroy or somebody, . . . whoever it was, . . . in charge of that particular job. . . .

Before every election we'd always have a city-wide rally. . . . The chairman of the party would give the speech, the whip-cracking speech as they called it, to get the vote out. . . .

Felix Payne was a good speaker, he was a rabble-rouser you might say, especially in the black neighborhood. They [even] used him at white rallies sometimes. . . . He was very active in politics. He was one of the few Democratic black people in those days. . . .

In those days we'd hire a neighborhood movie house for the night and after the movie was over we'd have speeches. That was common all over the city. . . . You had a movie house in practically every neighborhood, . . . nickel and dime movie houses. . . .

[As a precinct captain] you poll the neighborhood . . . door-to-door . . . to find out how the people voted, and if they were Democrat you saw that they got to the polls on election day, and assisted them in any manner that you thought they wanted. If somebody comes to you, needed something and you could help them, you helped them. . . . [If somebody new moves in] you go to meet them and ask if there's anything you can do to help 'em—before you asked 'em their politics.

Henry McKissick: There was around twenty-three, twenty-four [precincts] at that time [twenties and thirties] . . . in the Second Ward. It was a big ward. . . . We had . . . around 20,000 [voters], 'cause I got 18,500 votes when I ran; my opponent got 500. . . .

In my precinct I'd have ten or twelve workers and you'd get these rooming house operators and give 'em a twenty dollar bill, they'd keep everybody registered, and also they're responsible for 'em on election day, comin' down. . . .

We tried to get as many jobs for our workers as we could, and I did pretty good on that. ...

In those days the political boss in [the black] district was a fellow named Cas Welch. . . . He was a justice of the peace. . . . [A boss], it's just a fellow that has a lot of friends, knows the neighborhood and knows the people. . . .

I was indicted twice . . . for buying votes . . . [and] acquitted twice.

Lawrence Denton: Cas Welch, yeah, he was big time. He was a friend to the blacks, and he was one of Felix's [Payne's] friends. The blacks would vote for him.

Bernard Gnefkow: Every ward had a club, and most of 'em had two clubs, a Pendergast club and a Shannon club. See, there was two distinct organizations in those days. They call it the Pendergast era, but Shannon had an organization . . . that was still powerful in some wards, and it could beat the "goats" as we called ourselves. Those were the days of the goats and the rabbits [the Shannon faction]. . . . We'd have a primary fight about some inconsequential office to keep the enthusiasm up. . . . [The Republicans] weren't in power enough to do anything. . . .

[The Pendergast machine was powerful] because of Mr. Pendergast, his organizational ability and political sense. [Cas] Welch was the third faction. Pendergast's organization took two-thirds of the jobs, Shannon took one-third, and the Pendergast faction gave Welch one-sixth of their two-thirds [in return for Welch's votes]. . . . At the peak [the Jackson Democratic Club] had maybe six thousand dues-paying members. . . .

There's no doubt but that [Kansas City] was a wide-open town. I think everybody went out on the town quite a bit. There's always a certain amount of reformers that don't believe in people having a good time. . . . Some people believed you shouldn't have a drink on Sunday, or a can of soup on Sunday. . . . I don't believe in that myself, but then a lot of people do. And I respect their opinion.

Charles Goodwin: You see, guys like Johnny Lazia, . . . they were the big time and Pendergast, he was the big man, he was the big boss. They used to call our capitol down there [in Jefferson City, Missouri] Uncle Tom's Cabin, . . . 'cause he called all the shots throughout the state. If you knew him well you could do anything . . . short of murder, and get away with it.

The town was wide-open during Pendergast's days, and you could work, and you could make a living pretty well playing music if you was capable. It kinda folded down [after Pendergast]. You had to scratch to make it.

JAY "HOOTIE" McSHANN. *Born 1/12/1909, Muskogee, Oklahoma. Piano and vocals. Toured Southwest with Al Dennis and Eddie Hills, then moved to Kansas City in 1937. Organized first band in 1938, enlarged to big band proportions in 1939. Gained national prominence with blues hit "Confessin' the Blues," sung by Walter Brown, in 1941. Currently active nationally and internationally.*

Kansas City died after Pendergast, you know. It was lively when I first come in there. Kansas City was moving, you know, and then from what I heard previous from when I was there, it was moving [then]. All the cats were working you know, and they used to have plenty of bands around. Plenty of clubs, plenty of places to play and everybody's makin' it. . . . Everybody was doing something.[2]

Buck Clayton: You know, the laws [in Kansas City] were a little lax. Most of the policemen had been crooks, and everything was wide open, . . . particularly [a] lot of gambling, . . . prostitution and gambling.

Buddy Anderson: Kansas City was fast-like. Oklahoma City was just conservative-like. Kansas City was *screaming*, man. It's way through Las Vegas. It had all that glamour. They had cathouses lined up. This was a cattle center, see, and all that dough would be coming through here. . . . Pendergast had it going. The machine. And they was for where that money was. . . .

I didn't know what politician meant, really and surely, but I was made to know that the machine was in and that it . . . had a terrific influence on the town, and that they had it lit up; they had the town jumpin'. This thing was . . . just wide open. That's all. It was just wide open.

NOTES

1. The effects of this continued to be felt through the 1970s, but have since largely waned. From the Kefauver Commission in the early 1950s to the Don Bolles investigation in the late 1970s, Kansas City was frequently identified as a major Mafia center of influence. For example, significant portions of mob revenues from Las Vegas and the Teamsters Central States Pension Fund (once a major mob "bankrolling" vehicle) were reported to be controlled from or channeled through Kansas City. However, vigorous prosecution efforts that began in the late 1970s have by now largely removed this long-felt influence from the city.

2. Litwak and Pearson, *Goin' to Kansas City*, 35; used with permission.

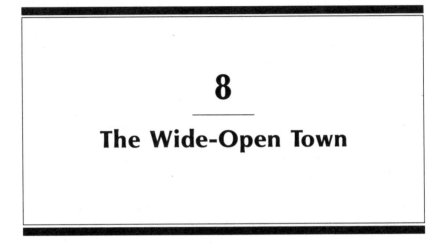

8

The Wide-Open Town

Kansas City in its jazz prime was a truly "hot" environment that gave rise to a remarkable body of exotic, sensual, and lurid tales. The city even seemed to take a measure of pride in its outrageous behavior, and stories of gangsters and bootleggers, prostitutes and gamblers, liquor and drugs are legion. Musicians speaking here have an interesting perspective on all that, enjoying the raciness of their tales, reveling in the memories, but they are also often quite matter-of-fact about occurrences that may be bizarre to the uninitiated but were commonplace to the Kansas City nightclub musician of the twenties and thirties.

This chapter is split into four sections, covering each of the major vices that were prevalent in K.C. during those years: gangsters; gambling and gamblers; prostitution and other open sexuality; prohibition, bootlegging, and narcotics. Each was common in K.C. then and each had positive (or at least relatively benign) and negative aspects. They all significantly colored the era, and are important to understanding the scene and how musicians lived.

Gangsters

These were the "Roaring Twenties" and their aftermath. Gangsters were sometimes folk heroes and were always fun to talk about and glamorize. The legends probably stretch reality, but it is clear that Kansas City was a relatively "safe" town for mobsters before World War II, and that Pretty Boy Floyd, the Barker Gang, and others frequented the city's innumerable nightclubs.

The relationship between gangs and mobsters and musicians in those days was mostly complementary. Musicians minded their business; the gangsters minded theirs, but also tended to take a paternalistic interest in the musician's (or the dancer's, or the prostitute's) well-being. Entertainers were both part of the gangster's own nighttime community and a drawing card for nightclubs, thus representing an important income source. It was in the syndicate's interest to keep its workers happy. Buster Smith speaks for most of his peers when he asserts that gangsters were "the musician's best friend." The cancerous vice that infected the city rarely harmed the musician, and often helped him.

HERMAN DAVIS. *Former Kansas City, Missouri, police officer and detective. Active in organized crime investigations, including that of the Kefauver Commission.*

What brought on almost all of the problem [crime in K.C.] was Prohibition. . . . This place in the early thirties was wide open for everything. There was no control whatsoever. There was no law. . . . Downtown was a series of gambling places and houses of prostitution. You go into . . . one of those gambling places . . . on Twelfth Street . . . [and] police in uniform would be shooting the dice. [At] Thirty-ninth and Main there was about five or six crap games, along with Fortune, which was a bingo place. And every election you could count on at least one execution of some kind. Somebody would get killed. . . .

There was some effort [by mobsters] to control the police department. This does not mean the police department was controlled, and I don't think it was, but certainly an attempt was being made. . . . There is no doubt at that time that there was a definite attempt to influence the Board of Police Commissioners. . . .

[In order to open a nightclub] in the thirties, now, . . . he'd have to go to somebody to get the money first, . . . and that would have to be Pendergast back at that time, and H. F. McElroy, the city manager, would be the one that you'd have to deal with, because at that time there was some laws that controlled occupational licenses. . . . And there would be liquor licenses at that time. Most of these things were ignored, but still somebody would have to pay to get started. Now, after you got started, then they would come and they'd say, "Well here, you're going to use these pinball machines." And then you're talking about Will Fryman. . . .

When pinball machines got to be popular, my first recollection of control was Will Fryman, and he dictated to especially the beer joints, what pinball machines they would use. He caught his at Fourteenth and Chestnut. He was down there to see A. J. Stevens . . . [who] was politically inclined, . . . and just as he left there to get in his car, six bullets

hit him in the back, killed him. . . . There's a lot of insulation between
the leaders here and the men on the street [who] are expendable. . . .
Narcotics and murder, and bribery, strongarm and terror tactics, and
gambling . . . were what they were doing. . . . North of the river they
have sort of a nest of houses there connected up with tunnels one from
the other. . . .
We probably ought to understand what we mean by organized crime,
first of all. . . . To me, organized crime is a confederation of people, two
or more . . . where they have established a monopoly of some kind,
somewhere in a criminal activity where there's a large profit. . . . Now
this could be anything. . . . Many people believe that this confederation
is the Mafia or the Cosa Nostra or something of that kind. It is not. It
involves other ethnic groups, Jews, the blacks. They're all involved and
so it's wrong to call it a mafia.

Sam Price: Back in Dallas I used to get guys out of jail and know people like that who were gangsters. . . . [In Kansas City] Ellis Burton [black
owner of the Yellow Front, notorious and popular K.C. jazz club in the
twenties and early thirties] liked me. I know he's supposed to be one of
the fellows that stuck up a train . . . but I knew Ralph Capone,[1] . . .
Pretty Boy Floyd, . . . Harvey Bailey, and people like that. . . .
They liked my music and I was their favorite. Aside from that, I'm
always friendly with people.

Eddie Durham: See, it's a gangster town, and they was hiding all the
gangsters. I met Pretty Boy Floyd there and I saw Baby Face Nelson.
Saw Floyd about four days before he got killed, because he came in the
Cherry Blossom. He was playing pool . . . and he come around to hear
the bands. Finally police came in and told him . . . to get out of here
because the police are looking for you, . . . the Feds. . . .
I played at one place, . . . a mobster come in with his big white hat on
and his four bodyguards. The boss come in and said, "All right, Johnny,
check the hardware." These guys would take a machine gun, . . . all the
guns, . . . lay 'em on the piano. . . .
They had it pretty well controlled. Only thing was . . . one particular
night . . . some fight started. Not between the gangs, something else. I
left [the club], jumped out the window and went home, about one
o'clock. Three o'clock, knocking on the wood . . . was the triggerman,
"Come on, he wants you back there." Got in the car. Felt good, . . .
nothing's going to happen to you; I got a friend. . . . Because you
couldn't quit one job and go to another. We worked for one guy. . . .
Those guys paid you double for anything you ever done in Kansas
City. They never owed a musician a nickel. The gangster always pro-

tected. . . . Those gangsters would always treat everybody right. If you touched a musician, or one of the girls, you'd go out on your head. Nobody ever harassed musicians.

Buster Smith: In Kansas City all them big clubs were [run by] them big gangsters, and they were the musician's best friend. They give you a job, and something to eat, and work regular. We didn't know nothing about their business, they didn't know nothing about ours, all they want us to do is play the music, and keep the crowd happy.

Ernie Williams: When [people] wanted someplace to dance, the [bands] would play pretty waltzes, and the jitterbug. Pretty Boy Floyd and them would come down to the Ritz Ballroom [in Oklahoma City] and shake a leg and do the lindy hop. . . . Wonderful man, used to come up, . . . hold them pistols and stuff. . . . No kidding. . . . The dude.

Orville Minor: [When gangsters were around] we'd just go on and play, because these guys, they didn't bother musicians. But don't cross 'em.

Jesse Stone: [At] the North Dallas Club in Kansas City, which is like a park, we had such a good band there, we were closing up most of the places around us. Then the gangsters threatened us. A guy came to the club and hollered through the window, "Jesse Stone, get out of town or else you won't be able to." That didn't work. We didn't leave. Then the guy came in and hired us to work in another place. Gave us a down payment.

It so happened that in a crap game I had rooked the manager of the place the week before. I won all the money and all the cash receipts for a Saturday and also his Packard. . . . So I took the job. When we got over there, there wasn't no such place.

So we went back again and got an apartment . . . for the whole band. We just kept going; we were having a ball off the money.

MYRA TAYLOR. *Born c. 1922, Kansas City, Missouri. Vocalist. Featured singer with the Harlan Leonard band, particularly for "I Don't Want to Set the World on Fire." Still active performer, mostly in Europe.*

I remember the time when if you worked here for some gangsters, in this club, maybe his friends that owned another club, which were also gangsters, would come in and say, "Okay, close the place up. We are buying the place for the rest of the night." . . . They just walked around to the customers . . . and put them all out. Then this man would bring all of his employees, his bands, entertainers, everybody would come in. The house doors would be locked and then you just drank all you wanted to drink. You could stay there as long as you wanted to stay and the gangsters would pay for everything. Then maybe next month the people we worked for would go to his place and do the same.

Clarence Love: I did get caught in a raid one time in one of the night-clubs. . . . Old Gus Gargotta [leading figure in one of K.C.'s biggest mobs] had it. . . . When I got down there [to the police station] I said [my name was] Jack Mortimer, and then you got to go to court the next day. But in his joints . . . you wouldn't have to go back there. Just tell him whose name you give to the man [and] . . . they would take . . . the rap [for you]. . . . If you got caught in his joint any time you didn't have to go to court, you'd go home. . . .

[And] every Christmas he'd feed two or three hundred people . . . in his club.

One night, . . . I can't think of the name of the club, . . . they [gangsters] all came running in . . . and they ran to the back of the club. Italian boys ran the club. They dug up the floor . . . and a lot of them come out with machine guns and ran out. I didn't know what the hell was going on. . . . Some guy was putting a guy on the spot and a different sheriff happened to be coming from a party and caught him and killed him. They just wanted a floor show, those old boys.

Gamblers and Gambling

It is evident from these recollections and other evidence that gambling to a great extent fueled the nightclub world. It offered large amounts of tax-free income, minus the inevitable percentage to the syndicate, and led many club owners to employ bands as a good crowd draw. Many musicians gambled, but the activity is primarily of interest to this story because it helped to support the music.

Lawrence Denton: My mother-in-law . . . was one of them old-time policy writers.[2] . . . She studied that dream book.[3] She caught [won] quite a bit too; she was lucky. . . . She'd play with certain policy writers . . . down there at that clothing store on Eighteenth and Vine. That was a big policy place in '39. You could go there and you could see 'em, you could turn the wheel yourself. Lots of people would. I used to go there and sit down there for hours. They'd draw every hour at that place. . . . Lots of old wash women would go out and work in the service . . . for white people and come back there and chance it on the policy wheel.

Felix Payne and Piney Brown

Probably the best-remembered and best-loved of all Kansas City's club owners were partners Felix Payne and Piney Brown. They epitomize the very strong link between gamblers, gambling, and the musician's world.

Payne was a politician, bon vivant, gambler, and club owner. Piney was less known to the general public, but much more visible to musicians, as the manager of some of Kansas City's most popular clubs, including the Sunset and the Subway, both headquarters for many notable after-hours jam sessions. The feeling for Piney is well expressed by the epitaph sung by Joe Turner in "Piney Brown Blues": "I dreamed last night, I was standing on Eighteenth and Vine. I shook hands with Piney Brown, and I could hardly keep from crying."

Sam Price: Kansas City was a good time . . . and we had some supporting fellows, like Felix Payne and Piney Brown . . . and Ellis Burton, and those were the kind of fellows that really helped to sponsor jazz in America. . . .

[Felix, Piney, and Ellis] were like godfathers actually for most musicians. People became friendly with them, they understood problems, financial problems. . . . They would feature the music [in their clubs]. . . . Felix Payne was a very wealthy man. And Piney Brown was wealthy, I guess. They made money gambling, you see, adjacent to the club, that was what it was, really, the gambling.

Lawrence Denton: Big Piney . . . had them great big games. Old Felix [Payne] would get to one side of the table and Big Piney the other side. They'd have games of hundreds of dollars. . . . I wasn't much of a gambler, but it was enjoyment just to watch them games, bettin' all that big money way back there in them days. Old Big Piney was Felix's partner.

Mary Lou Williams: We used to go to Piney Brown's place on Twelfth Street with Count Basie. He used to play, and there was a little bench. Everybody used to sit on the bench, and whoever was next, they'd go and play, and they just loved it. He'd give us money; he was very kind to the musicians.

Count Basie: Piney was sort of a gentleman about town. . . . I would say he was more on the inside. He knew everybody and everybody knew Piney. Piney was good to all musicians.

Eddie Barefield: Piney was like a patron saint to all musicians. He used to take care of them. In fact, he was like a father to me. . . . Most all the playing and jamming happened at Piney's place. Piney was a man, he didn't care how much it cost; . . . if you needed money to pay your rent, he would give it to you and take you out and buy booze. He was a man you could always depend on for something if you needed it, as a musician. . . .

The first time I met Piney, I went in there with Ben [Webster] and [Count] Basie and them, and I didn't know Piney, but they had friends and knew I was a country boy, . . . a clodhopper. . . . So we were playing, and was blowing away, and Piney came in and he started playing like he was a faggot. He said, "Oh, play it," [in an effeminate voice] and all that. I was getting madder and madder. Basie and Ben said, "Don't get mad, play up to him, he'll buy us all a drink." I would play up with him, and he would come over. Finally he got too close to me and I grabbed him in the collar. When I grabbed him in the collar, everybody just started to laugh, and he started to laugh, and from then on I couldn't do no wrong. . . .

He was older than we were. We were kids in our twenties and Piney must have been in his thirties. . . . He ran the numbers racket there. . . . I don't think he made any money off the Subway because he gave away too much. . . . When you went down there to play, you could go down there any night and get juiced and eat and play and do whatever you wanted to do. If you came there as a musician it never cost you anything.

Charles Goodwin: You really had more fun out of music than you do now. . . . There was guys like . . . Piney Brown. If a bunch of musicians would run into Piney Brown, well, the party is on, everything is taken care of, . . . and even though there is a segregated thing to these clubs,[4] well, guys like Piney they wouldn't turn him down, because he'd probably spend more money than anybody in the place. . . .

Felix [Payne] was behind Piney all the way. Anything that Piney would get into, Felix would . . . bail him out. Felix did have something to do with several clubs . . . and he was *the* big gambler.

Ellis Burton

Another popular and prominent patron of jazz musicians was Ellis Burton. Burton ran the Yellow Front Cafe in the mid-twenties and early thirties, a place notorious for being a dangerous dive in a time when many clubs were notably funky. Though more of a gangster and thus more dangerous than either Payne or Brown, Burton was still a steadfast musician's friend.

Dude Lankford: The Panama Night Club at Eighteenth and Forest was a great nightclub. And right up the street on the right-hand side Ellis had the Yellow Dog [slang, actually called the Yellow Front]. [It was] over a feed store. . . . Me and Everett Johnson, called him Joshua, played over at Ellis Burton's a whole winter. The whole building rocked when you danced.

Ellis Burton was bootlegging, he was selling the whiskey like pop. He was selling it for a quarter a drink out on Twelfth Street, with that little glass. [Burton would sell whiskey by the glass on the streetcorner, and was well known for the small glass he would use.]

Booker Washington: Ellis was a great man, as far as I was concerned. He was a little, chubby, brown-skinned fella. But if he liked you, he stuck with you. There've been times I went home [to eastern Missouri] and . . . I'd telegraph him [to] send me money. He'd send the money . . . and I'd play it out. . . .

[The Yellow Front] was sort of rough. You'd have some goings-on on a weekend. They were drinking nothing but corn whiskey then, and they get full of that and people start shooting at one another, and take a knife to each other. I remember one night he didn't want the band to stop [when a fight was going on], . . . so I got behind the piano [and kept] playing my horn. . . .

They would raid us occasionally. But no sooner do they take the people down, there was always a bond waiting for them to get out. . . . Burton had his connections. . . . I stayed downtown for about ten minutes, come on back, start all over again. . . . He had a strong hold politically to even operate that place.

Sam Price: [Ellis Burton] was the kind of guy that just liked musicians, and he had music around the clock. He had a gambling joint, and he'd have music from eight o'clock in the morning until like about two o'clock in the afternoon. And then from two 'till eight, and around eight o'clock at night he'd have two bands alternating until the next morning. Just like Monte Carlo or Las Vegas. Continuous music, and he was good to musicians.

If you went up to him and told him that you didn't have a job, that was right up his alley, 'cause he'd help you get a room, give you some food, give you some money, and really help you. And he really liked me.

I'd had a problem in Kansas City with a police officer. This guy was interfering with me, you know, that thing where a guy just don't like your looks. So I told Ellis about it. And Ellis sent for this man. This man was a policeman and everybody shivered when you called his name. . . . Ellis Burton never looked a man in the eye. He always had his hat down so that he's looking at your lips and nose . . . and you can't see in his eyes. He said to this man, "If you interfere with Sammy Price anymore, forget those favors that I used to do for you." And the guy left me alone.

Prostitution and Other Sexual Attractions

Although not directly associated with the jazz world, prostitution, drag acts, live sex shows, and other forms of open sexuality were important aspects of Kansas City's nightclub milieu.

Brothels were widely known and tolerated, and so widely dispersed that a well-defined red-light center like New Orleans's Storyville never lasted long. The girls were often also waitresses in the clubs, and were acquainted with many of the musicians. In fact the most common relationships between prostitutes and musicians were familial rather than sexual, and performers often protected the girls from abuse.

Various homosexual performances, including drag acts, were also widespread. As Edna Mintirn so vividly recalls below, the performances were colorful, and the performers were respected members of the professional world.

Many other club attractions were also primarily sexual. A semiclothed or naked shake dancer; a waitress or singer picking up tips with her vulva; heterosexual, homosexual, and bestial sex shows all could be readily seen in K.C. A particularly well-known spot in the late twenties and early thirties was the Chesterfield Club, a downtown businessmen's restaurant that featured four categories of naked waitresses, two Caucasian, two Negro, with pubic hair shaved to represent a heart, diamond, club, and spade.

Prostitution

Herman Walder: They had a red-light district down on Thirteenth Street. Red lights in all the windows. [They would] knock on the windows [at you]. The high-class Negro place was Anna Rhine, she had a baby grand piano in her house, and had all nations to choose from. . . . Hers was high-class. That's where all the big shots went. . . .

I know some cats tell me, down on Eighteenth Street, used to be [cost] a quarter. It went from a quarter to fifty cents. This was during the Depression time, man. Fifty cents, then seventy-five, then a dollar, and then the cats started hustlin', tryin' to cheat 'em down.

Charles Goodwin: Bennie Moten played in the houses. . . . played mostly blues, because that's what people like. The gals, they always have a hang-up, . . . feeling low. . . . Where the music would be going on there probably wouldn't be nothing in there but just a piano and a few chairs. [They were] sitting around, and sometimes they get raided, all of 'em go down to the can, but they'd get out right away. They [would] do whatever you wanted to do. But most of all you spend some bread. . . .

[They were mostly] down around Sixth Street and Independence Avenue. This is where the big happenings was on that kind of stuff. It was wild and rough, anywhere they serve booze. There's some guys that can't control it and there's going to be a whole lot of scrapping and fighting.

Eddie Durham: The clubs were very risqué. Like we'd have girls dancing, . . . one young girl [would] get nude and pick up the money. The guys would lay the money up there to see her pick it up. She'd do an hour, then the next hour she's going to go to another gangster club.

Henry McKissick: [There was a red-light district] in my ward, [at] Fourteenth and Thirteenth, and Cherry and Holmes. I always have thought that [it was better to have prostitution concentrated in one area]. That's what I told the Kefauver Committee. . . . They're never going to stop it, so . . .

I never attended any of 'em, [but] I registered and voted, got 'em to vote.

Other Sexual Attractions

John Tumino: I'll tell you this, they never closed any doors in some of those days, and that's a fact. There was a lot of places that never had a key. . . . A lot of places had gambling, . . . bingo upstairs and tables downstairs. . . . Every place had a slot machine. . . . The clubs all had shake dancers, . . . strippers really, only they were professional dancers, . . . shake their butts and their bodies and their boobs; . . . they were black. . . .

In a place called the Ship, they had these little old girls come at your table, and you'd lay a dollar on the goddamned corner of the table, and she'd come up and snatch it right up with her little old twat. . . . That's part of the show. . . . Everything went, no holds barred.

Ernie Williams: That's what burlesque is, . . . dancin', dancin' girls. . . . I know some of 'em used to . . . set a table up, see a sack of money, just like that, and roll it up like this and carry it up just right. . . . It was the show. . . . They didn't bother anybody and their numbers was clean. . . . I've seen 'em take dollar bills [and] pick 'em right off the table. . . .

That's a nightclub, . . . somebody'd say that's risqué, but some girls, some people would do that . . . the other way, that's art, the way they do. But these girls now [that] do it; it ain't nothin'.

Herman Walder: In the black clubs they had female impersonators' night . . . and everybody'd come to see 'em dance. It's like that big ball they have in New Orleans, for the Mardi Gras. They have a big drag act where all the gays in town come out and do their show.

Hell, man, we judge people by what they want to be themselves, you dig what I mean? Those people were good, they're always good to you. They'd fill up the kitty if they make some money.

EDNA MINTIRN. *Born c. 1912, Kansas City, Missouri. Singer, dancer, and entertainer. Performed in many K.C. and Chicago clubs through the 1940s.*

The Stork Club was more high-class than Dante's [Inferno, a nightclub where Edna sang]. The furnishings [were better], and they didn't have [female] impersonators. A lot of people didn't like impersonators, but I learned a lot from them all. They're wonderful people, very talented, and our crowd loved them. . . .

When we first got them, people were curious and didn't know what to make of them; the longer we had them, the more they [the audience] liked them. They'd invite 'em to sit, and buy drinks for 'em and everything. The only thing that we had trouble with 'em, the nigger boys would make cracks to them, and they slapped a couple of them around, which is bad. You don't treat those people like that because theirs is just a business. It's nothing personal, and it wasn't safe to have them around the nigs. . . .

This man performed all over the world, this Mr. Half-and-Half. See he had all the sequins and hairdo on this side, and he'd sing the soprano part, and then he'd turn around on the other side with the tux, and sing with a deep voice. And he had a high, coloratura voice. . . .

[For our uniforms at Dante's Inferno] we had a little devil suit with horns. We had tails, but that caused a little business. You'd go by with a tray of drinks and some sucker would get a hold of your tail and stop you. Red velvet shorts and satin tops, a skull cap with little satin horns on it. It was a very spectacular club, and it made a lot of money for them for a long time. We worked seven days a week. Didn't get nights off in them jobs. . . .

We went down in Nigger Town when we got off [work]. We'd go down and watch 'em jam. Twelfth and Vine, that's where the big shots were, and you could sit in there and get three or four drinks and there was so much marijuana in the air you'd get a buzz. Everybody had smoke comin' up off the ashtrays.

Orville Minor: I used to play smokers when I was working down in the Bottoms [the Missouri River bottoms]. In smokers . . . they bring in two men, you know, one guy sticks the other guy . . . that's just one of the acts. . . . Ain't no women, only woman involved is the one doing the act. They've been having those for years. Male and male. One time they brought a dog in . . . when I was working at the Antlers Club. . . . They probably charged guys twenty-five dollars a head to come in . . . around in '37, something in there. . . .

But they had phenomenal acts. . . . They would go get some cat out of the audience, try to stick this chick. . . . He couldn't raise one . . . and you'd just die laughing. He'd get up there and try and try and try. . . . They had women [that] smoked cigars thataway too. They did all sorts of things.

Gene Ramey: There was a club that I worked in that was two blocks down the street from where Basie was, and we had nude women working there every night. Now this was back in 1934. They had them large glass windows, but they had them painted up to, say, this high. . . . They thought they could paint it high enough where only the grown people could look, but it ended up everyday had to chase those teenaged boys away from the [window].

Prohibition, Bootlegging, and Narcotics

The link between the growth of organized crime in America and Prohibition has long been recognized. Prohibition (begun January 16, 1920) had the effect of channeling the supply of a durable public need to mobsters, who were willing to organize and develop the massive infrastructure needed to satisfy a demand of that proportion. In the process, organized crime became entrenched in the nightclub business because clubs were a convenient conduit for liquor sales, and developed the wealth, power, and greed to move into other areas, particularly narcotics.

The liaison between club management and narcotics distribution proved disastrous for generations of jazz musicians and black Americans. The mob began to shift into narcotics sales at the end of Prohibition (December 5, 1933), just as a new generation of musicians were experimenting with new musical ideas and rebelling against the manners of their elders. Charlie Parker led the musical revolution and also, in the minds of many of his contemporaries, was a tragically significant role model in leading black youths to heroin.

Parker was a musical genius and an enormously charismatic figure, in many respects the Louis Armstrong of his generation. For Armstrong, the diversion was marijuana. Parker found it in heroin, which was readily available in Kansas City in the mid-1930s. Much of a generation of black youth saw Charlie as a hero. His art was transcendent and many sought to emulate him, even his heroin use. Some of Parker's contemporaries thus attribute an important part of heroin's spread in black America to Bird's example.

Many of the accounts that follow treat the playfulness and excitement of intoxication, and accurately show an important and usually pleasant aspect of the scene, along with the sense of experimentation and adventure that jazz musicians felt. The dark side of the story only peripherally emerges, but cannot be ignored.

Prohibition and Bootlegging

Charles Goodwin: We played in a place called [the] Imperial Ballet with the twelve-piece band, and we got raided there [for] illegal sale of whiskey. This was still during Prohibition, hadn't been repealed yet. The G-men chopped their way in there one night. They'd been taking pictures of people going in. The people coming out be weaving, you know, and they found a weak spot in the wall and just chopped away. About six or seven guys came in, some of them with their pistols drawn.

They wanted to confiscate our instruments . . . [but] we were working on a job, so we talked them out of [that].

Eddie Barefield: Nightclubs were good for bootlegging . . . and they [the bootleggers] never bothered people, they only bothered themselves. They were fighting all amongst themselves. It was all over business. . . .

The speakeasies [in Kansas City] weren't really in the black neighborhood. In the black neighborhood they pretty nearly ran free.

Marijuana and Narcotics

Gene Ramey: Before I left Texas I smoked it [marijuana] a couple of times. . . . You could get a sack of marijuana right here in Austin [Texas] for ten cents, one of those full bags, . . . like of Bull Durham tobacco.

I remember when we were with the McShann band, and I'd say our front line got pretty much indulged. . . . You probably knew [that] Charlie Parker [used marijuana and heroin]. We used to go along the highway when we played up in Lincoln or Omaha, Nebraska, you'd see marijuana wild on that highway. We'd just get off and a guy would go off in the field [to cut it]. . . . Man, it looked like a man with a bale of hay comin'. The top of that car was covered with it. We'd say "Drive fast!" so it would dry out.

I remember in Kansas City, the guys used to go down to the river. . . . The weeds would be about this tall [a man's height]. The guys would go down there after they got off work at night . . . and they'd get themselves some marijuana in the dark. . . . It's a funny thing the cops never caught them, but you'd see about fifty cats breaking out of the weeds.

Buddy Anderson: You've seen people like that [on narcotics], you know them and they'll just be acting ordinary and then suddenly . . . he's not with you. . . . I don't think this was heroin [that] was comin' out [in the late thirties]. It was morphine.

I just really can't say [why Parker got involved]. It was a social thing that I haven't let never phase me too much, but I know that Bird influenced a lot of it. In fact, he is *the* influence on hard drugs in America. More than anybody, he popularized it, although Billie Holiday had made it [was known to be an addict] already.

So many young cats, just learning, went to the pen and everything. A whole generation of cats was done in. I don't believe there's anything as lethal as heroin.

John Tumino: [Pot] is the only thing they lived for I think, some of 'em in those days. Oh, they drank nutmeg, and this is the craziest thing I ever saw, they did Coca-Cola and nutmeg and aspirin. Now I don't know how they mixed it up, and get a high on. . . .

[Parker] and a couple of other guys that I know of, that's about all [that were involved in heroin]. Most of 'em were grass and juice. . . . Charlie Parker was always broke every morning. He was hocking his instrument every day to get the stuff. I'd have to go and get the money, get the horn and put him to work the next night, and make him promise not to hock it before he get [to work].

Herman Walder: I saw one cat do that [take large quantities of nutmeg as as intoxicant]. I've never done it in my life. He's a white fella, he was scared, he says, "Man, I drank a whole box of that stuff." . . . I've never indulged in nothing but the pipe, man. . . . Any cat's a fool not to get a little potted every once [in a while], it's just good for him, like on lemonade. . . .

[The pot was good,] depending on who you get it from, and where you get it. Mom's [a well-known dealer in marijuana] was a masterpiece. . . .

A long time ago . . . a fella come from Mexico looking for Hot Lips Page, couldn't find him. . . . He says, "Come here, you cats." Jesse Stone was with us then. We went out in the back. Says, "I'm going to light up, don't you all take but two drags apiece, pass it, pass it, pass it." . . . Boy, every time I looked at the cat, it was funny. . . . I went home, my kids was small, . . . they said, "Herman, what you laughing about?" . . . I just had a ball, man, that's the worst I ever been. He was looking for Hot Lips, man, and run smack into my lips.

JOHN HAMMOND. *Born 12/15/1910, New York City. Died 7/10/1987, New York City. Critic and producer. A member of a socially prominent and wealthy family. Hammond began writing jazz criticism in 1931, producing jazz concerts in 1932 and jazz records in 1933. From that time he was among the most influential and most respected figures in jazz, blues, and rock production, aiding the careers of hundreds of musicians.*

I'll never forget the first night [in Kansas City], I went to the Reno [Club, a popular K.C. spot where Count Basie had the house band]. . . . There was a whorehouse upstairs . . . and there wasn't enough money for liquor so obviously it would be, everybody grew pot in the backyard in Kansas City, this was how the band was able to exist. There was a window in the back of the bandstand . . . and people used to just shovel up pot through the back window and it didn't seem to affect the guys at all. It [the Count Basie band] was still the best band I had ever heard, and without that kind of stimulus they couldn't have done it.

NOTES

1. Ralph Capone was the brother of notorious Chicago gangster Al Capone.

2. "Policy" is a colloquial term for numbers racketeering.

3. Among the ways numbers players derive number combinations for betting is by consulting dream books in which certain features of dreams are assigned corresponding numbers.

4. Most of the better nightclubs of the period, even those run by blacks, were for white patrons exclusively. Blacks were often allowed into the balcony on certain nights, or to sit on the bandstand with the musicians.

"The Boss," Tom Pendergast, c. 1933. Pendergast is shown at the height of his power as political boss of Kansas City. (Courtesy of the Kansas City Museum, Kansas City, Missouri, and the *Kansas City Star*)

City Manager Henry F. McElroy, c. 1932. McElroy was Pendergast's "front man" in city hall from 1925 to 1939. (Courtesy of the Kansas City Museum, Kansas City, Missouri, and the *Kansas City Star*)

Johnny Lazia and Mrs. Lazia, c. 1932. Mob boss Lazia led Kansas City's North Side Democratic party faction and, by agreement with Pendergast, controlled political patronage appointments to the police department. (Courtesy of the Kansas City Museum, Kansas City, Missouri, and the *Kansas City Star*)

Food for the Needy of Kansas City's Fifth Ward, c. 1930. Among the positive aspects of boss rule in Kansas City were public services such as the distribution of free food and fuel to the needy, acts that helped provide the Pendergast machine with a strong, legitimate base of popular support. (Courtesy of the Kansas City Museum, Kansas City, Missouri, and the *Kansas City Star*)

"Building the Pyramid," 1933. *Kansas City Star* political cartoonist S. J. Ray frequently lampooned the maneuvers of the Pendergast machine. (Courtesy of the Kansas City Museum, Kansas City, Missouri, and the *Kansas City Star*)

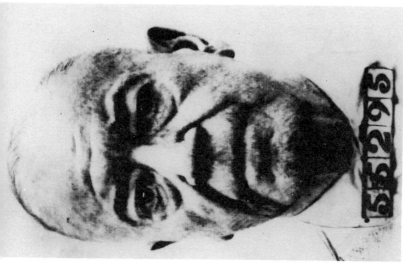

"The Boss" Behind Bars, 1939. Pendergast's conviction for tax evasion resulted from an investigation following his embezzlement of state insurance funds. Boss Tom served a sixteen-month sentence in federal prison and died shortly after his release. (Courtesy of the Kansas City Museum, Kansas City, Missouri, and the Truman Library)

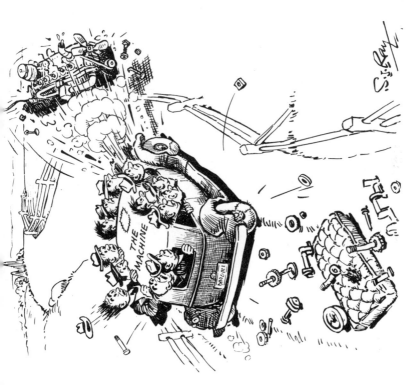

"The Machine," 1938. This S. J. Ray cartoon depicts the breakdown of the Pendergast machine. Blatant civic corruption and uncontrolled racketeering finally led citizens' groups to act against the machine, but even after Pendergast's 1939 conviction for tax evasion his organization remained a potent local political force until the mid-1960s. (Courtesy of the Kansas City Museum, Kansas City, Missouri, and the *Kansas City Star*)

Kansas City Nightclubs, 1935. The plain or even tawdry facades of clubs like those shown in this newspaper photomontage gave no hint of their exotic interiors. In 1935 over three hundred Kansas City clubs featured live music, and many also included floor shows. (Courtesy of the Kansas City Museum, Kansas City, Missouri, and the Kansas City Public Library)

Dante's Inferno, c. 1936. This well-known mob controlled nightclub featured unusual decor such as fire-breathing, smoke-spewing dragons, waitresses in devil costumes complete with pointed tails, and exotic entertainment. (Courtesy of the Kansas City Museum, Kansas City, Missouri, and Edna Mintirn)

Mr. Half-and-Half, c. 1936. Among Dante's acts was this singer/ comedian/female impersonator. (Courtesy of the Kansas City Museum, Kansas City, Missouri, and Edna Mintirn)

Female Impersonator, c. 1936. This female impersonator was another popular act at Dante's Inferno. (Courtesy of the Kansas City Museum, Kansas City, Missouri, and Edna Mintirn)

Orrie Brothers Dance Team, c. 1939. Sophisticated dance acts such as the Orrie Brothers were also crowd pleasers at the local nightclubs. *Left to right:* Raymond Orrie, Dorothy Poston, Frances Williams, Elmer Orrie. (Courtesy of the Kansas City Museum, Kansas City, Missouri, and Elmer Orrie)

9

Stepping Out and Sitting In: The Musician's Nightlife

In many ways the essence of the Kansas City jazz scene is best understood through accounts of the constant jam sessions and warm socializing that thrived in nightclubs. K.C. in the thirties enjoyed a remarkable musical community that largely existed in and around its clubs.

During K.C.'s heyday there was an extraordinary abundance of nightlife. Of literally hundreds of clubs that rose and fell, the most famous are the Sunset, the Subway, and the Reno. Of the countless performers making the scene, many achieved acclaim. Two of them, Joe Turner and Pete Johnson, merit special mention because they are so strongly identified with the joyous spirit of K.C. nightlife.

John Hammond and Jay McShann have the most detailed anecdotes here of Big Joe and Pete, but nearly every musician who ever spent time in K.C. recalls the performances of Turner and Johnson as among the musical highlights of the city. Joe was the greatest blues singer in town (probably the greatest blues singer in any town, and certainly among the fathers of rock and roll), and Pete was the local king of boogie-woogie piano.[1]

Joe and Pete usually played at the Sunset Club, located at Eighteenth and Highland, in the center of the black downtown of the early thirties. (At times Joe also played in other clubs, including the Lone Star and the Cherry Blossom.) Joe was the bartender and would sing from the bandstand, from behind the bar, and occasionally out in the street while the band rocked inside. Joe referred to the street sorties as "calling the children home." He would face first up one side of the street and then down the other, shouting the blues at passersby, encouraging them to come and swing inside.[2]

As Joe strolled the club and belted the blues, Pete would play strong boogie-woogie on the piano, and a drummer (Baby Lovett, K.C.'s best in those days, or Murl Johnson) would back it all up. Piney Brown, the musician's favorite club owner, ran the place. The combination of these riches was irresistible to other musicians, and for years the Sunset was the club of choice for jam sessions and general good times.

When Prohibition closed down clubs in other cities, it served to open them in K.C. The town jumped, and nightclubs were at the center of the action.

Count Basie: Oh my, marvelous town. Clubs, clubs, clubs, clubs, clubs, clubs, clubs. As a matter of fact, I thought that was all Kansas City was made up of, was clubs at one time. . . . I mean, the cats just played. They played all day and tomorrow morning they went home and went to bed. The next day, the same thing. We'd go to one job we'd play on, then go jamming until seven, eight in the morning. I don't think money was all that important then, actually. We never really thought too much about bread. Just wanted to play to make your rent, something like that. Everybody chipped in; it was good times. . . .

Truthfully, I never heard the blues until I did go, have the pleasure of visiting Kansas City, which was in the very, very early days [c. 1925], even before [I joined] the Blue Devils and Bennie Moten's band. We were through there with a burlesque show which I was traveling with named Hippity Hop. And I got a chance to wander over on Eighteenth Street.

At that time it was blazing. I mean, everything was happening there, it was beautiful. Wonderful trumpet players, and clarinet players, and banjo players. You could hear the blues from any window or door. And it's the most remarkable thing I ever heard.

That's when I first got a good taste of listening to a blues singer. I don't know anyone's name, but I do know they were belting out these blues. And great piano players, blues pianists. . . . I'd never seen anything like it.[3]

John Tumino: Kansas City had the cream of the musicians in those days. You know why? Because the town was wide open and every joint had a band. Well, hell, everybody, the rest of the country, was in the Depression. It really was. Now I'm talking about deep depression. They couldn't afford three dollars a night for a musician. But in Kansas City, every damn little old joint had musicians. They came from Oklahoma and New Orleans and Omaha and . . . the whole Midwest. They all came to Kansas City because every joint had a place for 'em. . . . Every joint had music, every joint. And every joint had, every music stand, had a kitty, right in front of it, with a light blinking, you know, put some money in there.⁴

Jay McShann: We had so many different kinds of kitties, you know. . . . We'd always try to fix up something that might be attractive to the customers. And sometimes they'd get a kick out of throwing money into . . . the cat.⁵

Herman Walder: [At the Spinning Wheel we'd play] dance music and novelty music. . . . We'd have a show . . . about four times a night, see. We was going to work at nine o'clock and getting off at four o'clock in the morning. . . . We wasn't making very much money, but we were making more than anybody. . . . This was four dollars a night, we made. . . . And our tips at night . . . when we'd check up, six of us now, sometimes eight dollars, ten dollars, twelve dollars apiece. We had a big cat down there, blinking his eyes, blinking his eyes, when you drop your money in that thing.

Sam Price: They had, like, parties, and we used to go out in the county,⁶ you know, outside of the city [where] they'd have road houses. The only time a guy went to bed is when the sun comes up, and [it'd] be like one of those guys getting back in a casket. . . . I'll bet you there are more [Kansas City] musicians who can tell you how the day breaks.

Jay McShann: We used to have those spook breakfasts. It was a funny sight to see. People would be on their way to work, sittin' out waiting for the streetcar, and they step inside and start listenin' to the music . . . and they put the dinner bucket down and don't go to work. Stay there and ball.⁷

Orville Minor: You're talking about the things called spook breakfasts, because people from everywhere went, no matter who they were, would come in to set in. Of course you might get your head cut, musically.⁸ [Then] they would leave there [the Reno Club] and go down to the Sunset. . . . Right across the street was the Lone Star, where Joe Turner was, and they had a band there. . . .

You came on down to the Barley Duke, and went on up the hill to the Spinning Wheel, another joint, and then you're ready to get into the black area. From there on there were nothing but little clubs. . . .

Everybody would go to the Sawdust Trail, that was a restaurant. That's where I met everybody. . . . There was another place which was a knock-down and a drag-out, I mean. It had a whole lot of names, [one

was] Havana Inn. That's where you just take your life in your hands. . . .
In every block there was a club. . . .

I mean, it was really all music up and down Twelfth Street, from
Cherry all the way down to Troost [the de facto dividing line between
black and white Kansas City]. . . . You could just walk that distance and
get all the music you want.

Charles Goodwin: Now Eighteenth Street, from about Charlotte up to
Prospect, was mostly joints. You know, booze houses. The corner of
Eighteenth and Vine there, that's the most celebrated street in Kansas
City. All over the world you can hear about Eighteenth and Vine. There
was a nightclub on the northwest corner and there was one on the
southwest corner, one was Wolfe and the other was Fox. . . . In the middle of the block was the Subway, this was down in the basement, this is
where any musician of any consequence [who had] come to Kansas City,
well, he'd have to come down there and blow, you know.

Kansas City was so full of talented musicians during that time that a
guy would come here and they would just blow his socks off, just blow
him right on out. If a guy come out of Duke's [Ellington] band or
Fletcher's [Henderson] or something like that, we'd go wake some guy
out of bed, [who] we thought was good enough to blow them out . . .
[and] we'd have jam sessions [to do it].

Buck Clayton: They used to have jam sessions like they were gunfight-
ers. . . . Lips Page used to go around and write notes, and find out where
this trumpet player's living, and slip a note under his [door], like he did
Cootie [Williams, trumpet star for Duke Ellington] one time. Lips
slipped a note under Cootie's door and dared him, he said, "Meet me
tonight at such and such club." . . .

All of Kansas City was swinging at that time. And Joe Turner and
Pete Johnson, they were the stars in the Sunset Club.

Jay McShann: The first time I came to Kansas City I'd never been ex-
posed to anything like what was happening then. Joe Turner and Pete
Johnson and Murl Johnson [drummer] were working together [and] I
would go down . . . the street and listen to Joe sing.

I had no idea that sometimes he'd be making up the words as he'd go
along. The thing that really amazed me was that Joe would keep singing
for thirty or forty minutes straight through. . . . Between times he'd tell
Pete to roll 'em [play a boogie-woogie piano solo], and Pete would . . .
roll 'em on piano for maybe ten minutes, then Joe would come back
[and] sing ten or fifteen minutes. You know, they'd play one tune and
it'd last forty-five, fifty minutes and that was the set. A one-tune

set. . . . I'd never seen anything like that. I didn't know when to go to bed. I was afraid I'd miss something.[9]

Mary Lou Williams: [Kansas City] was such a great city for the music, when anyone visited they always stayed! They never left. That's where I met Thelonious Monk, and Joe Smith, the great trumpet player. Fletcher Henderson stayed there, married a girl. It was just so joyous to go out every night, around seven o'clock and jam and play the piano and mingle with people all [through the] morning. . . .

Anybody that came through town, they'd come and get me. If I was home and somebody was in the city, Ben Webster or somebody would come and scratch on the window and say, "Come on out, everybody's jammin'," and I'd get up and go out with 'em. [There were] just thousands of clubs. I've never seen so many clubs in all my life. On Twelfth Street there must have been fifty. They were clean clubs, but not anything classy.

John Hammond: I didn't actually get to Kansas City until late March or early April [1936] . . . and I'll never forget the first night. I went to the [Reno Club]; Basie had a show at eight o'clock at night, eight P.M. to four A.M. They did three shows a night. There were about four chorus girls, there was a whorehouse upstairs, and Basie got eighteen dollars a week and the guys got fifteen dollars a week. . . .

So there I was at eight o'clock and I stayed until four that night. Then afterwards Basie said to me, "Come on, John, I'm gonna take you to the Sunset." I had never heard Pete [Johnson] and Joe [Turner] at that time. Joe Turner was singing at the bar and Pete was in the back room playing, and while Pete was playing Joe would be singing. A room apart, and it was unbelievable. Joe's invention was just endless. One blues could take a good half hour or forty minutes if it was slow and twenty minutes if it was fast. . . . He was just marvelous. Then after that, Basie says, "There's still another place, John."

This was all night. By about seven o'clock we ended up in a place . . . on Eighteenth Street, and there . . . was another wonderful boogie-woogie piano player from Kansas City who never got recorded, unfortunately. His name was Clarence Johnson. I got there, and there was Lester Young, sitting in. This is a very primitive piano player, but wonderful, and there was Prez[10] sitting in [at] this bar. The Paradise, I think. It got to be eleven o'clock in the morning and I was kind of beat, but I got to know some very fascinating people in Kansas City.

Sam Price: I think the thing that fascinated me so about the town was that everybody was so friendly, everybody would eat, almost at the same time. . . . You'd have thirty, forty musicians eating at the same time . . . in a restaurant . . . before they went to work, because you had a lot of bands. . . . You had a lot of great piano players [there, too]. It was just a beautiful kind of thing.

You had Thamon Hayes, you had the Twelve Clouds of Joy, Andy Kirk and Bennie Moten and Harlan Leonard. Plus those big bands had so many piano players. . . . and they'd gather and they were nice and friendly. You rarely ever had a misunderstanding among the musicians. . . .

Kansas City was the kind of place, you didn't make a lot of money, but everybody took care of everybody, and you had one helluva time.

NOTES

1. We are fortunate that many excellent recordings exist of Joe and Pete. Their first and possibly greatest recording was "Roll 'Em Pete," a boogie-woogie and blues anthem that captures the wild exuberance of Joe's incredibly strong blues voice and lyric invention joined with Pete's unstoppable boogie piano rhythms. Many others followed. One to look for is "Piney Brown Blues," Joe's ode to the deceased club owner and friend.

2. Joe was not only a brilliant blues singer, sensitive, swinging, and inventive; he was also the loudest singer I ever heard. My first personal encounter with Big Joe was in 1976 at Barney Josephson's Cookery in New York City. Joe was sixty-five years old and no longer the big, well-built lady-killer of his youth. He must have weighed at least three hundred pounds and could barely walk (later he was forced to use crutches and a wheelchair because of his weight), but he could still sing. He held the microphone down below his waist, and raised his voice to the crowd. People in the first few tables were deafened, but everybody was impressed. In his prime, at the Sunset Club, he must have been truly awesome.

3. These remarks are quoted from an interview with Count Basie by Ralph J. Gleason on "Jazz Casual," a KQED (San Francisco) television program, in 1968.

4. Club owners were not only often patron saints of musicians (as noted in chapter 8); they also used the abundance of talent and good feelings in the city to their own advantage. Many clubs never had to hire a full-time band. Instead they could either hire only a core rhythm section—piano and drums, possibly with bass—or no one at all, and count on the ambiance of the club, the club owner's good reputation among musicians, the ever-present "kitty" that collected tips for the performers, and the prospect of free food and drink to attract musicians for all-night jam sessions. Many clubs, including some of those most favored by musicians and crowds, thrived in this fashion for years.

5. Litwak and Pearson, *Goin' to Kansas City*, 36; used with permission.

6. "Out in the county" refers to areas beyond Kansas City's limits in Jackson County, where the already lax enforcement of vice laws, particularly closing times, became nonexistent. It is particularly remarkable that many of the county clubs, which specialized in after-hours entertainment that was often of a rowdier nature

than that in K.C., also were among the most racially open (if not tolerant). Many musicians recall those clubs fondly and mention a mixing of black and white patrons that was rare in Kansas City. This is remarkable because rural Missouri (even today the "county" is often rural) was notably racist.

7. Quoted from "Hootie Blues," a 1978 Nebraska Educational Television (NETV) production. Used with permission.

8. Having one's "head cut" refers to "losing" in a jam session.

9. Quoted from the *Kansas City Star*, September 30, 1983. Copyright *Kansas City Star*. All rights reserved.

10. "Prez" or "the President" was Lester Young's nickname.

10

Kansas City Jazz Style

The Kansas City style is most strongly identified with swing. K.C. swing is founded on a strong 4/4 rhythm, fluid soloists, and, most important, riffs. Although not unique to Kansas City, these brief, repetitive, harmonic passages played in strong rhythm became so important to K.C. jazz music that "setting riffs" (creating the riff structure), building new compositions through riff-based improvisation, and using the base of swinging riffs for extended solos were all part of a musical ethos and were a splendidly effective way to blend dance music with improvisational jazz.

Dance music requires consistent and strong rhythm. Constant performance of even the most interesting dance music, however, often becomes boring for talented musicians who want to experiment, learn, create, and grow. Riffs became the Kansas City musician's primary release from potential artistic stagnation.

Background riffs set by rhythm, horn, and reed sections provided a foundation for both dancers and soloists. The persistence of the dance rhythm gave the soloist freedom to depart from it, to weave his musical concepts in relatively free time around this rhythmic core. Riffs are the device that gave such brilliant instrumentalists as Lester Young, Buster Smith, Charlie Christian, Ben Webster, Lips Page, Buck Clayton, and Charlie Parker opportunities to develop fresh concepts in music while still playing economically viable dance music.

Of course, the essence of Kansas City jazz style is found in more than just riffing. A strong feel for the blues was fundamental, as was an innate sense of showmanship. Many fine composers and arrangers also had key parts in producing the K.C. sound, but most acknowledged that their creative inspiration primarily came from their fellow musicians, who were

114

creating new riffs in orchestras and during jam sessions, or stretching musical boundaries in solos emerging from swinging dance music.

The following descriptions of this sound are grouped by major elements—rhythm, riffs, and jam sessions—and conclude with observations on the overall sound that resulted. Most important, these comments also describe a foundation of shared musical sensibility that characterized Kansas City's major jazz orchestras of the thirties—Bennie Moten, Andy Kirk's Twelve Clouds of Joy, Count Basie, George E. Lee, Thamon Hayes's Kansas City Rockets, and Jay McShann.

Rhythm

Charles Goodwin: As far as Kansas City jazz was concerned . . . it was just a beat, . . . we called it the Kansas City beat, . . . and I think the man responsible for this more than anyone else was Bennie Moten. . . . It was a simple, two-beat thing, but it was such an effective thing that everybody was Bennie Moten-oriented. . . . You could tell a Kansas City musician.

Booker Washington: Kansas City has a certain beat of music, and anybody plays here knows that beat. If you're jamming, it's that same beat, you can feel it. And people that knew that went wild. They would . . . go up and down the street, whistling "Moten's Swing."[1]

It's kind of a 4/4 beat backsway. Bennie [Moten] started that [with] his left hand. That left hand, that drum, and the bass fiddle player can carry a solid beat. If you hear Basie, you hear Kansas City. There wouldn't be no boogie-woogie stuff, just straight beat, but he added little extras. I can't describe that, but it's something like a backbeat.

Mary Lou Williams: The Kansas City style was a swinging left hand. . . . If a pianist didn't have a strong left hand, well, he was not considered very good at all. Nobody would play with him. . . . They had quite a number of good piano players.

Gene Ramey: Let me give you my definition . . . of the forms of jazz. New Orleans, which is the original jazz, you know, was . . . built off of marching band, parade band [music]. The drums swung the band. . . .

You go to Chicago-style jazz, which was the same thing, but they put a little organization in the front line. In other words, the three horns, instead of just going for themselves . . . would play some little old arrangement. One guy played the lead, another played the tenor, another played the alto, but they played organized.

Now comes Kansas City, which is like an old-time revival, . . . like an old camp meeting. . . . You hear the people shouting, you hear that in Basie's band, you know. It's just a happy-go-lucky thing. The trumpets are going one way, the saxophones another way, the trombones are still going a different way, and that rhythm section is just straight ahead. . . .

[With a Kansas City band] the rhythm section is supposed to be free. . . . For example, [in] the Basie band, the rhythm section never read the music after the first time. . . . This is why Basie's band has always been famous, and it still sounds the same. The rhythm section is not harnessed. And don't forget, the rhythm section is the food [of a band]. . . . There never was a band that was great unless it had a great rhythm section. . . .

The rhythm section [has to] sound together. In those days they didn't have an amplifier for a piano or for a guitar. The drums were the loudest one in there. Now all four of us got to play, and we've got to play so that the loudest instrument is no louder than the softest instrument. . . .

The drummer's foot was never supposed to be so loud, . . . it's called a "big foot" drummer, . . . anybody'd go crazy after a while, you know, jump out of windows. The Kansas City rhythm sections got together.

Riffs

Jesse Stone: There was a different Kansas City style because the horns themselves played with the rhythm section, like Count Basie's band plays now [in the 1970s]. . . . They can play in rhythm without a drummer. They have that sense of rhythm feeling and that's where the change [to a Kansas City style] happened. When we started transferring the rhythm power from the rhythm section into the brass and reed sections and then played. We practiced that sound.

Gene Ramey: We don't need any [written] music. What we play is on . . . a riff. . . . Kansas City jazz is supposed to be more freedom. . . . But you didn't go too far with the solos. . . . [When] the McShann band went to New York we had the first chorus and the last chorus . . . written. All in between was nothing but riffs. . . . It was [the same] with the Basie band, too. You're getting more to the people because you're going to play those little simple things that they can understand. The rhythm section's got to be swinging. . . .

The less piano you play and the more room you give the bass player to walk and the guitar player to play his chords [the better off you are]. . . . That's why Basie's just swinging. He stays out of the way. . . .

We'd have a jam session, this guy sets a riff over here and this one sets a riff over here and another one sets a riff, and the guys just go on swinging. Each chorus, they'd build it up.

Booker Washington: Riffing is just a pattern that builds from the type piece you're playing. You can play a certain number, and all it requires is [a] harmony background. You take a swing number; to give it more punch you got to add a riff. That's between you and various sections. Your trumpets get together, [and with] somebody else, just build it right from there. . . . But keep it as simple as possible so that you are free jamming. . . . The more simple it is, the better all of it [will] sound.

Buck Clayton: Kansas City music is mostly where they set riffs behind you. No matter who's playing a solo, the guys would get just as much kick out of setting a riff. Like Prez [Lester Young] . . . or Joe Smith . . . if you heard them playing behind somebody. . . . The first one that set the riff, we all had to follow. If you could think of a riff quicker than anybody else, then we'd all follow you. You play it first, then the whole group would play it with you underneath the soloist. And he's just blowing away. . . .

That's what used to make Kansas City music stand out. Nobody else did that. It's the solo playing and the moving background below it, and a strong rhythm section. . . . Swing music. . . . I'm sure it wasn't planned, but it just became the style in Kansas City.[2]

Jam Sessions

Myra Taylor: [At the Sunset Club] musicians would come in and . . . sit and talk with their friends. Their instrument would be down at their side. If . . . they wanted to play, they would just pick up their instrument and play from where they were. . . . You might hear a trumpet from way over there, a trombone from way over here. But they always managed to play a background for whoever was playing a solo.[3]

Sam Price: Jam sessions is just where . . . guys get together and . . . start playing. . . . I remember one night I went in the Subway about nine-thirty, Hot Lips Page was playing "Am I Blue?" or . . . something with Ben Webster or some other musicians, and I stayed there . . . till about twelve or one o'clock and . . . I went home and came back a couple of hours later. They were still playing the same song.

Herman Walder: [A jam session] will wear a drummer down and a piano player and a bass man. . . . I've seen Big [Walter] Page . . . play so long one night . . . [that] his bass just crumbled, looked like toothpicks.

William Saunders: One guy would take fourteen or fifteen choruses before he'd stop. . . . [and] you'd steal passages [from him]. . . . They might be trite to the guy that was playing them, but to you they were different things that you could relate to your playing.[4]

ERNEST DANIELS. *Born 1911, Little Rock, Arkansas. Drums. Moved to Kansas City in 1925. Played in local bands until joining Harry Dillard's WPA band in 1934. Active through the 1970s.*
   What the jam sessions did to a person was acquaint them with new ideas, and you got the chance to play with the best, and so by playing with the best some of that rubs off on you.

T. Holder: In [Kansas City] it seemed like all the boys was musically inclined, because they always had something going. . . . They always was working on some kind of job. . . . They had a whole lot of that [jamming] there. And I loved to jam. I loved to blow cats out. [I'd go down] to the Subway, the Yellow Front. I went to all the clubs, man. Most of them boys would go hide when I came to town. Even if they catch me drunk, they still won't get me.

Gene Ramey: Even to this day, I can . . . tell you that Kansas City is the only place where the musician wants to battle each other with all guns blazing.

Buck Clayton: I remember the first time I went to Kansas City. The first time I took out my horn. There's a place called the Sunset Club, and all those . . . trumpet players looked like they came from behind the walls; they came from under the rug; they came all the way from Kansas City, Kansas, because they knew I was going to be there that night and they all want to cut you.

Mary Lou Williams: [In a jam session] we'd improvise. Somebody'd say, "Let's play 'Georgia Brown.'" You improvise, and I've heard arrangements that were sensational; an arranger couldn't do as good. . . . That's the type of band that Count Basie had. . . . You see, there's an awful lot of love in the music. . . . There was quite a bit of love [in Kansas City]. That's what made it so wonderful.

Buster Smith: There wasn't nothing but jamming then. There wasn't but one band that would come there and wouldn't jam, and that's Duke's boys [Duke Ellington]. But all them other fellows, Fletcher Henderson was the main one. He'd come there, Coleman Hawkins would come there, wouldn't be nothing but tenor players, and Lester Young and Dick Wilson, Ben Webster, Herschel Evans, all of 'em went down there and started jamming, jam all night long. Lester Young and Ben Webster would [come out on top]. See, "Body and Soul" was the main tune [for jamming]. Wasn't but one man made it there and made it back out, that was Chu Berry,[5] all the rest of 'em was run out of town. . . .

Kansas City had the big name, they reigned down here. . . . Some guys didn't think about nothing but Kansas City. All them bands hung out around there.

Jay McShann: Kansas City is at the center of the United States, so when . . . musicians gathered here the styles evolved to . . . the loose, relaxed . . . improvised style.[6]

William Saunders: We'd go down every day and . . . have little sessions down at the union.[7] And everybody knew every out chorus together.[8] . . . We listened. We didn't have radios or television to interrupt us. . . . That developed the Kansas City style because you would hear in a cluster and the style just developed between your ideas coming in here from Texas and Oklahoma and possibly Nebraska and Colorado, and there's a fusion of all those ideas together, and over a period of years and a period of sessions it became obvious as the Kansas City style.[9]

NOTES

1. "Moten's Swing" was a 1931 composition by Eddie Durham based on "You're Driving Me Crazy." It became the theme song of the Moten band, and, eventually, of Kansas City jazz.
2. K.C. was not the only jazz center where riffing was popular. In somewhat different fashion riffs were also commonly used in New Orleans, and by other prominent 1930s swing bands elsewhere.
3. Litwak and Pearson, *Goin' to Kansas City*, 30; used with permission.
4. Ibid.
5. Tenor saxophonist Leon "Chu" Berry followed Coleman Hawkins, Lester Young, and Ben Webster with the Fletcher Henderson Orchestra in 1935. He joined Cab Calloway's band in July 1937 and remained there until his death in 1941. Berry was widely regarded as one of the most accomplished if not distinctively innovative saxophonists of his day.
6. Quoted from "Hootie Blues," a 1978 Nebraska ETV production. Used with permission.

7. Local 627 of the American Federation of Musicians, K.C.'s black musicians' union hall.

8. The "out chorus," or theme, of a tune was often used as the foundation for riffs. Shared knowledge of such basic musical building-blocks gave Kansas City musicians a common vocabulary of key musical phrases that in turn permitted the exuberant jamming that characterized the city.

9. Litwak and Pearson, *Goin' to Kansas City*, 24; used with permission.

Dave Lewis Jazz Boys, c. 1922. Dave Lewis led one of Kansas City's earliest jazz bands. (Courtesy of the Kansas City Museum, Kansas City, Missouri, and Lawrence Denton)

Chauncey Downs and His Rinkey Dinks, c. 1927. This popular Kansas City band flourished in the mid-to-late 1920s. (Courtesy of the Kansas City Museum, Kansas City, Missouri, and the Mutual Musician's Foundation)

Julia Lee Trio, c. 1948. Julia Lee, sister of bandleader George E. Lee, remained active in Kansas City after her brother's Singing Novelty Orchestra disbanded. She was extremely popular locally, made several successful recordings, and was a favorite of Harry S. Truman, which led to several White House performances during Truman's presidency. (Courtesy of the Kansas City Museum, Kansas City, Missouri, and the Mutual Musician's Foundation)

Herman Walder Swing Unit, c. 1946. Typical of the many small jazz bands in Kansas City was this ensemble that played at the Paseo Boulevard Room. *Left to right:* Herman Walder (alto saxophone), Mabel Marshall (piano), Edwin "Little Phil" Phillips (drums). (Courtesy of the Kansas City Museum, Kansas City, Missouri, and Herman Walder)

Curtyse Foster Band at the Reno Club, c. 1942. Foster was active in Kansas City from the early 1930s through the 1970s. The "kitty" perched in front of the reed section was the ubiquitous repository for tips. The Reno Club was where the Count Basie Orchestra first performed and made radio broadcasts that led to Basie's "discovery" by John Hammond. (Courtesy of the Kansas City Museum, Kansas City, Missouri, and Charles Goodwin)

Hot Lips Page with the Bus Moten Orchestra, c. 1937. Star trumpeter and vocalist Hot Lips Page is shown in a guest appearance with Bus Moten's orchestra at the Reno Club. This band and the Buster Smith-Count Basie Barons of Rhythm formed from the remnants of Bennie Moten's orchestra after his death. By the time Bus Moten's group was booked into the Reno Club, Basie had left for New York and stardom. (Courtesy of the Kansas City Museum, Kansas City, Missouri, and the Mutual Musician's Foundation)

Big Joe Turner, c. 1945. Big Joe was Kansas City's best-known and finest blues singer. (Courtesy of the Kansas City Museum, Kansas City, Missouri, and Jimmy Jewell)

Jam Session at St. Mary's Church, Kansas City, Kansas, c. 1939. Impromptu jam sessions were the hallmark of Kansas City jazz. This one included several local musicians who were then featured with Jimmie Lunceford's Orchestra: Joe Thomas (tenor saxophone, far left), Snooky Young (trumpet, next to Thomas), and Jimmy Crawford (drums). (Courtesy of the Kansas City Museum, Kansas City, Missouri, and John Randazzo)

Musicians' Union Local 627, May 4, 1930. The opening day of Kansas City's black musicians' union at 1823 Highland was a major event. Band battles had been staged for years to raise money for the building, and all the major local bands turned out for the celebration, including George E. Lee's Singing Novelty Orchestra, Bennie Moten's Orchestra, and Paul Bank's Rhythm Aces. The building is still used as a musicians' clubhouse and was designated a National Historic Landmark. (Courtesy of the Kansas City Museum, Kansas City, Missouri, and the Mutual Musician's Foundation)

Nightclub Advertisements, 1936-37. Nearly every club had special attractions and gimmicks designed to draw a crowd. "Spook breakfasts" were held for incorrigible nightowls who stayed up until dawn, or for those who wanted some good jazz before beginning the workday. (Courtesy of the Kansas City Museum, Kansas City, Missouri, and the *Kansas City Call*)

11

The Bennie Moten Orchestra

Kansas City jazz is noted among jazz enthusiasts for many things, including the birth and rise of the Count Basie band, and the development of Charlie Parker, progenitor of modern jazz. Among Kansas City musicians, however, the city, the style, and the era of its flowering are virtually synonymous with the Bennie Moten Orchestra.

Moten led the first jazz band in Kansas City and kept his orchestra in a dominant position in the city until his accidental death in 1935. The Count Basie orchestra, a direct outgrowth of Moten's band, continued to carry important elements of the Moten sound through to the 1980s. Bennie was a good but not remarkable pianist by the standards of his day. A well-known bon vivant, he was most of all a canny, generous, and sensitive bandleader with a strong musical sense and the wisdom to consistently employ the best musicians in the region.

Fortunately for jazz listeners, Moten recorded often and became a major star for RCA Victor in the 1920s with his recording of "South." By following the changes in his band's sound on recordings one can trace the development of K.C. jazz. In the early twenties Moten had a relatively crude, "stomping" style, not particularly distinguished from that of his contemporaries. By the late twenties Bennie had raided much of Walter Page's Blue Devils and was playing hard swing. Moten's final recordings, from 1932 (including his and Kansas City's theme, "Moten Swing"), are quintessential big band swing—powerfully rhythmic, woven with several complex themes, characterized by superb timing, and performed by musicians whose sensitivity and group interplay border on the telepathic. It is a pity that the band's final three years, when Moten had his greatest musicians playing at their peak, were not recorded.[1]

Among the Moten alumni were: Bill "Count" Basie, Jimmy Rushing, Lester Young, Eddie Durham, Hot Lips Page, Ben Webster, Walter Page, Buster Smith, Eddie Barefield, Dan Minor, Joe Keyes, Harlan Leonard, Thamon Hayes, Woodie Walder, Ed Lewis, Booker Washington, Jack Washington, and Willie MacWashington—an extraordinarily rich sampling of the greatest Midwestern musicians of the period.

The following accounts trace the beginnings and rise of Moten's orchestra—its transformation when Territory-band musicians from the Blue Devils and elsewhere were hired in, and its dissolution upon Moten's death. It begins with the account of Parris "Dude" Lankford, the drummer in Moten's first band. Following Dude, the accounts are framed by Booker Washington, prominent K.C. trumpeter, who was featured with Moten during the orchestra's most prosperous years and who left after Moten added new musicians in the early thirties.

Moten's First Band: B. B. and D.

Dude Lankford: [When] I first met Bennie, he was playing around town, little old joints here, some of 'em just little fronts, a bar and a gambling room in the back. Just have piano and drums in there. [Dice] and pool tables back there. . . . Bailey [Hancock] was a blues singer; we picked him up [in 1918]. . . . Everybody knew us real well, B. B. and D. [We] always used to call it Big, Black, and Dirty. We'd get that dago wine, just have a ball. . . .

The Labor Temple . . . was the big dance hall [in town] . . . [and] Ted McCue [was the manager]. . . . His sister, Jeanette McCue, had a dancing school up there. . . . We, Bennie, Bailey and myself, played for the school up there from time to time. . . .

We went up there and got [our first job] on a Friday night [December 1918]. It was our first dance, we had the bills all up, tacked up all them posters in windows and things, "Labor Temple," "Labor Temple." . . . "Bennie, Bailey and Dude," we had big placards made up, in great big letters, would put 'em all up in windows and things for our dances. Now we got cold feet, 'cause a streetcar strike was on, [it was] snowing, cold. . . . Now it was so bad we were scared to go up in the hall, and we didn't think no one was coming, scared we wouldn't make the limit, and we didn't have no money to pay Mr. Ringling [the owner].

In those days you could get dago red, dago wine. Well, we used to go to the North End [then and now Kansas City's predominately Italian district] and get that dago wine, a quart bottle for a quarter, and 'twould knock you out.

We went over there and got that wine, got a little nerve [to] go on up there to the dance. A few people are standing outside, and say, "Look here, these people must be fools to come out on a night like this." But the dance hall is so nice, big nice dance floor. . . . We went on in. Took the elevator on up to the second floor, and still was kinda shaky but that wine kept us going.

We had one of them [attendance counters] you press like that, to count people. We had a fellow would press that thing every time a couple would come on in, and at one time we had twenty-three hundred on the floor. . . . Things was on in them days. That place was packed, you couldn't get in, the first floor and the second floor. . . .

I'll tell you we was blowed, knocked us out. Got about seventy or eighty dollars apiece. That was during World War I. . . .

B. B. and D. didn't last too long, but I'll tell you, we didn't think there was going to be a B. B. and D. at all that first night we opened.

We stayed there for over a year I guess. . . . We had three nights up there, Monday night, Thursday night, and Saturday night. . . . We gave Bailey a dollar and a half for singing them three nights, and of course me and Bennie split the spoils. I wouldn't tell a lie, God strike me dead. I wasn't [ashamed] then, I am now. [Bailey] didn't care, just as long as he was singing, and there was a lot of pretty girls. . . .

It was the only dance hall in town and it was just crowded every night. . . . They'd have a sign written in the window, "Learn how to dance." . . .

We got to be big shots on account of making money. A hundred and something apiece [per night]. . . . We knew a fellow that was in show business and a pretty good friend of ours, got to be a car agent; he sold me a car and he sold Bennie a car, a Chalmers, and a Peerless. Then we were big shots then, sure enough. . . . We'd parade all up Eighteenth Street. People would say, "Look at them big niggers." . . . We used to wear old big celluloid collars . . . and a big cravat tie. . . .

We'd go [attend shows] in all the big theaters. Down at Fifth and Walnut was the Joyce, great big theater. Then we'd go up to Seventeenth and Walnut and there was the Grand Theater; they all was great big theaters, with them musical comedies going on. Then you come on to Ninth and Holmes, there was the Auditorium Theater. We had pleasure going to all of them. It only cost us a quarter. At the Century Theater, Twelfth and Central, [they] had burlesque shows. Then to enjoy the big shows, like Ziegfeld Follies, we'd go to the Willis Wood at Tenth and Wyandotte. They had a balcony [for the black people]. At Twelfth and McGee was the Empress Theater. We enjoyed ourselves. But them was the happy days. . . .

We played waltzes, schottisch, all kinds of things. We never did practice. Most of the time musicians [would] just come, sit in, blow their heads off. . . . In them days they could play with each other. Different people would come to sit in, just to be blowing, you know, and sharpen their stuff up. . . .

The white dances would have two-step and things like that; they wouldn't have fancy dances. The colored dances had schottisches and waltzes, one-steps. . . .

Bennie wasn't much of a manager, 'cause there wasn't much to manage. Just the three of us all the time, playing together. It's a great thing to be a manager, and be a manager right, but Bennie didn't have no idea of doing that. . . . That was his downfall there, wine, women, and song. . . . Bennie wasn't a musician; he was a piano player. When you say "musician," you've said a mouthful.

Dude was probably thinking more of himself than Bennie Moten when he asserts that "wine, women, and song" were Moten's downfall. Dude left the apparently good life in K.C. in the early twenties to hit the road with TOBA, vaudeville, and carnival shows. He stayed on the road, returning home occasionally, until the early forties when he moved back to Kansas City.

Howard Litwak and I located Dude in July 1977 after some detective work. Many of our musician friends believed that Dude might still be around, although he was certainly blind, but no one knew where he might be, in Kansas City or elsewhere. Howard discovered that Dude was still in the city by searching through local social service records for elderly, blind, welfare recipients. This source could not release his address, so we then persuaded a social worker to call Dude and tell him that some folks wanted to talk. Ten days later his daughter called us.

Dude was an impoverished, lonely man, but blessed with a vivid memory and a storyteller's gifts. His greatest interest was in chasing women, and he regaled us for hours with tales of exotic days on the road. Particularly interesting was his winter-long interlude as the house guest of a Montana brothel. It was too cold to go outside.

Booker Washington: Dude was an excellent drummer in those days. In fact he was one of the top drummers in those days, 'cause he had the experience and the knowledge. . . . Bennie started out as B. B. and D., Bennie, Bailey, and Dude, and then he kept adding to the orchestra. He come up with five [pieces, by 1922], then he come up with seven, until he got to fifteen pieces.

The Moten Band in the Twenties

JERRY WESTBROOK. *Born 2/2/1904, Westpoint, Mississippi. Piano and vocals. Active in Kansas City in the twenties and thirties. Achieved considerable local prominence by being the first black performer to have local radio broadcasts. Continued to perform with the Little Jerries through the late 1970s.*

Bennie Moten always wanted me to go as his second band [in the twenties]. That would have meant that . . . whenever he got more jobs than he could do, he would call me.

So he had two or three jobs. He was going to be playing at Labor Temple hall at Fourteenth and Woodland, and he gave me the job playing down here at Lincoln High School for this junior-senior reception that they were having. . . .

He had a nice, round face, dark brown skin, was a nice piano player, and the first records he put out . . . were called "Elephant Wobble" and "Crawdad Blues." [These recordings were made in 1923, the first by a K.C. band.[2]] I taught Woodie [Walder] to solo in those pieces. I hummed it to him on the kazoo, and he caught it on his clarinet, and that's what he used.

Eddie Durham: Bennie Moten was the king. He was the king all out. Only person, maybe, who could play with him would be guys like Duke [Ellington]. He didn't ever battle with those guys, because he was his own promoter. . . . It was a commonwealth band, everybody got the same money, leaders and all.

Bennie had a funny kind of swing. I don't know what you would call it back in those days. Wasn't no Dixieland; . . . those guys had a funny style that [no one else] played much. I often think about this tenor guy, Woodie Walder, that was in Bennie Moten's band. No other tenor player in the world ever sounded like that guy. . . . He could swing that stuff. . . . It was commercial the way he would do it, enough so you could keep up with him.

Booker Washington: I first met Bennie when I was playing with this school group [from Western University, Kansas City, Kansas] . . . and one evening [in 1929], one Sunday night, Bennie come up and said, "I have an opening, I'd like you to take it." I'd heard of him, but I'd never heard him, or seen him. . . . I said I didn't want to go noplace. . . . I was well satisfied . . . So he said, "Meet me down at ---." It was a bar, large place, and Bennie was treating at that every day. . . . You just could gather in there. . . .

I met him the next day. He said, "Washington, I want you to go with my band. I need a trumpet player." Paul Webster [had] left the band and went . . . to Chicago with some band. Later on he joined Cab Calloway; later on he was with Jimmie Lunceford.

But I told Bennie, "I don't think I want to go with you. You play different-type music than I play, number one, [and] I'm not ready to go out of town." 'Cause I was thinking of getting married then. . . . So, we had a little taste together. Pretty soon I said I'd let him know tomorrow.

I was sitting in the Lincoln Theater, looking at a show down there, somebody'd page Booker Washington. I got up and went to the front and there was Buster Berry [Leroy "Buster" Berry was Moten's banjoist]. Buster said, "Bennie want to see you right away." So I left the show [to] go there. Bennie said, "We leaving tomorrow, sent Buster up to . . . help you pack your clothes. We are leaving for Oklahoma tomorrow." Didn't ask me did I want to go or not.

I went up to where I stayed and [got] my little grip, put clothes in it, go on out. Next morning I caught the bus to Oklahoma City. [I] hadn't even heard the band, don't know what they're going to do. . . . [But] Bennie Moten had one of the greatest names in Kansas City, and if anybody didn't take up a chance to join Bennie Moten's band, he was just pretty silly. . . .

After I got straightened out . . . Bennie called rehearsal to see if I had memorized my stuff, the music. So I started playing and he says, "You take [the solo on] this number we're playing. [Then], slow down, I like it." So I'm in now.

We started to play there and played there [in Oklahoma City] all summer. This was in 1929. . . . I was about nineteen, the others could have been twenty, twenty-two. That was practically a young group except [for] fellas like Vernon Page and Thamon Hayes and Bennie. Those were considered elderly. . . .

At those places like Oklahoma City, we exchanged two cities. George Lee played one week in one town, in Tulsa, and we'd play a week in Oklahoma City. Then George would go to Oklahoma City and we'd go to Tulsa. Bennie was paying anywhere from fifty-five dollars up [per night, per man]. That was good money then.

So I stayed with Bennie. We left Oklahoma and made a tour through the South, Texas and Louisiana . . . during the off-season. Then we was going back home. We played right here [for] all the different dances, big dances, at Fairyland Park, at the El Torreon Ballroom. Bennie was one of the most popular bands around here then. He had just about all the jobs [and] I grew to love it.

The Moten Band—Personnel and Style

Booker Washington: [The band then] was, percussion section, Willie MacWashington, Bennie, and Leroy Berry [banjo], they had three percussions, and a tuba, Vernon Page. The saxophones were Harlan Leonard, Jack Washington, and Woodie Walder. The trumpets was Ed Lewis and myself, Thamon Hayes on trombone. Had ten pieces. . . .

Now when we were playing Oklahoma City with Bennie there was a famous fella that we couldn't pull off [from the Blue Devils] . . . and that was [Count] Basie. . . . [Even so] pretty soon he ended up playing piano [with us, by late 1929]. . . . On the big jobs Basie and Bennie would play the piano, had two pianos going.

Buster Smith: Basie used to be with the Blue Devils. In '28, Walter Page was heading the band and Bennie [Moten] wanted a piano player; he got tired of playing the piano by himself all the time, because he had Buster [Moten, Bennie's nephew, performed vocals, accordion, occasional piano, and was the orchestra director] in front of the band playing accordion. So he stole Basie from me right here on State Street [Dallas, Texas]. 'Cause we got Basie out of Kansas City when we went there the first time. He came there with a show, Gonzelle White, and the show ended, he got stranded in town. So Basie just barnstormed around town, and so we got him and brought him on down with us. He wasn't down here a month before Bennie sent for him to come back to Kansas City.

Jesse Stone: Count Basie really got into that band because Bennie was such a businessman. He had to spend so much time taking care of business. He would work on the door and watch the ticket office and all that sort of stuff and the band would be playing without a piano.

In reality, Count Basie came in this band like a valet. He was hanging around with the band,[3] and all the guys were wanting him to play because he could play. Count Basie played a whole lot more piano then.

Booker Washington: Then he added more pieces and we made a tour. He added Hot Lips Page [and] he added James Rushing.

Jay McShann: I caught . . . the Bennie Moten band [when I was growing up in Muskogee]. . . . The first time I ever heard [Jimmy] Rushing . . . he was using a megaphone. . . . He'd stand up, put it to the side of his mouth and he would sing the song about "when the leaves bid the trees good-bye." And that was a waltz. . . . He impressed me more with that number than anything he did that night. . . . I never did forget that. . . . I liked the tune and I liked the way he was slurring those notes, what he did with it.[4]

Booker Washington: We [started traveling] mostly in individual cars and later on, when we started growing, we bought a bus. . . . I think the longest jaunt I had was . . . from New York, clean down to the Virginias on a six-band tour, Cab Calloway, Andy Kirk, Bennie's band, and three others. . . .

We bought uniforms every so often. We had different combinations of uniforms. One was a Spanish-type uniform, and one was a frock coat, yellow striped trousers. . . . You'd better be neat at all times. . . .

The bus driver would take care of most of [the valet duties]. His name was Layman Dorton; he was the driver and the handyman. . . .

Our repertoire was quite large then. We didn't have to depend on no five or six tunes, 'cause we had a variety of different tunes. We had soft ones, . . . jump music; we had medium music; . . . we had waltzes, fox-trots, one-steps, and swing. . . .

Do you know what people in New York said when they first heard Bennie's band? They said [to every other band], "Why don't you move over, we got a band from the West coming up here." There's something about the music that just drove them frantic. I don't know whether it was the beat, or what it was. . . .

I made up a tune during a recording session. . . . We'd sit down and plan until we have an idea . . . and we would get together [and the band would] riff around. You created this theme, saxophone would take it down first, brass would add something to it, . . . then different solos come in and when you got it all together it was a number. . . .

[In the brass section] we would trade ideas and we would try for effects. We were trying to get a blend, where it would sound like one horn, with four different sounds [including the trombone]. . . .

We [the trumpets] were just three of a kind. We each played our own music, our own voice. Ed [Lewis] had a specific part to play. . . . He was the lead trumpet player and I was the second player and Lips [Page] was third trumpet player. We called Lips the "hot man." He was the take-off man [the soloist]. . . .

[Lips Page] was a good section man [too]. He just had natural ability. . . . He started singing more as we went on. . . . He and Louis Armstrong were almost identical. . . .

We had plungers and we had mutes and we had derbys [in the band]; just about everything [for sound effects and showmanship] that there was. We had a rack of instruments. . . . So we had motion, everything was a picture [on stage]. When one would do one thing, we'd all be together.

Saxophones would move their bodies, sway or swing up and down, and fellas like Bus Moten . . . was the champion as far as being in the spotlight. He had personality. And Basie . . . was a show-off on the piano. . . . Just be playing a whole lot of piano. . . .

We rehearsed all the time. In fact . . . if we open up [on tour] on a Monday . . . we would start rehearsing at eight o'clock in the morning, just like it's supposed to go down. 'Cause the show go on at two-thirty, three o'clock and you gotta be ready.

We had a special rehearsal man, Eddie Durham. . . . He would do the stomping-off in the beginning. That's the most difficult thing I ever tried to do, 'cause you have to have a knowledge of music, a knowledge including everything to play a show. . . .

Bus [Moten] was the director. When he wasn't playing accordion he was directing with that baton. . . . [And] Bennie was important. . . . Whether he played a little bit or whether he'd play all night . . . he had to be there.

The only thing about it is, if Bennie would lose his left hand, wouldn't be no Moten style. That's key to that. His rhythm, combined with the percussion, the bass especially. Bennie was one of the best [piano players] in his line at the time that he played.[5] . . .

He was one of the biggest sellers that [RCA] Victor had ever in their record [catalog]. . . . He had a contract with Victor for ages. [They] even sent a crew to record us here in Kansas City at Lincoln Hall. They came here . . . and we recorded for about three or four straight days.

Jesse Stone: There were a lot of sharks out there [in the management of orchestras in the twenties and thirties] and they were taking advantage of every sucker that they could get their hands on. That's why T. Holder's group [the Twelve Clouds of Joy, failed], because the band showed no interest in the business end. You could tell them anything and they would accept it.

Bennie was a shrewd man in a different sort of way, because he was a promoter. Bennie would give those dances. He would have good timing. He would know when to go into a town, like if the railroad yards in Falls City paid off on the first and fifteenth of each month, he'd time it. He would rent a hall and give a big dance there and people were flush with money. This was the thing that he was noted for.

Eddie Durham: Bennie Moten was one of the greatest leaders that ever was. . . . He just knew what to do and how to treat the men, everything like that. And he was the same with the men, exactly, 100 percent.

The Transformation of the Moten Band

Booker Washington: Some [of the songs we played] were memorized and some [played] by charts, most of them by charts, especially when Eddie Durham got in the band. Eddie Durham joined the band right here in Kansas City [in 1929, staying in until 1933, and] started making arrangements then. He added to [the band's sound].

Eddie Durham: I knew how to voice individual harmony up to six parts when I went in [the] band, but they were using three. . . . They could read, but you had to coach them on how to make a true tone. . . .

I made [the band's theme] "Moten Swing" in the theater. We needed it for a show in Philadelphia. . . . We took a lot of encores . . . so the band said, "You got to get some more songs because we're playing the same things over and over." So I took off and went downstairs to make "Moten Swing." I based it on "You're Driving Me Crazy," because we had an arrangement. . . .

Basie came down and started it [but then] got out of there. . . . When he came back he said, "Go ahead, use this [line from] 'Driving Me Crazy' " because he wanted to play that. Then when the band played he took [that line], because he wasn't sure of the chord I run the other stuff against. He knew the melody all right. He helped create that.

Buster Smith: Bennie Moten was great. He was buying arrangements off all them cats, and then they had Eddie Durham doing arrangements too in the Bennie Moten band. Eddie Durham, he was a genius. Eddie Durham made "Moten Swing" up one day. . . . He always did experiment on stuff he was writing.

Druie Bess: Bennie had a band of musicians that stuck together. Nobody could get into his orchestra . . . all through them years [until 1929, when Moten began to raid Walter Page's Blue Devils]. They kept the same bunch. They had such a big name and all. . . .

[Then in 1929] they [several Blue Devils, including Eddie Durham, Lips Page, and Count Basie] went to Kansas City. The reason they got in Moten's band was that . . . Moten went to New York with his old band . . . where there was a booker said, "You've got to change names [in the band], you got a good name but that band stinks." Well now, the Blue Devils come in just blowin' so much, every time one of them Blue Devils come in he'd go in and grab them. . . . He tried to get everybody. Got all them guys that blow. . . . I had a chance to get in there [but I didn't take it].

Booker Washington: [Then] Walter Page joined [in 1931, after Count Basie]. Walter Page was an asset to anybody. [He] brought a better and different sound. The only thing you ever heard beforehand was just a tuba, but Vernon Page had a very mellow and beautiful sound out of the tuba. [But] Walter Page played upright bass [and] gave you a broader sound . . . playing chords.

Buster Smith: So Moten sent all them cars over there [to St. Louis] to pick us up [the remnants of the Blue Devils, after hoboing from West Virginia in 1933] and we joined his band. [When] we got in his band, he wasn't doing nothing much, and so he went around there and had that old place called Cherry Blossom, right on Vine Street there, between Eighteenth and Vine, and he got that job working in there for eleven dollars and a quarter a piece. We played six nights a week. [We had] Bus Moten, Basie.

Buck Clayton: Bennie Moten had the best band [in Kansas City]. . . . That's when he had Eddie Durham and Barefield. He had everybody at one time or other. . . . Basie was with Walter Page and the Blue Devils down in Oklahoma. . . . Lips [Page] was with [Walter] Page, Jimmy Rushing was with Page. So Bennie got a chance to hire just the whole group of them, and he just took [Walter] Page from his band and all the rest of the guys and put them in the Moten band. . . .

It was a hit band all the time, but it was better when Basie and Lips [Page] got into it . . . it just turned Bennie's band around. They played music, it was a nice band, but it didn't swing like it did when Basie came.

Count Basie: [When I joined the band] they were playing swing, that's what I would call it, because that's what Bennie Moten was playing, was swing . . . and it was sort of a Western swing if we would place it that way, 'cause it certainly had a beat. It was real foot-pattin'.

Booker Washington: [I left Bennie in 1932 because] of a misunderstanding. Eddie Durham wanted some specific fellas in the band. Joe Keyes is one, Ben Webster is another. So on our way back [from New York] they come back to Kansas City with us. . . .

[When] we got back to Kansas City, Ed Lewis, Thamon Hayes, Woodie Walder, Vernon Page, and myself said, "Something's happening. I heard them talking in Chicago that they's going to let Booker go and let Woodie go." I was home then. I didn't care. Well, we got together and we formed this other band that was known as the Kansas City Rockets. . . .

[Bennie and Eddie Durham] wanted the best musicians they could find . . . but when Bennie's band went right back to New York, after he formed his new band, people asked, "Where is Booker, where is Woodie [Walder], where is Ed Lewis?" We could sit on the stage at the Pearl Theater and you could hear us in the back. But this new band they took up there, they couldn't hear them in the back. They didn't go over so good. So after they got on the road for about a month, they come back. . . .

When Bennie went back to New York, New Yorkers were playing Bennie Moten's style of music, and Bennie was playing New York's style of music, so it didn't make sense! If you've got something going, you should keep it.

JIMMY JEWELL. *Born c. 1914, Omaha, Nebraska. Club owner and booking agent. Father owned the Dreamland Hall, Omaha's finest black club, which Jimmy took over in 1930. Continued to operate the hall for many years, and booked acts around Omaha.*

When Bennie Moten took his band to New York, with Basie playing piano, they took New York by storm, they'd never heard nothing like it, that Kansas City beat. Then . . . Bennie Moten made a big mistake, he started buying arrangements from those guys in New York till he sounded just like the other bands. They played and had to walk back, they were killed.

The Dissolution of the Band after Moten's Death

Buster Smith: The way the band fell to Basie, we went out in Denver and Bennie got sick. A friend of his was a doctor, named Dr. Bruce. Bennie had adenoids trouble, and he operated on him and he didn't wake up.[6]

Bus was Bennie's nephew, and the band fell to Bus. We came back to Kansas City and Bus went out on Troost there, got a little old job out there, but he was hard to get along with. He'd holler at the boys 'cause somebody'd make a note wrong or somebody'd be late. He'd fuss and raise sin. Bennie was fine, a skillful [leader]; he was very cooperative. Know how to talk to you, never would get mad whatever you did. He was a good fella.

After Moten's death the band split in two. His nephew Bus tried to continue leading the band, but lacked the personality or musicianship required. Where Bennie was steady and good-natured, an excellent judge of talent, and a skilled promoter, Buster was volatile and often ill-tempered. As a result, Buster was unable to attract the best players, and had few solid contacts for bookings. Although several fine musicians including saxophonist William Saunders went with Buster to the Coconut Grove nightclub, most soon went to the lower paying Reno Club with Buster Smith and Count Basie. This band, initially called the Barons of Rhythm, was the true inheritor of the Bennie Moten heritage.

Moten's untimely demise left a void in Kansas City's musical life. He was a remarkable jazz maestro, able to organize and maintain excellent musical organizations through good times and bad. Had Bennie lived to see the return of national opportunities in late 1935 and 1936, he would have been able to present a truly extraordinary band. The lineup of Basie, Walter Page, Buster Smith, Lips Page, Eddie Durham, Lester Young, Ben Webster, Dan Minor, Eddie Barefield, Jimmy Rushing, and others would have been unparalleled.

Fortunately, most of that ensemble is shown off in Moten's final recordings, made on December 13, 1932, in Camden, New Jersey. That session produced a stream of spectacular recordings, among them the first, and greatest, version of "Moten's Swing," "Prince of Wails," "Toby," "Lafayette," and "Milenburg Joys." They represent the apex of Moten's recording career and, for many, the height of Kansas City jazz. Their excellence makes it particularly frustrating that the band performed continuously for another two and a half years without having another opportunity to record. These last recordings also clearly show that the roughness reported by Booker Washington and Jimmy Jewell was long gone. This was a superb, thoroughly polished swing band.

Count Basie later made the Kansas City style and sound famous to jazz listeners everywhere, but his great first recording orchestra was largely derived from Moten's, and it lacked several of the performers most prized by Moten's fans, particularly Lips Page, Buster Smith, and Ben Webster. We can still be grateful for the joy that Moten's recordings give, and for the memory of a big, round, friendly man who grew from being one of a naive trio known as "Big, Black, and Dirty" into the premier bandleader in America's hottest jazz town.

NOTES

1. Moten's absence from the recording studio during his last, and greatest, three years is entirely attributable to the Depression. Between 1932 and 1935 relatively few recordings were made, and record sales plummeted from the high levels they had reached in the late twenties. Recognizing the fate that befell Moten, by far K.C.'s best known black bandleader, one realizes how isolated Kansas City truly was from the jazz mainstream and the possibility of reaching a national audience during those years. This was also an important reason why Count Basie had such

a striking impact nationally when he "broke through" in early 1937. His "steady rollin' " rhythm was fresh and powerful. Combined with several brilliant soloists and a great singer in Jimmy Rushing, all of whom were relatively unknown, Basie hit listeners and fellow musicians like a thunderbolt.

2. Nineteen twenty-three was not only the year of Moten's first recordings, but also the pivotal year in the growth of jazz as a nationally popular music. Only a handful of jazz bands had recorded prior to 1923, but many recorded in that first big year. The early date of his initial recording and the regularity of subsequent releases attest to Moten's popularity and his ability to adapt to suit the changing tastes of his audience.

3. Jesse Stone is probably incorrect in stating that Basie was just hanging around the Moten band before he was taken in. Most other accounts agree with Stone that Basie was well known to the other band members before he joined (due in part to his prior experience in Kansas City), but also assert that he was vigorously recruited by Moten. Stone is correct in implying that Moten recognized his own limitations as a pianist, and wished to devote more time to leading the orchestra. Basie was the perfect and much sought-after choice to take his place at the piano bench.

4. Litwak and Pearson, *Goin' to Kansas City*, 22; used with permission.

5. Despite near-universal agreement that Bennie was responsible for popularizing a distinctive rhythm that became known as the "Kansas City beat," not everyone thought of him as a particularly gifted pianist. Buster Smith asserts that "Bennie was a mediocre piano player, old timer you know"; and Mary Lou Williams noted that Moten's "style as a piano player was more of a slapstick kind of thing."

6. Moten died at the age of thirty-nine of heart failure following a simple tonsillectomy performed by a surgeon-friend who is said to have been hung over during the operation, after all-night clubbing with Moten.

Bennie Moten's Radio Orchestra, c. 1925. This earliest known photograph of the Moten band shows a five-piece ensemble that had evolved from his original trio but was still smaller than his later jazz orchestras. *Left to right:* Willie Hall (drums), LaMar Wright (trumpet), Bennie Moten (piano), Thamon Hayes (trombone), Woodie Walder (clarinet). (Courtesy of the Kansas City Museum, Kansas City, Missouri, and Herman Walder)

Bennie Moten Orchestra, c. 1926. Now with eight pieces, the Moten band steadily grew in both size and sophistication. *Left to right:* Willie MacWashington (drums), George "Banjo Joe" Tall (banjo), Vernon Page (tuba), Thamon Hayes (trombone), LaMar Wright (cornet), Bennie Moten (piano), Harlan Leonard (saxophone), Woodie Walder (saxophone). (Courtesy of the Kansas City Museum, Kansas City, Missouri, and Charles Goodwin)

Bennie Moten's Victor Recording Artists at Fairyland Park, c. 1932. This fifteen-piece orchestra was Kansas City's most star-studded jazz band, but personnel changes under Eddie Durham's guidance soon led several members to leave to form the Kansas City Rockets. *Left to right:* Oran "Hot Lips" Page (trumpet), Eddie Durham (trombone and guitar), Ed Lewis (trumpet), Bennie Moten (piano), Thamon Hayes (trombone), Booker Washington (trumpet), Jimmy Rushing (vocals), Willie MacWashington (drums), Bus Moten (accordion), Buster Berry (banjo), Harlan Leonard (saxophone), Vernon Page (tuba and bass), Jack Washington (saxophone), Woodie Walder (saxophone), Count Basie (piano). (Courtesy of the Kansas City Museum, Kansas City, Missouri, and Corrine Walder)

BENNIE MOTEN Musical Crown in DANGER

Jesse Stone Defies Bennie
For Orchestra Contest

$500 Side Bet— Bennie Posts $250.00 Stone's Money is Up.

Bennie Accepts Challenge

THURS. NIGHT FEB. 3

15th & Paseo **RECREATION HALL**

Who Will Win?

Come Out and See!

Bennie Says--

This contest is going to be a horse race. My boys claim THE CHAMPIONSHIP and will defend their title against any orchestra.

This is going to be a bloody battle of jazz music. There can be no dead heat. I am going to win; I have the greatest orchestra in the world.

Stone Says--

I have heard much of Moten's orchestra and if he beats me he'll know he has been to a dog fight. I am going to grab those honors if I have to blow Bennie out of the hall.

I have played all over the East and my 10-piece orchestra has made a hit every where. Watch me win.

The Battle Is On!
Two Stages — Two Pianos
• Two Orchestras •

"Bennie Moten Musical Crown in Danger," c. 1928. This advertisement illustrates the drama that concert promoters tried to create. In this case the attraction is a "battle" between two fine bands, Moten's and Jessie Stone's Blues Serenaders. (Courtesy of the Kansas City Museum, Kansas City, Missouri, and the *Kansas City Call*)

Count Basie, c. 1942. (Courtesy of the Kansas City Museum, Kansas City, Missouri, and Jimmy Jewell)

Count Basie and Lester Young, c. 1941. Basie and Young examine Young's clarinet, his second instrument after the tenor saxophone. Young was Basie's best-known soloist. (Courtesy of the Kansas City Museum, Kansas City, Missouri, and Gene Ramey)

Count Basie Orchestra, 1940. *Left to right:* Walter Page (bass), Count Basie (piano), Buddy Tate (tenor saxophone), Jo Jones (drums), Freddie Green (guitar), Tab Smith (alto saxophone), Buck Clayton (trumpet), Dan Minor (trombone), Earle Warren (tenor saxophone), Dicky Wells (trombone), Harry Edison (trumpet), Lester Young (saxophone), Al Killian (trumpet), Ed Lewis. (Courtesy of Duncan Schiedt)

Portion of the Count Basie Orchestra, c. 1938. *Left to right:* Buck Clayton (trumpet), Herschel Evans (tenor saxophone), Ed Lewis (trumpet), Earle Warren (alto saxophone), Harry Edison (trumpet), Bennie Morton (trombone), Jack Washington (alto saxophone), Dicky Wells (trombone), Lester Young (tenor saxophone), Dan Minor (trombone). (Courtesy of Duncan Schiedt)

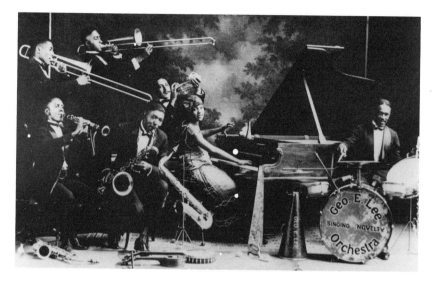

George E. Lee and His Singing Novelty Orchestra, c. 1925/26. During the late 1920s George E. Lee was Bennie Moten's most significant rival for popularity in Kansas City. *Left to right:* Thurston "Sox" Maupin (trombone), Robert Garner (clarinet), Charlie Ross (trombone), George E. Lee (saxophone), Chester Starks (trumpet), Julia Lee (piano), "King" Henry Smith (drums). (Courtesy of the Kansas City Museum, Kansas City, Missouri, and Charles Goodwin)

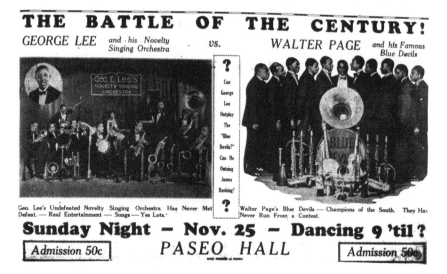

"The Battle of the Century," 1928. This advertisement for George E. Lee's appearance in a battle of bands is notable for including the only known photograph of Jimmy Rushing and Count Basie with the Blue Devils (seen at far left in the Blue Devils photo). (Courtesy of the Kansas City Museum, Kansas City, Missouri, and the *Kansas City Call*)

12

The Count Basie Orchestra

The best known and longest lasting big band to emerge from Kansas City was the Count Basie Orchestra. It was formed by Bill Basie and Buster Smith as the Barons of Rhythm in the tiny Reno Club after Bennie Moten's death in 1935, although Basie had led a band briefly under Moten's auspices in 1934.

The nine-piece Reno Club band was heard on evening radio broadcasts over an experimental short-wave radio station, W9XBY, beginning late in 1935. In March 1936, record producer John Hammond heard one of these broadcasts and was drawn to K.C. to hear this remarkable band. Hammond engineered the enlargement of Basie's band to full big-band scale and booked them on a tour leading toward New York. After initial difficulties with the larger ensemble and some personnel changes, Basie emerged with a core of all-star musicians. From his first recordings in January 1937, Basie was a star, and quickly brought the Kansas City style to the forefront of jazz.

Bill Basie, a Red Bank, New Jersey, native, learned piano literally at the feet of Fats Waller, who played both organ and piano in Harlem in the early twenties. By the mid-1920s Basie began touring with TOBA road companies, and was finally stranded in Kansas City when the Gonzelle White show broke up in 1927. After a period as a pianist in small clubs and as an accompanist for silent movies at the Eblon Theater, Basie joined Walter Page's Blue Devils in Oklahoma in 1928. Bennie Moten began his raids on the Blue Devils in 1929, and Basie was one of the first he grabbed.

Aside from his considerable keyboard skill (which he never acknowledged, always referring to himself as being "just in the rhythm section"), Basie was blessed with good organizational instincts, an even temper, and

135

an uncanny rhythmic sense. Everything he played swung, and his ability
to "stomp off" a band with the proper tempo was unparalleled. By most
accounts Basie was very creative musically, although a somewhat lazy
songwriter who usually left completion of a song idea and scoring to others,
such as Eddie Durham and Buster Smith.

Basie was also blessed with both luck and a good sense of timing. When
the Barons of Rhythm were organized in 1935 the Depression affected even
Kansas City musicians by sharply limiting their touring possibilities. Basie
took the available opportunity and organized a club band, allowing him
to lead a significantly smaller, tighter ensemble than a road band would
permit. The only apparent weaknesses in Moten's last orchestra were those
of occasional flabbiness and lack of precision due to the size of the ensemble.
Basie avoided these in his Reno Club band by having fewer performers,
and by having all of them be stars.

The Barons of Rhythm included, in the rhythm section, Basie, piano;
Walter Page, bass; Jesse Price (later, Jo Jones), drums; Clifford McIntyre
(later, Claude Williams, later still, Freddie Green), guitar (and violin);
reedmen Buster Smith, alto; Lester Young and Herschel Evans, tenor; Jack
Washington, baritone (Smith and Young both doubled on clarinet); trumpeters Joe Keyes, Carl Smith, and Lips Page (Page was replaced at the end
by Buck Clayton); and trombonist Dan Minor. The full complement was
not reached until Basie's last days in the Reno Club.

Bill Basie was a gentle, affable hipster who inspired admiration, envy,
and loyalty among his comrades. The story of his band is also the story of
the world discovering the power of Kansas City jazz, which Basie continued
to exemplify in his big band, if often in diluted form, until his death on
April 26, 1984, in Hollywood, Florida.

Count Basie: Really the main guy that influenced me is Thomas, that's
Fats, Waller. That was the man that I really did idolize, 'cause Fats
taught me to play what little bit of organ that I do know. I used to
watch him, lay around him long enough to style a little piano after him,
which was quite difficult. . . .

I do like to do things where you can halfway pat your feet. . . . So I
simplify it [my songs] so I could do it. . . . This is me, this is what I like,
a tempo that's danceable. . . . I never get tired of playing the blues, or
listening to the blues. . . . To me, the blues is the start of an awful lot of
things. . . . Blueswise, there's one guy . . . that I can remember, Pete Johnson. Pete was a guy that I really idolized as far as blues playing is concerned. . . .

The beat's changed quite a bit [with my band now, 1968]. We've been
experimenting with different styles, but basically we haven't changed.
We have some soloists [now] that lean towards the modern side, but we

remain the same. We play the blues; and I'm pretty sure that's from that era. That goes back a pretty good little taste. 'Way back in the early thirties.[1]

Basie and a fellow musician named Harry Smith were stranded in Kansas City in 1927 by the Gonzelle White vaudeville show. After playing odd jobs for a few weeks, Basie was hired to replace Tiny Parham as pianist for the Eblon Theater orchestra. This was a conventional "pit" band of the day, playing filler music for silent movies and keeping the audience entertained between shows. Also in that band were William Saunders (saxophones), Booker Washington (trumpet), and Baby Lovett (drums). Western University's music director Guiou Taylor led the band. Saunders recalls that Basie kept alive his devotion to his mentor by playing a Fats Waller composition, "Honeysuckle Rose," whenever someone in the picture died.

Soon after finishing the Eblon Theater job, Basie became ill. Following his recuperation he joined another vaudeville act, the Whitman Sisters, which worked locally rather than following the TOBA circuit. In July 1928 he joined Walter Page's Blue Devils in Dallas (see chapter 5), and then returned to Kansas City in 1929 to join Bennie Moten.

Gene Ramey: Lester Young . . . and Herschel Evans were playing with Basie when I first came . . . to Kansas City. They were playing with Bennie Moten's band . . . when they broke off into two sections [c. 1933], they were each trying to form a band. Basie took a little band . . . and got stranded in Little Rock, Arkansas. Buddy Tate was living down there then. Buddy kind of helped to feed them, and sit in with the band on a couple of dates, something like that. This was the usual routine, for musicians in those days to get stranded. . . .

Bands in those days tried to spread out all over . . . but then Basie came on back to Kansas City . . . [to get] back with Bennie Moten. . . . [When] they came back they were just hustling around town. . . .

Now it was during this time that Basie had patches in his pants, and holes in his shoes, and you see him walking down the street, trying to be a dignified beggar.

Druie Bess: Well, then Bennie had his throat cut, you know, and he died. Well, Basie was playing in there with him . . . and Basie grabbed the band.

There was a chance for Basie, see. Now, Bus [Moten] was telling me [that] . . . he should have grabbed the band himself, but Basie grabbed it . . . and he put a whole lot of [Blue] Devils in there. Old Devils and all kinds of Devils, and he got it started. He tried to get . . . all them guys that could blow. Lester [Young] and all of them.

Buster Smith: So Basie, he left [Bus Moten's orchestra after Bennie's death] and went down in the Reno Club. The first man who went on down with him was Joe Keyes, and he finally made about four or five pieces and we all got together and he made it up to eight pieces. But the hours were so long. You started working down there at eight o'clock at night and didn't get off until five in the morning. [Pay was] twenty-one dollars each.

[The Reno] wasn't nothin' but a hole in the wall. Just mediocre people mostly went in there, a lot of the prostitutes and hustlers and thugs hung out down there. And the house was packed. They had a show down there [that] we had to play. Dancers and comedians and things like that.

Claude Williams: The Reno was a little club up there on Twelfth Street. It was sort of down a little below the street [but] it was a pretty big place after you got down there. . . . I never did go down there much until I come in with the Count.[2]

Buck Clayton: [At] the Reno, beer was a nickel, scotch was fifteen cents, and the other whiskey in there was a dime. That's all it was. We'd go to work about ten o'clock, play to about four. And it was great, you know, it was really nice. You didn't have to wear any clothes [uniforms]. You just put on a shirt, whatever you wanted to do, but it was hot as hell.

If you wanted to get up for something, you just get up and walk out in the back and the band would keep on playing.

Count Basie: While we were at the Reno, it was very special. I looked forward to going to work. It was just wonderful, it really was. It was more than just a thing, you know. . . .

I was pretty happy with my nine pieces in Kansas City. We had a lot of fun with it. It was later that we started to augment it . . . [but] we wouldn't play in the bigger dance halls [then]. We were just right there at that club . . . [and] played seven nights a week. . . .

We were just working, very happy to be working, and work was plentiful, if you wanted to work. . . . Beautiful work.

We were very young then, it didn't matter. All we wanted to do was just play, have a little taste, just finish playing there all night and go somewhere else and play the rest of the morning. . . . [We played at the Reno until] three o'clock, but the clubs never closed.

Buster Smith: We needed a drummer and we got old Jesse Price, 'cause Mac [Willie MacWashington, Bennie Moten's drummer], he stayed with Bus [Moten]. Some of the old boys, they all stayed out there, but most of the Blue Devil bunch went on down there with Basie. Lester Young, . . . Jack Washington, Lips Page, . . . Joe Keyes, and we didn't have no trombone player. Eddie Durham was still out there with Bus. He finally come on down there with us. . . . Jesse Price [was] on drums [but] he and Basie couldn't get along. Jesse was temperamental. He got mad, walked off and left the job.

So I got Jo [Jones]. [He] was in Omaha, Nebraska, playing with Lloyd Hunter. . . . So I called up there to get Jo.[3]

Walter Harrold: Jo was in Omaha about three years, but he lived in our house two of those years. . . . He took my job, I was working with Lloyd Hunter's band. . . .

He come to Omaha with a carnival group; they were playing in Lincoln at the state fair. . . . Jo was playing piano at that time, he wasn't playing drums. . . . My Dad told Jo to come up to Omaha, he was organizing a band, he'd give 'em a tryout, so they'd all come up. . . . He got his band mostly from penitentiary and stuff like that, . . . but not Jo Jones, he come up with the carnival. . . .

So he said, "This is a talented guy. He's got the beat and got the feel, I think he'd make a better drummer." So he started talking to Jo and Jo said, "Yeah, I like the drums anyway." So my Dad started to teaching him, . . . just give him free lessons.[4] . . . I taught him how to use the sock cymbal,[5] and he got to be a genius with that sock cymbal. . . . Then he joined Lloyd's [Hunter's] band and I think they went out East someplace; I think they went to New York. . . .

He was a cymbal man. He'd stay up all night long polishing those cymbals. . . . And he could tap dance, he could do all those things. He loved to play the piano but he just fell in love with the drums.

Buster Smith: In the Reno Club, Basie, it's no telling what he's liable to play, 'cause he's just sitting down on the piano. He didn't know nothing about no music or nothing, just played by ear. He'd sit down there, . . . he'd get to playing in F (F is his main key), get to playing the blues, he'd say, "Prof (they all called me Prof), set something." He'd leave it to me.[6] I'd be playing the horn and the other boys would be following me, way on down the line. Every time we'd change choruses I'd set a different riff. That's the way I made up the "One O'Clock Jump."[7] They liked it so well . . . we all called it "Blue Balls." I named it the "Blue Balls."

At the same time Basie had made the band up and we went down into Arkansas and played down there several weeks. That's when Buddy Tate got in the band. . . . The man at the radio station wanted us to come up there and play one night. We got up there and he said, "I want you all to play that tune that's got all that fire in the thing." We had to have about six numbers to play about thirty minutes. So we run down it; he said, "What's the name of that?" We hollered, "Blue Balls." "Oh no, you can't say that over the air." He kept looking around, at the clock, said, "It's near one o'clock. If you don't mind just call it the 'One O'Clock Jump.' " . . .

After I left the band to go with Claude [Hopkins] the first thing they recorded was that tune. . . . And Basie put his name on it. . . . [Later on] he said, "Don't sue me, it's a long story. I'll treat you right." He sweet-talked me there.

Count Basie: [The "One O'Clock Jump"] happened in Kansas City while we were at the Reno Club. In those years, you didn't have to program a number, clear it, you know [for broadcasting]. You could just play anything that you'd like to play and it would be perfectly okay. . . .

So each Sunday night we used to have, like a two-hour broadcast, and we sorta run out of tunes, and so had, I guess we must've had about a half hour, and we'd light out and play, the announcer would come out and say, "What's the name of that?" Well that's . . . So we just had about fifteen minutes left, and I just started something in there, and then we went to D-flat for a solo. So he asked, "Do you have a title for that?" I looked at the clock, it's about ten minutes to one, I said, "Yeah, the 'One O'Clock Jump.' " And it sorta stuck, because the guys remembered the riffs they were doing, and it laid there.

Eddie Durham: He's [Count Basie] got some fantastic ideas but nobody's ever got them out of him, he would never hold still long enough for you to get them. He'd always give me an idea for a couple of measures, then he'd find a little girl and go out and drink, or do something else in order to be gone. And I'd have to build from that. I could never tie him down. . . . People don't know he had a talent like that today. He smothered it, because you could never get him to do anything.

Jesse Stone: Count Basie played a whole lot more piano then [in the thirties] before he got [famous]. When he was hanging around the Subway Club in Kansas City he played a whole lot of piano. He used to stump all the piano players around. When he went commercial he simplified his piano playing.[8] . . .

He used to play like Oscar Peterson, . . . all over the piano. Both hands. All keys. He used to demonstrate playing thirteen keys. He'd play anything, any tune. . . .

I remember one time he and James P. Johnson[9] hooked up in Kansas City, down at the Subway Club, where all the musicians come to show off. J. P. came down and when Count Basie got through with him he got the surprise of his life.

Buster Smith: So then we played on down there [at the Reno Club] for three or four months, and Benny Goodman heard the broadcast, we broadcast at 12:30 every night, . . . and that's where John Hammond came in the picture. [The night John Hammond came] Lips [Page] was in the band and I was in the band.

So many guys [had] said, "You guys all right, I'll be back there to get you all" that we never did hear from no more; so we thought it was just a fancy [bringing the band to New York] he [John Hammond] had, just one of them things.

So before he could get back there and pick us up, Lips had left and went with Andy Kirk, and I got tired of that twenty-one dollars a week. I had to do all the arranging, 'cause Eddie [Durham], he wasn't writing nothing much during then 'cause the band was too small. He always liked to write for a big band. So Eddie went with Jimmie Lunceford and I left and went with Claude Hopkins. He offered me seventy-five dollars a week and I went off with him.

John Hammond: When I was in prep school I got a record . . . on the Vocalion race label,[10] and it was Walter Page and his Blue Devils. One side was "Squabblin' " and the other side was "Blue Devil Blues" and the pianist was Bill Basie, and [it was] marvelous. Walter Page on "Squabblin' " I guess had the first bass solo that was ever recorded.[11]

I first heard a Kansas City band live in . . . November 1932 . . . at the Lafayette Theater in New York, and that was Bennie Moten's band. . . . I thought it was a very stiff, very square band [on their previous recordings, but] . . . then they made these records, "Lafayette," "Prince of Wails," in Camden [New Jersey, in 1932, Moten's last recording session]. . . . They were unbelievable records. It was incredible to me how . . . Basie and Eddie Durham . . . really transformed that band to an extraordinary degree. . . . I used to just play those records to death. . . .

There was a wonderful speakeasy behind the Lafayette Theater called Covan's Morocco Club . . . and Basie used to come in there between shows. . . . I got a chance to hear a little of Basie in the flesh at that time. . . .

In '34 . . . I was producing Fletcher Henderson[12] . . . and Fletcher said, "You know, John, I just feel like chucking the whole band business. . . . I was out in Wichita [Kansas]. I heard a band that were the remnants of Bennie Moten's band. . . . As far as I'm concerned I'd like to fire my whole band and take this band over. . . . They got a saxophone player that you just wouldn't believe[13] [Lester Young] and . . . as good a trumpet player [Hot Lips Page] as you'll ever hear, and they've got one hell of a rhythm section. . . . It was a different kind of a band from Moten 'cause it's a smaller one." . . .

In '35 I was very busy in the recording studios [producing artists such as Benny Goodman]. . . . I had some money from a trust fund . . . so I didn't charge anybody for producing records. . . . So I got out to Chicago . . . by car. I had a Hudson and I had a wonderful radio, the Motorola Golden Throat. . . .

One night . . . I went out to my car and I turned the dial all the way at the end of the dial at 1560 kilocycles and I heard some music that I couldn't believe. They said, "This is radio station W9XBY. . . . We are broadcasting from the Reno Club with *Count Basie and His Orchestra."* As far as I could tell it was a nine-piece band. . . . They were on for an hour every night and on Saturday nights they were on for four solid hours.

[They had] Lips Page, who was an incredible trumpet player, the best Basie ever had, . . . and a drummer I'd never heard of called Jo Jones, Basie on piano, and the saxophones were Jack Washington on baritone, Lester Young on tenor, [and Buster Smith on alto], and there was Joe Keyes on first trumpet who played kind of flat. . . . Then there was a trombone player, Dan Minor, just one. . . . Little Jimmy Rushing sang most of the vocals and there was a comedienne there called Hattie Knoll . . . who sang pretty good. I would listen to this band every night.

I didn't actually get to Kansas City until late March or early April [1936]. . . . It was the best band I had ever heard. . . . When I heard Basie's rhythm section I've never been satisfied by any other rhythm section before or since. . . .

I was able to get a table right next to the piano 'cause I wanted to hear . . . and the rhythm setup was absolutely perfect. Basie was on the floor, then Walter [Page, bass player] was a level up, and then Jo Jones [drums] was on a top level. . . . On Jo's left was the brass section. The three saxes were on the middle, because they wanted to have as much room for dancers as possible. . . . God knows where there was a dressing room for Jimmy Rushing and the four chorus girls and Hattie Knoll.

Count Basie: John Hammond is, well, let's say he's responsible for me. He's right in my private little room, of thoughts, dimensions. Everything is wrapped right around Mr. Hammond.

He's done so much for so many people, and asked for nothing in return. And he's uncovered so many people [including Bessie Smith, for her last recordings, and Bob Dylan and Bruce Springsteen for their first] that have been covered up for years, and he uncovered them and brought them right back to light again, made them start all over again. . . .

We're the greatest friends. Sometimes John likes my band, sometimes he don't. But that never stopped our friendship . . . [and] we're pretty much agreed on music. John liked the blues, so did I. We're nuts on the blues.

The first step of Hammond's plan for bringing Basie to New York required him to build his band from the nine-piece Reno Club ensemble to a full orchestra. Their first test was at a major dance hall, the Grand Terrace Ballroom in Chicago. While preparing for that engagement, however, Basie met some initial setbacks as he sought more musicians, the most severe being Buster Smith's departure. After years of frustrations with the Blue Devils, Smith had little faith in the promises of a young producer named John Hammond. Others felt the same way, including William Saunders who Basie tried to take from Bus Moten's struggling group. The result was some initial shakiness as the Basie Orchestra grew from a tight, medium-sized group, to a full big band.

Buck Clayton: I met Herschel [Evans, widely admired saxophone and clarinet player, featured with Basie; Evans died in 1939] in California [and] we played together a lot. He used to always tell me about this band in Kansas City, Count Basie. . . . He says there's this cat back there named Lester Young. He walks around with a pipe in his mouth, and Jo Jones, and Basie. . . . Herschel had played with these guys before. I [only] knew them all by name. And he told me about Lips Page. . . .

Herschel used to call them on the telephone and just let me listen. He said, "This is the band I've been telling you about all the time," and I listened. It was only nine [pieces] then. . . .

So when I went back to Kansas City [from California] I met Basie and Walter Page in the street. Lips [Page] had just resigned from the band because Joe Glazer was going to bring him to New York and feature him like Louis Armstrong. . . . There was a spot open, and Basie asked me would I make it.

I said, "Well, I'm on my way to New York." He said, "We're going to New York . . . in two months." This was about August, and they was playing in the Reno Club, making two dollars a night.

They were swinging. The band was swinging so nice. I never heard a group swing so much with Lester [Young], and [Walter] Page, and Jo Jones. . . . Basie had a band swinging the minute they sit down until the minute they got up. . . . Every number was a swinger, and Jimmy Rushing was singing the blues. . . .

We didn't get big until we had to go to the Grand Terrace in Chicago, and they had a show there that you had to have fourteen featured [performers]. So we had to add five guys and it made the band real sluggish. Like some of them we found out later couldn't read very well.

John Hammond: When Basie left Kansas City and went to the Grand Terrace in Chicago half the band couldn't read, including Basie. . . . Buck Clayton read beautifully, Caughey Roberts, who was the first alto man who replaced Buster Smith, read very well. . . . Herschel [Evans] couldn't read at all, Lester [Young] was a marvelous reader. Jack Washington was pretty good. The second trombone player, Rabbit [George Hunt], read pretty well. Dan [Minor] read well but slowly. Joe Keyes was so drunk most of the time it didn't matter whether he could read or not. Jo Jones's instincts were so good, that saved him. Walter Page was a very good reader, and the guitar player he had, Claude Williams, was a pretty good reader 'cause he was a fiddle player.

Claude Williams: I was in Chicago . . . and Count came up there looking for me. . . . that's when he was enlarging his band and we worked at the Reno until he got his band up to twelve pieces, what he wanted. Just got different musicians from different parts of the country. . . .

We got on a bus and made a tour, on through Tulsa . . . Nashville . . . and [for] our first steady job we opened up at the Grand Terrace in Chicago. . . . It was kind of ragged because the band was new. He didn't have too many good arrangements and we had trouble playing the shows.

Basie wasn't reading any too good then. [He] had to hire another piano player to play the shows. . . . That was the only trouble we was having in Chicago.

We had Joe Keyes and he was one of the best in the world. . . . Joe was one of the only fellas that could sit up there and sight-read that book. . . . We had some good readers, Herschel Evans and Lester Young and Caughey Roberts. . . . Caughey left the same time I did . . . and nobody could fill Caughey's place 'till they got Earle Warren. . . .

From Grand Terrace we . . . went on into the Roseland. . . . We did some recordings while we was at the Roseland.

I wasn't with Count just about a year. Part of '36 until the beginning of '37.

Buck Clayton: Some of them came from Texas, like Buddy Tate, he took Herschel's [Evans] place, . . . but it was heavy [with the larger ensemble] because we had been used to light music. . . . We caught hell in that nightclub. We weren't playing the music right. . . .

We had vocalists, and dancers, and things [at the Grand Terrace], chorus girls. We had to have the fourteen pieces, and they used to fight every night. These singers used to be so mad at us when we'd goof up the music. . . .

We changed one by one [after we left the Grand Terrace]. We brought in Dicky Wells [trombone] from New York. We brought in Bennie Morton [trombone] from New York [and] as we bring in better guys the band started getting better. . . .

We got in New York around a little bit before New Year's Day, because I remember I never seen anything like so many people on Broadway on New Year's night. You couldn't walk . . . and Roseland [where we played] was right in the middle of it.

Downstairs there was another club where Erskine Hawkins's band was, and upstairs with us was Woody Herman's band on another bandstand.

[The band] was getting better, but it didn't really start getting better until later when we started having some rehearsals, and finally getting new guys like Earle Warren [saxophone] in. . . . Billie Holiday came out to Pittsburgh [before we got to New York] and sang with us for a little while.

Claude Williams: Our best stuff was what you call head arrangements. . . . Count had some real good ideas. I remember some rehearsals we had at the Roseland, Count would just get on the piano and [say], "Saxophones, you all play this." And the saxophones would get that riff together and get their four parts. And he said, "Brass, you all play this." He'd play this by head and put that together. . . . That's the way some of the best arrangements we had [were put together].

Eddie Durham: When I went to Basie [in 1937] he was in New York, engaged in playing the Park. I arrived there that Monday morning. But when I took the train in, Ben Bott, the manager, said, "Get enough sleep. . . . Better sleep all night. I'll bet you fifty dollars you'll have a song when you get here, arranged for the band."

So sure enough I got on there and I got . . . some sort of tune, slightly Latin, and I just took my guitar and I played it low. . . . When I got there that morning with Basie's band, Buck Clayton was in the band, Harry Edison [trumpeter who played with Basie from June 1938 through 1950], those kind of fellows, so they had a rehearsal at twelve o'clock. I had the thing about half-finished, no score, just the parts. I said, "Anybody want to help me copy some parts?" Everybody just stood there. I went out in the Park [and] that's how they got "Topsy" [among Basie's first recordings and a major hit]. That's the first tune they put in the book.

Buck Clayton: Benny Goodman had set everybody on fire with his swing music. And Benny was using Fletcher Henderson's arrangements. Actually our band outflanked Benny's band, but we didn't have any arrangements. We was all playing from heads. . . . That's why when we came along we fit right in. They was looking for swing music, and we played more swing music than all the bands in New York. . . .

[But] we didn't start making money when we first got there. We was making thirty-three dollars a week. That was union scale.

Count Basie: As far as I'm concerned, my piano playing is a little bit dated. I'm just in the rhythm section, [and] I'm just happy the guys will allow me in there. And that's as far as my piano playing will go.

NOTES

1. These remarks are quoted from "Jazz Casual," a KQED (San Francisco) television program hosted by critic Ralph J. Gleason in which he interviewed Basie in 1968.

2. The Reno was like most Kansas City clubs in that the main floor was for whites only. A balcony and the small space behind the band were the available spaces for black patrons.

3. Jo Jones was a key element in Basie's powerful sound. A former tap dancer and pianist, Jones "lightened" the swing beat considerably by accenting primarily with cymbals instead of the bass [foot] drum. This, coupled with Walter Page's powerfully percussive string bass playing and Basie's subtle piano accents, resulted in an extraordinarily propulsive rhythm that remained airy and flexible, the perfect beat for big band swing.

4. Although Walter Harrold's father undoubtedly played a significant role in Jo Jone's development as a drummer, other researchers and Jones himself state that he first learned drums in the mid-1920s from Wilson Driver (born 2/29/04) in Birmingham, Alabama. Jones also was a proficient dancer, pianist, organist, and trumpeter by the time he arrived in K.C., although by then he devoted himself to drums exclusively.

5. The sock cymbal, also known as the hi-hat, is a set of two cymbals on a stand that can be played with a foot pedal, with sticks, or in combination. As a result of the variety of ways it can be manipulated, it can produce a wide range of percussive and tonal effects. Jo Jones's skillful and innovative use of the sock cymbal was the essence of his famed cymbal work, which is widely recognized for playing an important role in making orchestras swing more freely in the late 1930s and as an important stylistic building-block of modern jazz.

6. Eddie Durham also contributed many songs to the Basie band repertoire in a similar fashion.

7. "One O'Clock Jump" became Basie's theme and, after "Moten's Swing," a K.C. anthem.

8. Count Basie's piano style became increasingly spare throughout his career. By the 1960s he played so little that he was often caricatured. In spite of this, as many K.C. musicians note, Basie in his early years was a formidable performer, as well as a canny bandleader.

9. Pianist James P. Johnson was a New Yorker and along with Willie "The Lion" Smith was the leader of a group of "stride" pianists. The stride style featured a broad, rolling left-hand bass with elaborate right-hand ornamentations. In some ways it was a transitional style between formal ragtime music and rollicking boogie-woogie. Johnson was certainly among the best known and most respected pianists of his day.

10. "Race" records were produced and distributed primarily for Negro audiences. This kind of segmentation of the record market was once commonplace—many ethnic communities had entertainment media focused on their specific tastes.

11. "Squabblin'" and "Blue Devil Blues" were recorded in 1929. Blue Devils band members disagree over whether Basie or Willie Lewis played piano on those sessions, but most assert that it was Lewis. Also, although Walter Page was without question among the most important and influential bass players in jazz history and an extremely significant figure in the development of Kansas City jazz, he did not record the first jazz bass solo.

12. At the time, Fletcher Henderson led the most highly regarded black jazz band, after Duke Ellington, in the country. Henderson later arranged many of Benny Goodman's best known songs.

13. Basie's first tenor saxophonist at the Reno Club was Lawrence "Slim" Freeman, later replaced by Lester Young. Among the first players Basie engaged when he began to enlarge the band past nine pieces were tenor saxophonist and clarinetist Herschel Evans and trumpeter Wilbur "Buck" Clayton.

13

George E. Lee and His Singing Novelty Orchestra

Through the 1920s George E. Lee was Bennie Moten's major rival for supremacy among the black orchestras in Kansas City. While Moten primarily led dance bands, Lee was best known for performing in variety and stage shows. His orchestra was thus more akin to a vaudeville troupe, although it always featured several strong soloists, including at various times trumpeter Albert Hinton, trombonist Sox Maupin, alto saxophonist Herman Walder, tenor saxophonist Budd Johnson, pianist Jesse Stone, and drummer Baby Lovett.

Lee and his vocalist/pianist sister Julia were born in Kansas City and played together through the mid-1930s. They organized their first band around 1920, within two years of Moten's first jobs in 1918. Both Lees were strong singers as were several band members, particularly Herman Walder, and singing was always featured in the band. This distinguished the group, as no other black band in Kansas City had comparable vocal skills. Singing versatility also enabled Lee to do well in band battles, since audiences always enjoyed a well-sung song.

Lee's major failing was that he lacked the organizational ability of Moten. Band turnover was always high and ensemble playing was consequently spotty. On at least one recording, however, "Ruff Scufflin'," from 1927, the band plays a complex arrangement skillfully and features an extraordinary instrumental solo by Herman Walder. Walder was among the strong early influences on Charlie Parker, and some of the similarities of their styles—such as unusually rapid note cascades and complex harmonies—are demonstrated in this tune.

Lee's popularity was consistent through the early 1930s. He and Moten often toured jointly, alternating engagements in cities in the Territories. In

1933 Lee was hurt by the defection of several of his stars, particularly Herman Walder, Jesse Stone, and Baby Lovett who joined performers let go by Moten during his band's reorganization to form the Kansas City Rockets. In 1934 Lee and Moten briefly co-led a band in an effort to economize in tough times. By 1935 the Lee orchestra had disintegrated.

Lee had intermittent success during the remainder of the thirties, but he still failed to keep a strong band together, even though he always had a good ear for talent. Notable in his bands of this period was Charlie Parker, who learned the fundamentals of musicianship with Lee. George Lee retired from music in 1941 and moved to Detroit where he operated a tavern until his death in 1959.

Julia Lee remained very active in Kansas City, usually teamed with the brilliant percussionist Baby Lovett, until her death in 1958. During the 1940s and 1950s she was the most popular performer in town. Her popularity was heightened by a series of successful recordings in the early fifties that featured all-star K.C. musicians.

The George E. Lee Orchestra is primarily of interest to us now as a well-regarded period orchestra that illustrated the enduring popularity of vaudeville during the jazz age, as the major local rival to Bennie Moten, and as a prominent musical training-ground, notably for many of Thamon Hayes's ill-fated Kansas City Rockets and, briefly, Charlie Parker.

HUGH JONES. *Born 1/23/1910, Pine Bluff, Arkansas. Trumpet. Performed with many Territory and show bands, including June McCarr's Ragtime Steppers, Drake and Walker's Review, the Bronze Mannequins, and Jimmie Lunceford.*

I made up my mind I wanted to be a musician when I was in grade school. One reason was because it was enjoyable . . . and [because] the fellas always looked so nice back in those days. They dressed nice . . . and I liked the work. At that time a band I was particularly interested in was George E. Lee. That was about 1922. . . .

I was working at a big [shoe] shine parlor down there [in K.C.'s black downtown], shining shoes. . . . Sometimes George Lee would come in there and his band would play. They'd play it, man. . . . He would play in there once or twice a month at least. . . . I liked George Lee's band best [over Bennie Moten] because it played more popular music. Bennie played mostly arrangements [instrumental pieces].

Clarence Love: Old George E. Lee had a band that had the style I liked. Julia Lee was on piano, . . . Tweety [Clarence Taylor] on saxophone, and . . . that old drummer, Baby Lovett. Boy, and they didn't have mikes in those days. He used a megaphone [to sing]. . . .

The Lincoln Theater was on this corner and they had a bunch of apartments [across the street]. I lived in those apartments. We were kids, I guess I was about six or seven years old, and they'd have to leave the windows up [in the summertime]. We'd dance out in the street when old George would be up there. You could hear old George from here to back up town. He had a set of lungs that were terrible, and Julia. They had a novelty band. They played everything.

They did novelties, like sing different songs and get up and do little acts, somebody may get up and dance. Like I had . . . a preacher act one time . . . in my band. I stole my old man's frocktail coat . . . and people liked that kind of stuff, you know. . . .

He played the waltz, two-step, one-step, hesitation, schottisch. . . . Those were dances. Then we had dance directors on the floor. . . . You couldn't dance all over the floor like you do now. One guy was all dressed up with a baton. He stood in the middle of the hall and he directed you around . . . just like a skating rink. If it was a waltz you had to stay in line. If it was a two-step, one-step, you had to dance around. . . . He'd guide you just like an orchestra leader.

John Tumino: They had a great band. George E. Lee was just like Bennie Moten in those days. Those two bands out of Kansas City were the greatest in the Midwest. [They played] very commercial music. For a black band he was the most commercial guy, next to Duke Ellington, around.

He would play novelties and he would play the ballads. He would take care of the ofays [whites], play their music, that's the way he was commercial.

Herman Walder: I played around [Kansas City], done so well on the saxophone[1] [that] Sox Maupin, one of the best trombone players . . . says, "Man, you'd better get this man [George E. Lee], you ain't gonna find nobody else you can depend on." I got with him and stayed with him for quite a while. That was '27. . . .

We went all through Oklahoma, trailing Bennie Moten, and he's trailing us, one of them kind of things. . . . We'd switch and go like this summer and winter. . . . Budd Johnson was with us, by the way. . . . We was getting paid, the first time we went down there, fifty-five dollars a man. . . .

We was on the Falkenburg tour. . . . Falkenburg is the cat that owned the parks in the summer and the dance halls in the winter, Tulsa and Oklahoma City. . . .

We had an instrument truck where two cats kept . . . our cases. . . . George Lee's sister's husband, Harry Auburn, [drove the truck], and they got a car, pink with gold wheels. . . .

He changed men so many times, man, half of Kansas City was on there. . . . He used to call himself a big shot; he'd fine his sister. He was pretty overbearing. . . . He was a different kind of cat altogether from Bennie Moten. I was jealous [of] the way Bennie Moten's band was getting paid more than we was getting paid. That made me feel awfully bad. When they'd give their dances, they'd split the money. . . . They'd make fifty and sixty dollars apiece. When we'd play a dance we'd get paid union scale, which was nine dollars. . . . But it was a good band. . . .

After they caught onto my style, Budd [Johnson] and I was the only two take-off men in the band, outside of the trumpet man. . . . That band was terrific on them records. . . . We recorded down at the Kansas City Star [newspaper office] on a Brunswick record. . . . The people's favorite . . . [was] "St. James Infirmary." . . . It was real popular then. . . . I never did have a favorite [song, though]. What the people wanted is all I wanted, dig? And get paid for it. . . .

We battled a band down in Texas the first time we went down there . . . in a great big hall . . . and, man, we tore them cats up. Everybody wanted to hear a band from Kansas City. We beat Bennie Moten down there [too].

Don Albert: I played against the George E. Lee band . . . [when I was] with Troy Floyd [a prominent Texas band of the mid-1920s]. I always told Troy that they cut us to pieces that night. . . . George Lee was such a tremendous singer, and he had some great, great musicians in that band. . . . They were fantastic.

Herman Walder: You see, George Lee had what you call a novelty band. He called it George Lee's Novelty Band. . . . Jess Stone had us doing all them kind of things, . . . singing and so on. . . . Like you're going to school, he come out there with some kind of thing going on. Just entertaining the people . . . [with] all this personality stuff you see the cats doing. . . .

A novelty tune would be like George Lee and Julia would sing "Bring it on down to my house baby, ain't nobody home but me." And a lot of times I'd chime in with 'em and [sing] "Last night. . . ."

We broke up [when] we was in New Orleans, we went down for Mardi Gras [in 1933]. [We played] for special dances . . . at the Pelican Garden. . . . Then we played for them society dances. That's when I met some of them old-time New Orleans cats. . . .

But, man, they found that Bennie Moten's band broke up in New York [Moten replaced several Kansas City musicians], and [then] our band broke up in New Orleans. . . . Hell, we wasn't getting nothing to eat. He wasn't getting the gigs. All the gigs he went down there to play, was run out, and he wanted to go towards Denver. . . .

These cats formed the Thamon Hayes band, and they sent for us, three of us, Jesse Stone, Baby Lovett, and myself. . . . He [Thamon Hayes] sent us a ticket for five dollars apiece. [It was] nice down in New Orleans and we come up here and like to froze to death in the back of the bus. . . .

He [George Lee] heard about us getting these tickets and we had to hide out from him. . . . We saw George Lee pulling up beside us, like he's gonna make us get off the bus, or something like that. But man, we got dug down in the seat . . . and slipped out.

Williams Saunders recalls that he joined George E. Lee in 1934 at the Harlem Nightclub in Kansas City on one of Lee's last major engagements. Times were hard for big bands in that year, so Lee and Bennie Moten joined forces for the job. Lee hired several musicians from Tommy Douglas's orchestra, and Moten contributed the rest. The joint band performed for an unusually elaborate floor show, with dancers, comedians, and a chorus line imported from New York. This was apparently too big a production for K.C. at that time, and the club soon failed, with Lee and Moten separating to reassemble their own orchestras.

Saunders also recalls that while Lee was a good leader, he was not generous with his musicians, and that later road trips with the Lee Orchestra were usually "starvation tours." At the first opportunity, Saunders left for a more profitable gig.

John Tumino: He [Lee] was a good businessman, but he goofed up his money worse than any of them. He had kind of a taste for white girls . . . and they would take him for all they could have. He died broke. Julia had to send him money all the time . . . [to] keep him clean as possible. . . . Keep him in a good pad anyway. She was a very big-hearted girl. Big gal with a big heart. . . .

Julia Lee was a very great artist for Capitol Records. I managed her. She was a great, great entertainer. . . . She had made a big hit with Capitol records called "You Got to Give Me What You Got," and "Tonight's the Night." You ought to hear some of those.

She was a big fat black colored girl who was just great, and could play any request you wanted to hear. She knew it all. She could do the ballads, the blues, and the swing. . . . She made a lot of money, . . . a thousand dollars in one night, stuff like that.

As has been true for so many artists, prominent in their prime but lacking durable qualities, George E. Lee and His Singing Novelty Orchestra live only in the memories of a few—the dwindling number of musicians who knew him well or played with him, K.C. jazz fans and students, and assorted seekers of nostalgia and curiosity. His sister Julia left a much stronger legacy due to her considerable skill as a singer and pianist, her many excellent recordings, and her deep generosity of spirit. It is less of a legacy than most would have predicted in the swinging twenties and thirties, but, at least for Julia, one that is quite respectable.

NOTE

1. Walder had played trumpet until an automobile accident in 1925 seriously damaged his lip, leading him to switch to alto saxophone, a less physically demanding instrument.

14

The Kansas City Rockets: Thamon Hayes and Harlan Leonard

Music from the twenties, thirties, and forties exists for most of us via recordings. Through them we can readily appreciate the surging power of Bennie Moten and Count Basie, and the vaudevillian approach of George E. Lee. Unrecorded groups suffer a twilight existence, recalled by memory but not verified by recordings. There are many such ensembles in jazz history, including all the early New Orleans bands and many others, mostly from the early years of jazz.

Kansas City musicians are justifiably proud of Moten, Basie, and McShann, but many of the leading performers from the prewar period recall the Thamon Hayes Kansas City Rockets most fondly of all. This band is their "if only" legend, and it represented a most heartfelt attempt to establish a musical legacy.

When Bennie Moten, with the urging of Eddie Durham and Bill Basie, decided to restructure his band in 1931, he cast out many of his best known musicians. These included Booker Washington and Ed Lewis, trumpets; Thamon Hayes, trombone; Harlan Leonard and Woodie Walder, saxophones and clarinet; and Vernon Page, tuba, sousaphone, and string bass. All were very well known performers to audiences both in Kansas City and the Territories, and all were at the peak of their musical skills.

Led by Thamon Hayes, the eldest among them and Moten's former assistant, this core of ex-Moten musicians proceeded to form their own band, the Kansas City Rockets, recruiting Herman Walder, alto saxophone; Jesse Stone, piano and arranger; and Baby Lovett, drums, from George E. Lee; and Charles Goodwin, guitar and vocals; Vic Dickenson, trombone; and Richard Smith, trumpet, from other local groups. With this lineup the band was, at least in the eyes of contemporary K.C. musicians and fans,

154

superior to any other in the area, including Moten's. (Moten's recast ensemble went through a painful period of restructuring and growth before returning to its accustomed position as the premier K.C. jazz orchestra.)

Of particular importance was the presence of Jesse Stone who, along with Eddie Durham and Buster Smith, was among the most creative and experienced arrangers in Midwestern jazz. Stone and Herman Walder shared arranging duties in the Rockets, and Stone took the additional task of schoolteacher. Jesse held forth almost daily in an available hall, either the musician's union building or Thamon Hayes's home, and instructed the band in nuances of orchestration and performance.

The Rockets rehearsed with a clear goal in mind—making a surprise appearance at the annual spring musician's benefit/battle of bands at the Paseo Ballroom.[1] When it came time in May 1932 they were ready. Harlan Leonard's wife and mother-in-law had paid for new Eton-style uniforms (several other costumes, including Toreador-style suits, soon followed), and Stone's arrangements were hot and tight. The combination of surprise, style, and swinging jazz that they presented that night succeeded in accomplishing what most observers remember as the most clear-cut band victory, and possibly the biggest musical upset, in K.C. history.

After opening to wide acclaim, the Rockets appeared to be headed for ever greater success until the Depression and bad luck took their toll. Crooked bookers at Chicago's Club Morocco, in league with local union officials, precipitated the loss of important work and Jesse Stone's departure from the band. Upon returning to Kansas City, an unfortunate disagreement with the band's own union local led Thamon Hayes to quit the music business entirely, and many of the standout musicians—Herman and Woodie Walder, Booker Washington, Rozelle Claxton, Baby Lovett, and Jack Johnson—to leave the group for a more reliable job in a local club. When Harlan Leonard reorganized the Rockets and finally did record in 1939 he had a fine organization, but one that bore little resemblance to the Rockets of Kansas City legend.

The failure of the Rockets to make it took on more importance to its members than might otherwise have been the case. These were experienced, proud musicians who, through luck or circumstance, had previously felt shunted aside in their search for greater success. This was their band. After its demise few among them ever again aggressively sought wider horizons than club bands in and around K.C. This is a pity, for much of the greatest talent of the era was present in the Rockets.

Booker Washington: After Bennie's band broke up, after we left Bennie's band . . . we got back to Kansas City, Ed Lewis, Thamon Hayes, Woodie Walder, Vernon Page, Harlan Leonard, [and I]. . . . We got together and we formed another band. We were the nucleus of this band, just the few

I named. Then we got Herman Walder, we got Jess Stone, and Baby Lovett to join from George Lee's band.

We picked [Thamon Hayes] as leader because he was an assistant to Bennie in Bennie's band. He was kind of what you call the right arm of Bennie Moten. He had this experience. We felt that he knew, and he did know, quite a few of the names of people to contact. That's why we elected him as the leader. . . .

And we formed this other band that was known as the Kansas City Rockets. . . . We rehearsed every day for about a month, next door here at Thamon Hayes's house [then as now, Hayes's home was adjacent to Washington's]. . . . Our wives would get together, they would fix a pot so we'd have something to eat, and we rehearsed. The brass section would go in the dining room, the reed section would rehearse in the living room. After we got the two sections together, . . . Jess Stone would arrange it. . . .

He could write music like you could write a letter. Knew everything about chords. . . . He had schools that we had to attend an hour every day, learning the fundamentals, the basics, and all that stuff. He would teach us anything about harmony, and he even had three or four fellows arranging that didn't know anything about it. He just put the band together and we had one of the greatest aggregations as had ever hit Kansas City, just from his patience.

Jesse Stone: We were rehearsing from the beginning I think three days a week, finally added another day, and then as we neared our first time playing we rehearsed five days a week.

Every rehearsal was from a half hour to an hour of class. [We covered] progressions, chord instruction, and all types of things. They would ask me questions and I would try to answer. They would even ask me musical history, how things evolved, and I taught them scale formation, and how the scale is based on steps, how chords are derived from the tones on the scale. I made them as simple as I possibly could. . . . I drilled them more than I did George Lee's group because we had such a short time to get ready. . . . We had something to look forward to.

Herman Walder: By that time I was writing [music] and Jess Stone was writing and Richard Smith was writing. We had a variety of stuff. All the cats could play, but we had to get used to each other. I hadn't played with Harlan before and I hadn't played with my brother [Woodie Walder] before. That's the first time we joined together.

Harlan Leonard's stepmother, his wife's mother, let us have enough money to buy some new uniforms and we rehearsed until this big dance was coming up, where they have a battle of bands once a year. . . . Man, we fell in with these uniforms on, man, double-breasted, with a sash around here, stripes all down here, . . . all shoes just alike, shirts just alike. Oh man, we was the sharpest *everything.*

Booker Washington: Harlan Leonard's mother, Mrs. Pennington, bought the clothes for the band. We had some brown Eton suits, yellow lapel, yellow stripes on the leg, everything.

Charles Goodwin: We were doing a kind of underground thing. We didn't want anybody to know about this band, this is supposed to be a Cinderella thing. And it was.

Jesse Stone: They had a contest [battle of bands] for the benefit of the [union] local. They were buying this building that they have now. . . . We was trying to make an impression up against Bennie Moten's band, because we had it in for Bennie Moten's band and then for George Lee's, because George Lee's band played there too that night. . . .
     That night we showed up in our uniforms and when we got on the stand it was just before the master band went on, which was Bennie Moten's band. Now Bennie Moten had been weakened because he had lost some of the guys and he had substituted with new players, but they were playing the same stuff. We were playing stuff they had never heard before. We were playing with a sound that they had never heard before, voicings and everything was new, and we tore up the hall. Bennie Moten didn't want to come on the stand after that.

Booker Washington: We come up to the Paseo Hall, everybody was watching this new band, looking to see what this new band gonna be. So, come time for us to play, we have introduced "Thamon Hayes and his Kansas City Rockets." We all pull off our coats, get our horns out, go to the bandstand, and we start playing. And from the start to the finish everybody got up on their chairs, the crowd was cheering more than anything we ever heard in my life.
     Bennie [Moten] got up on the bandstand after we finished playing, and his band got into a fight. The trumpet player, Joe Smith, and another person in the band at the time, got in a fight up on the bandstand. . . .
     From then on every club in Kansas City, every society, every social club in Kansas City hired us for the whole year. Sometimes two or three times a week. None of the [other] bands had any jobs, we sewed the whole thing up. . . . We played that whole summer. . . .
     We did have a monopoly on anything that went on in Kansas City. Then we stretched out on a Southern tour. Oklahoma, Texas, Louisiana,

and back another way. We did pretty good on that tour. . . . We went to Chicago twice. Both places they built a new building to bring us in, a new nightclub. . . .

We stayed there about four or five weeks and the union said we couldn't stay there any longer because we were a traveling band. . . . They refused [to let us in the local union]. . . . We did give a farewell dance, but they just finally said, "That's the end of it." So we had to come back home again. But this time, the last time we were in Chicago, the band broke up. . . .

We hired a boy, a youngster, to be a director.[2] We were making union wages at the El Torreon [a major K.C. ballroom], but we were taking so much out of our pockets to pay him a decent salary a week. . . . He had personality, and he's kind of tall, good-looking in a uniform and everything. We took about three dollars apiece out of our salary, give it to him. . . . But anyway he turned us in down at the union, to the president. He wanted to make the same thing we were making.

The next contract he would have [made more], . . . [but] we just give him so much out of our pocket. . . . So they fined Thamon Hayes five hundred dollars. Thamon didn't pay it. They fined us all a hundred dollars. Well, then Thamon [quit], he went into business [as] one of those salesmen for Jenkins Music Company [in Kansas City] . . . and Harlan Leonard took over. [The director] skipped town in a hurry.

Charles Goodwin: It was just a plain case of paying under scale. What it means is kicking some money back. We had been to Chicago and we had taken a guy to front the band. Then they had guys that wasn't conductors, they were more or less dancers and things like that. They would have personalities with the band by being in front of them and pretending to direct. . . . It didn't hamper the band any because they didn't pay any attention to him. It was a good thing to show. . . . He could run across the stage and make a big split, you know, added things to the band, introduce the numbers. . . .

Well, he was a smart aleck. . . . He goes to the union and turns this whole thing in. For which we wanted to kill him. We wanted to do him in for doing it because we had a good thing going. . . . Herman [Walder] decked him right out in front of the union there. He got up from there and he didn't get hit but once. He took off. In 1946, I believe it was, I saw him in Chicago. He wasn't doing anything to amount to anything. . . .

They fined Thamon five hundred dollars, which he said he wasn't going to pay. And he didn't. He just got out of music.

Herman Walder: That cat was standing out in front of the place down there [the musician's union]. And says to me, this dancer, "Man, I'm sorry about that, man. I'm sorry I turned you cats in." I said, "What do you mean, sorry, man? That's my living, man! My kids might go hungry by this." BAM! I knocked that cat down and he started running, and Harlan [Leonard] trying to catch him, and we run him out of town. Haven't seen him since.

Jesse Stone: When I got into Chicago with the Thamon Hayes band, they chased Thamon out of Chicago and I stayed. . . . Both these places [where we played in Chicago] were owned by gangsters. So the Morocco was getting all the trade, so they put a bomb in the Morocco . . . and Thamon was excitable and scary, and they wrote threatening letters, telephone calls, and he decided to pick up the band and go.

Now all the arrangements of the Thamon Hayes band were made by me. So without me, they wouldn't have had any music. So I made a deal. I let them take all the arrangements, and I kept the scores. I just went to the man that owned the Morocco and told him that I was going to stay. He said, "OK, organize another band." So that's what I did.

Booker Washington: We could've gone much further, 'cause we had the brand of music that people wanted to hear. The fellow that was writing for us after Jesse Stone was Rozelle Claxton, and he was writing screaming music, just as high as you could go on a horn. . . . [But] there really wasn't much here to look forward to. You'd have to stay on the road. . . . and you could've gone further, after you managed to break into that category, . . . just like Basie. They went to New York. . . .

We had a promise of a recording session, but it never did turn out. . . . But when Harlan Leonard took over the band when the original Rockets broke up, he took our repertoire and made recordings, . . . you can distinguish Jess Stone's music [in the recordings]. . . . That was a hard-luck band.

Herman Walder: Actually, the name of Thamon is the only one that went out of the band [at first]. We just didn't need no two trombones, we just used one trombone, four brass. It was all ready for [Harlan Leonard to take over]. . . .

[But after we went to] Chicago . . . and broke up . . . I says, if I ever get back to Kansas City, man, this stuff is gone with me, this traveling. I had enough with it.

I called a cat, name of Moon Eye, he owned the Spinning Wheel, and he sent us money for six cats. . . . The six was Rozelle Claxton on piano, and little Jack Johnson on the bass, Baby Lovett on drums, Booker Washington on trumpet, my brother Woodie on tenor [saxophone and] clarinet, and myself [on alto saxophone]. . . . I held that job down for three years. I said, the road never get me no more. . . .

Man, that second band couldn't have touched the first band. . . . He [had] to get a whole new crop [of musicians]. Would nobody else go.

Harlan Leonard's Rockets

Leonard's Rockets are distinguished by having achieved prominence through their popular recordings and extensive tours in the early 1940s ("I Don't Want to Set the World on Fire" was first recorded by Leonard). Among jazz enthusiasts, however, these "second-edition" Rockets are notable for bridging generations of Midwestern musicians and for showing early suggestions of modern jazz, much as was also true of Jay McShann's band.

Two of the most important arrangers in the Midwest, Eddie Durham and Buster Smith, worked extensively for Leonard, lending characteristically sophisticated and swinging tunes to his book.[3] In addition, two arrangers who became noted for their modern jazz work, James Ross and Tadd Dameron, also worked with Leonard, helping to shape the band's sound to a newly evolving jazz aesthetic.

Several strong new soloists were featured with the group, most notably a very young Charlie Parker (who never recorded with Leonard), and Fred Beckett (generally acknowledged as the first "modern" jazz trombonist). Featured vocalists were Ernie Williams, the former Blue Devils stalwart, and Myra Taylor.

The Leonard Rockets broke up in 1944, and Harlan Leonard retired from the music business to do civil service work in Los Angeles.

Charles Goodwin: [After the Thamon Hayes band broke up] Harlan's mother-in-law had some money, so he just picked up there. A kid named Jimmy Keith was a good musician, he could write and arrange and compose and what-have-you, and he had the band, and Harlan just took his band over. . . .

They were doing good then, recorded and everything, but Harlan finally goofed. Got so he couldn't take care of business anymore, and he was a good businessman, he had a good head on him. But he just couldn't cope with what was going on.

Ernie Williams: I started directin' [Harlan Leonard's] band about in '35, [and] left there in '41. . . . We didn't have no jobs then. He worked but he took the wrong jumps. He took the jobs, but he missed the money. . . .

Harlan managed the band, but I did a lot of running around for him. I had to do all of the dirty work. He was too lazy.

John Tumino: Harlan Leonard was very good, very pleasant to do business with. Easy to work with. He was a taskmaster to his men, though. . . . He was the one that came closest [of the black Kansas City bands] to featuring the sweet music. He would try to cater to the masses. . . . He got a contract with RCA Victor and made a helluva big hit record, which he didn't get the hit on, . . . "I Don't Want to Set the World on Fire." He played it in a jump, fast tempo, and it didn't do nothing. A few years later Al Hibbler came out with Duke Ellington [with the same song at a slower tempo and had a hit].

Eddie Durham: Harlan played it ["I Don't Want to Set the World on Fire," an Eddie Durham composition] too fast. That was the first recording that was ever made on it, though.

Gene Ramey: They sent Harlan Leonard's band after Basie, Harlan Leonard's band went to New York, and they came right back. Flopped the first night.

Now there's a case where you didn't really have the Kansas City thing. Didn't have a real Kansas City style, although they were all Kansas City musicians, but everything was written, even if you make a slur, it had to be on the music. The Basie band never read the music after the first time.

Myra Taylor: I was singing with Harlan Leonard's Kansas City Rockets. We had fifteen pieces then, but it was so loud, you just couldn't talk [in a nightclub]. The man kept telling them to bring the music down. . . . So Harlan took his band to the [musician's] union, upstairs there. They rehearsed for two weeks straight from early morning until late evening, every day except Sunday, and they got where they were the smoothest band you ever heard in your life. You could sit at your table and talk like this with a fifteen-piece band playing. That took work, but it was either that or be fired. . . .

You couldn't have told me nothing bad about [Harlan Leonard]. I loved the ground he walked on, that's how I worshiped him. And I shouldn't have. I went on a starvation tour with him that we left the last of May [1941], and we came back the first of September, and this is the honest to God truth, I never received one salary the whole time we were gone. He told me he was going to pay me at the end of the trip. He was giving me a dollar fifty a day to eat on, and it dropped down to a dollar. He had one dress cleaned for me one time while I was out and that was it. When we came [back] to town, I owed him eleven dollars. Now, can you figure that out?

I think he paid the men. I was the only dummy. I was the only one that didn't know. It hurts me today to think about it because I loved him so. . . . I guess maybe [other] people got tired of being used too, I don't know. I don't know what happened, but all of his men mostly came back to Kansas City. . . . If he had been all that outstanding they would have stayed with him and his band would have continued.

NOTES

1. Battles of bands were held in May at the Paseo Hall (also known as the Paseo Ballroom), located at Fifteenth Street and Paseo Boulevard in Kansas City (the building is now a church). They featured every K.C. band of note and were used by booking agents to determine the best, most popular bands to book in the coming year. The battles were the high point of the year for many musicians.

2. A band director was often no more than a sham orchestra leader, hired to provide an entertaining and attractive presence.

3. A "book" is a book of arrangements. A large and varied book was immensely valuable to a big band.

Kansas City Rockets, c. 1933. The Rockets were photographed at the Fairyland Park band shell in new uniforms provided by Harlan Leonard's mother-in-law. *Left to right:* Vernon Page (tuba and bass), Booker Washington (trumpet), Harlan Leonard (alto, tenor, and soprano saxophones), Woodie Walder (clarinet and tenor saxophone), Vic Dickenson (trombone), Thamon Hayes (trombone), Herman Walder (alto saxophone), Richard Smith (trumpet), Jesse Stone (piano), Baby Lovett (drums), Ed Lewis (trumpet). (Courtesy of the Kansas City Museum, Kansas City, Missouri, and Corrine Walder)

Kansas City Rockets at Fairyland Park, c. 1933. *Left to right:* Harlan Leonard, Vic Dickenson, Herman Walder, Thamon Hayes, Woodie Walder, Richard Smith, Booker Washington, Ed Lewis, Charles Goodwin (guitar and banjo), Baby Lovett, Vernon Page, Jesse Stone. (Courtesy of the Kansas City Museum, Kansas City, Missouri, and Corrine Walder)

Musicians Ball, 1933. This advertisement promoted the band battle where Thamon Hayes's Kansas City Rockets made their triumphant first appearance. (Courtesy of the Kansas City Museum, Kansas City, Missouri, and the *Kansas City Call*)

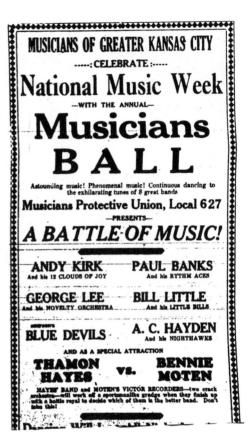

MUSICIANS OF GREATER KANSAS CITY
-----: CELEBRATE :-----

National Music Week
—WITH THE ANNUAL—

Musicians
BALL

Astounding music! Phenomenal music! Continuous dancing to the exhilarating tunes of 8 great bands

Musicians Protective Union, Local 627
—PRESENTS—

A BATTLE OF MUSIC!

ANDY KIRK
And his 12 CLOUDS OF JOY

PAUL BANKS
And his RYTHM ACES

GEORGE LEE
And his NOVELTY ORCHESTRA

BILL LITTLE
And his LITTLE BILLS

BLUE DEVILS

A. C. HAYDEN
And his NIGHTHAWKS

AND AS A SPECIAL ATTRACTION

THAMON HAYES vs. **BENNIE MOTEN**

HAYES' BAND and MOTEN'S VICTOR RECORDERS—two crack orchestras—will work off a sportsmanlike grudge when they finish up with a battle royal to decide which of them is the better band. Don't miss this!

Rocket Swing Unit at the Spinning Wheel, c. 1938. After the Kansas City Rockets disbanded, several of the original members formed their own club band. *Left to right:* Elbert "Coots" Dye (piano), Booker Washington (trumpet), Herman Walder (clarinet), Woodie Walder (saxophones), Jack Johnson (bass), Baby Lovett (drums). (Courtesy of the Kansas City Museum, Kansas City, Missouri, and Corrine Walder)

Jay McShann, c. 1937. (Courtesy of the Kansas City Museum, Kansas City, Missouri, and Charles Goodwin)

Jay McShann Orchestra, c. 1939. This early McShann band was a group sized for nightclubs rather than for dance hall appearances. *Left to right:* Harry Fergenson (saxophone), Jay McShann (piano), Gene Ramey (bass), Taswell "Little Joe" Baird [?] (trombone), Bob Mabane (saxophone), Gus Johnson (drums), Harold Bruce [?] (trumpet), Orville Minor (trumpet). (Courtesy of the Kansas City Museum, Kansas City, Missouri, and the Mutual Musician's Foundation)

Jay McShann Orchestra, c. 1940. McShann's thirteen-piece orchestra earned considerable but short-lived fame when it achieved national prominence through hit recordings. *Left to right:* Bill Nolan, Walter Brown (vocals), Charlie Parker (alto saxophone), Bob Mabane, Buddy Anderson (trumpet), Harold Bruce, John Jackson (saxophone), Harold Fergenson, Orville Minor, Taswell "Little Joe" Baird, Gus Johnson, Gene Ramey, Jay McShann (piano). (Courtesy of the Kansas City Museum, Kansas City, Missouri, and Charles Goodwin)

Jay McShann Orchestra at the Apollo Theater, New York City, c. 1942. By the early 1940s McShann was established in New York as an important up-and-coming band. *Left to right:* Orville Minor, Bud Gould (trombone), Harold Bruce, Buddy Anderson, Taswell "Little Joe" Baird, Jay McShann, Al Hibbler (vocals), Gus Johnson, Leonard "Lucky" Enois (guitar), Harry Fergenson, Charlie Parker, Gene Ramey, John Jackson (saxophone). (Courtesy of the Kansas City Museum, Kansas City, Missouri, and Gene Ramey)

Charlie Parker and Gene Ramey, c. 1940. Parker is shown playing with bassist Gene Ramey while still with Jay McShann. Ramey was Parker's friend, mentor, and occasional guardian both during and after their days with the McShann band. (Courtesy of the Kansas City Museum, Kansas City, Missouri, and Gene Ramey)

Lester Young with the Count Basie Orchestra, c. 1939. (Courtesy of the Kansas City Museum, Kansas City, Missouri, and John Randazzo)

15

The Jay McShann Orchestra

Jay McShann, an Oklahoma-born pianist and (later) vocalist, was a latecomer to Kansas City. He arrived in 1937 at the age of twenty-eight after touring the Southwest with a variety of bands, including those led by Al Dennis and Eddie Hills. In 1938 he first led his own small band and soon after obtained financial backing from Walter Bales (a local insurance executive who had previously sponsored Count Basie) to enlarge the small group to big band size. Jay accomplished this by raiding the Nat Towles band in Omaha. After a number of successful engagements, including a long stint playing for a walkathon, McShann began touring. Eighteen-year-old alto saxophonist Charlie Parker was the centerpiece of the ensemble.

In 1941 McShann engaged blues singer Walter Brown for a Decca recording engagement in Dallas. Decca co-owner Dave Kapp disliked and initially refused to record McShann's jazz specialties, but did accept several impromptu sides with a small ensemble featuring Brown. One of them, "Confessin' the Blues," became a national hit, one of the biggest sellers from a black band in that period, and established McShann's band, although not for the style of music they preferred to play.

With this success McShann was booked on a tour to New York, opening in a band battle against the Lucky Millinder Orchestra at the Savoy Ballroom in January 1942. Millinder was very popular locally, but McShann, with a devastating performance from Charlie Parker, "blew Millinder off the bandstand," and his success seemed assured.

The McShann band was thus nationally known by early 1942, and had several widely admired performers—Charlie Parker, saxophonists John Jackson and (later) Jimmy Forrest, trumpeters Buddy Anderson and Orville Minor, vocalists Brown and Al Hibbler, bassist Gene Ramey, drummer Gus

Johnson, guitarist Leonard "Lucky" Enois, and McShann himself. Contemporaries assert that McShann led the only post-Moten K.C. band that ever challenged Count Basie musically, and that the McShann band at its peak may have surpassed Basie.

There is little doubt that Jay had one of the most exciting bands of the day, filled with young musicians, fresh ideas, and enormous energy. But, like the Blue Devils years before, bad luck and bad timing haunted them. World War II devastated the music industry, eliminating opportunities for dance bands more quickly and decisively than the Depression ever had. With few young adult men about, fewer women were interested in dance halls. An entertainment tax that affected ballroom attendance; a strike by the American Federation of Musicians against the recording industry that banned members from recording from August 1942 through 1943; and gasoline rationing that made travel difficult and more expensive, all contributed to sudden hard times for orchestras.

The final blow to the band came when Jay himself was drafted off a bandstand (literally) in 1943. Upon his return in 1945 his irreplaceable "book" of tunes had been lost, and many of his best musicians were gone, either to the military, other bands in New York, or drug abuse.

McShann continued to perform, as leader of small groups and as a soloist, adding singing (in the style of Walter Brown) to his talents in the early 1950s. By the late seventies Jay was again a major national and international attraction, recognized as among the finest jazz/blues piano stylists.

McShann's featured performers took several paths: Charlie Parker was the leading figure in the development of modern jazz and be-bop; Buddy Anderson went into semiretirement due to health problems and returned to active performing in Kansas City in the mid-1970s; Gene Ramey was one of the most sought-after bass players in New York until his retirement to Texas in 1976; Walter Brown remained active through the early fifties; Gus Johnson is still active in Kansas City, as is Orville "Piggy" Minor; Al Hibbler was Duke Ellington's featured male vocalist for many years and continues to perform occasionally. John Jackson acquired a non-musical trade as a die setter in Kansas City, and also remained semi-active musically. He died in 1984. Parker Brown, William Scott, and Bob Mabane all died young, primarily due to heroin abuse.

Although eventually ill-starred, the McShann Orchestra was the last great big band of the Kansas City Jazz era. Most important, in its musicianship and personalities it embodied the transition from danceband swing to modern jazz, and provided the first genius of modern jazz, Charlie Parker.

Buck Clayton: The closest one [band] that came to us [the Count Basie Orchestra] was Jay McShann. Andy Kirk had a nice band, but Jay Mc-Shann was red hot. . . . Jay McShann is the quintessential Kansas City jazz pianist, . . . even more so than Basie.

Jay McShann — Beginnings

Jay McShann: It was four kids in the family, three girls and one boy.... It was sort of a church-going family but not necessarily musical. My sister, she studied music.... The old man, he [would] just kind of fool around on the piano, you know, and the same thing with my mother, but ... he only had one tune that he knew and he taught me that tune.... That was the only musical [thing] happening around in the family with the exception of ... singing in church....

Musicians use to come through town back in those days.... If they were having a dance they used to ... take five or six musicians and put them on a truck, and they'd drive all over town.... Very ballyhoo like; that is what you would call it.... They used to bring bands from Kansas City to Muskogee [and] I was very impressed with the Clarence Love band....

I was in school then but sometimes the bands would come over to the school and do two or three numbers for what we would call assembly. But of course my folks were pretty Christian-like, and they didn't ... want me to go to dances. If I went I would have to do it in another manner, like sneak off or something.[1] ...

I always wanted a horn, but my folks was too poor. They had a piano around the house, so that's all I could settle for.[2] ... [I was] just fooling around on the piano, I never thought anything about it.... My sister used to take piano lessons.[3] ...

After I finished high school and went off to college I decided I wanted to try to work my way through college playing football, but that didn't work out too good. There was too many other guys out there trying to do the same thing. So finally one night the guys wanted someone to play for a party, and they couldn't find a piano player. One fellow told them, "That guy that was out there playing football, ... we can probably get him. He knows a couple of songs." So the guys ... came and got me and said, "Listen man, we want you to play for this party." I said, "But man, I don't know but two or three songs. I couldn't play for no party." He said, "Well, you know what you do, you just play those two or three songs over and over all night." ... So this is what I would end up doing, and they paid me. After they paid me for playing I decided [that] this is about time for me to start learning some songs.

I started to learn a few songs and ... after leaving school I went to Tulsa, Oklahoma. I thought I would get me a job doing anything, you know. Jobs were few and far between [c. 1930]. So I happened to hear a band rehearsing one day. It was rehearsing upstairs, and you know how when you hear music and horns and all that stuff you follow the sound, like a parade....

I followed the sound and . . . these guys were rehearsing and they didn't have a piano player. The guy says, "We don't know what we're going to do . . . we have to have a piano player for Saturday night." I couldn't read no music, so I sat and listened to them. . . . After they got done I told one of the guys, "If you all still need a piano player I think I can make it." . . . So I went along just like I was reading music. . . . They put all this big orchestration out in front of me, but I'd heard 'em rehearsing so I just went ahead on and played along with them. . . . When we finished the tune they says, "Man, we got a piano player that can read and fake." They thought I was reading but I was just faking. . . . I couldn't read a note as big as a house. . . . That was Al Dennis's band. He had about a twelve-piece band. I started out with them.

They finally found out that I couldn't read because we had some music that had an introduction for piano only. . . . I asked the horns, "What is the matter, why don't you guys come on in." They said, "No, all this is you. . . . You got the first four bars, piano solo." . . . So I [said], "Fellows, I can't read." So instead we just kept the introduction out.[4] . . .

Jay worked with the Dennis band for a few months, then moved to Arkansas City, a small Kansas town just across the Oklahoma line, where he performed with a guitarist at a local nightclub. When the club closed McShann enrolled in a junior college, and spent most of his time in its music room. This was probably good training, but not particularly lucrative. His landlady was especially interested in his finding work, and referred Jay to the Eddie Hills band out of Shawnee, Oklahoma (her son also performed with Hills), and McShann signed on.

After a brief road trip the band arrived at its base, Silver's Resort in the mountains near Albuquerque, New Mexico. The ten-piece group played the broad repertoire of a territory band, featuring mostly dance songs but ranging from "Rose Room," "You Can Depend on Me," and "Sweet Georgia Brown" to waltzes and even cucarachas for Mexican patrons.

It was, however, a short-lived engagement. A conflict between the resort owner and his wife erupted when she had him evicted, which led him to shoot his wife and kill himself. The club closed and the band was stranded. The members scattered, and Jay returned to Arkansas City where he had been promised work. That job only lasted three weeks. McShann and a saxophone player in the band decided to head north to Omaha, where family and friends could put them up. While en route in 1937 McShann used a three-hour bus layover to see some of Kansas City.

The Jay McShann Orchestra

Jay McShann: When I first came to Kansas City, I didn't have any bread. . . . I guess I probably had about sixty or seventy cents on me.

Well, I ran into one of the guys that I knew from Tulsa [Bill Hadnott].
He was playing bass with Bus Moten's band, and he's the one that gave
me the idea to stay in Kansas City. He said, "Man, this is where you
want to stay. This is where the music is. You don't want to be going to
Omaha. Come on here." I says, "Man, I don't have no money for no
room here. I got people in Omaha." He says, "Forget it, come on and
take my room. . . . I stay at my girl's." So that's what we did.[5] . . .

Within a few days of moving in with Hadnott, McShann got his first K.C.
gig as pianist with drummer Elmer Hopkins at the Monroe Inn. Soon after,
trumpeter Ed Lewis, a much better known performer than either Hopkins
or McShann because of his experience with Bennie Moten, joined to make
the group a trio.

Jay McShann: Ed was undecided what to do. He had offers from Count
Basie and Andy Kirk, and he didn't know which one to take. Both Elmer and I told him we thought Basie had the better band and a few
weeks later he left.

I was making $1.25 a night, playing from 8:30 to 1, six nights a week.
Sometimes we picked up much more than that in tips, but on slow
nights that $1.25 was about all we got.

I was new in town and went everywhere, listening and having fun.
But no matter how much fun I was having I always set aside a dime so
that I'd have streetcar fare the next night to get to work.[6]

After several months with Hopkins, Jay moved up to Dee Stewart's band
at the Continental Club, earning $2.50 nightly. This was an excellent group,
with such local stars as alto saxophonist Buster Smith, drummer Jesse Price,
and McShann's friend Hadnott. It was, however, only a part-time job. A
Denver pianist named John Riggin had the regular piano job, and Jay was
only filling in. Still, it was a major step up for the twenty-seven-year-old
newcomer.

Jay McShann: When Riggin showed up [to play with Stewart's band] I
got a job at Wolfe's Buffet at Eighteenth and Vine with drummer Harold Gadson. The owner would add a singer from time to time, including
Joe Turner. Those were some great sessions.[7]

From Wolfe's Buffet (which was located in the heart of K.C.'s still-swinging black downtown) Jay joined a new band led by Buster Smith. While walking home from this job McShann first heard alto saxophonist Charlie Parker. This was a pivotal meeting for both men, as Parker would become the instrumental star of Jay's big band and there gain his springboard to New York and much greater prominence.

Jay McShann: I made all the spots where you meet all the musicians. One night I was passing by a club and I heard a lot of sounds coming out—it was a different sound, though. I went to see who was playing. So I walked up to the man and said, "I thought I met all the musicians in town. What's your name?" "Charlie Parker." So I said, "Where you been?"[8] . . . He says, "You haven't met me because I've been down in the Ozarks with George E. Lee's band. . . . I wanted to do some woodshedding[9] so I went down there." . . . The first time I got a small group together I hit on him. . . . Bird's just one of those cats, he just overnight put it together.[10]

Jay's opportunity to hire Parker would come soon, partly because of the support he received from Walter Bales. Bales was president of a local insurance company and a devoted jazz fan. He had previously befriended Count Basie, and the two had spent many hours playing piano duets in Bales's home. Since Basie's departure for New York Bales had been searching for a new musical comrade, and McShann's playing appealed to him greatly.

Jay McShann: William Shaw [then president of black musician's local 627] stopped in at Wolfe's, gave me Bales's phone number, and told me to call him. I went out to his place the next day and we had quite a session playing his piano. We got together quite often after that, some-times at his place, other times at Jenkins Music Company [a large local instrument, record, and sheet music outlet], where he would rent a cou-ple of pianos for an hour or so.

I was a pretty wild kid then. Mr. Bales would get after me about set-tling down and really working on my piano. When you play in a small club, particularly in a duo, you're inclined to just hammer away at the piano all night long. He was always getting after me to back off a little and to think out what I was doing. He sure knew what he was talking about. I learned a lot from him.[11]

Bales was a key factor in McShann's getting his first job as a bandleader at Martin's-on-the-Plaza. McShann's was both the first black band and the first jazz ensemble to play at this prestigious, conservative club. Jay began with a quintet that included his cousin Pete McShann, drums; Allen An-derson, trumpet; "Popeye," alto sax; and Bill Hadnott, bass. Within a month he replaced most of these men with Gene Ramey, bass; Gus Johnson, drums; and Charlie Parker on alto sax. This was to remain the core of both his soon-to-be-famous rhythm and reed sections. He also acquired a manager at this time, booking agent John Tumino.

John Tumino: Martin's had a club there, right by Forty-seventh Street . . . and Jay had a five- or six-piece band there. That's when I got ahold of Jay and put him in the Century Room. [Dave] Dexter[12] put me onto him; . . . he's got a tremendous ear for jazz. . . .

Jay McShann: Dave (Dexter) is primarily the cause for me playing music.[13]

Jay's Martin's-on-the-Plaza band was soon augmented further by Orville "Piggy" Minor, trumpet; Earl Jackson, alto sax; William Scott and Bob Mabane, tenor saxes. Charlie Parker had temporarily quit.

As the band expanded so did McShann's opportunities. He was now able to play occasional college dances and other outside jobs, and was a reliably popular attraction at Martin's.

John Tumino: Jay had what you would call the jumpingest band around. It was a real tight group; it wasn't a big band at the time when I got 'em. It was a real close, tight group and then he expanded. He had Charlie Parker in the band at that time at the Century Room when I opened it up, after Harlan [Leonard] left.[14] He got several guys . . . from Omaha. . . . At that time we were paying Jay about eighty-five dollars a night;[15] . . . just plain dirt scale. . . .

Early in 1938 McShann had his first opportunity for broader recognition, largely due to the efforts of *Down Beat's* Dave Dexter. Jay left his band under the joint leadership of William Scott[16] and Gus Johnson, hired a temporary pianist (Nick Payne), and went with Gene Ramey and a Pittsburgh drummer and vibraphonist named Honeyboy to an engagement at the Off-Beat Club[17] in Chicago. This two-week fill-in job was extended to six after Dexter published a glowing review in *Down Beat*, followed by a longer, equally favorable article by Sharon Pease, *Down Beat's* technical writer and musicologist. Thus through both the strength of his talent and the unflagging support of some key friends, McShann's fortunes began to rise.

McShann stayed at Martin's until August 1938 when he moved to the Century Room, a larger club operated by his manager. This venue required a full jazz orchestra (usually eleven to sixteen pieces), so Jay needed to recruit some additional talent.

His target was Omaha bandleader Nat Towles who had a reputation both for hiring excellent musicians and for losing them because of his notoriously tyrannical and stingy habits. So in September 1938, with about fifty dollars of financial backing from Walter Bales, Jay went to raid the Towles band.

Jay McShann: I knew you had to make a big showing to get some kind of attention. The guys were having a jam session at the Blue Room [in Omaha] that night and every time a guy blew something I liked I'd send the waitress up there. She'd take him a couple drinks and tell him to come to my table after he finished blowing.[18] . . .

Then I got down to business. I told him I was Jay McShann from Kansas City and I needed some musicians to fill out my orchestra, and he was just the man I was looking for. When he went back to the stand, he'd tell the others and pretty soon I was getting more attention than anyone.

Someone called Nat Towles and told him, "Some rich cat from Kansas City is trying to steal your band." Towles just sloughed off the idea, [and told him that], "All those boys owe me money. They aren't going any-place."

But by nine o'clock that night I had four guys from his band and another from [Lloyd] Hunter's and was ready to head on back to Kansas City.[19]

With the addition of the Omaha musicians (including trumpeter Harold Bruce, trombonists Leo Williams and Bud Gould, and guitarist Lucky Enois), some changes in his core band (notably the return of Charlie Parker), and other additions (including trumpeter Buddy Anderson), McShann was ready for the Century Room. The job was very successful, and was followed in turn by one of McShann's most unusual engagements, a several-months-long walkathon at the Pla-Mor Ballroom.

Buddy Anderson: Lord yes, that was an experience [the walkathon]. It was the only one of its kind. . . . The contestants were the whole show, and all of them could do some kind of act. They had to or else they didn't need 'em out there. . . .

A lot of them were pros, actors and singers, whatever they could do [to] just stay on the floor. Then they made it real dramatic, and they had the people really going with it. Big crowd in the arena, every night packed, and doing all the dances, stragglin', they'd be resting, but eve-ning comes, everybody come alive again and do the show. . . .

It involved endurance. Partners are allowed only to really lay down maybe a couple of hours at night and then they have to hit the floor. This place is open all night. Performers would have to come out on the

floor and one would sleep while the other one was holding up and keeping moving.

Days and days of endurance. Finally the eliminations came about.
Some would get to be famous with the people and when they would be
eliminated, oh, they'd just have a fit when their favorites went down.

They'd drag on until the last when just two couples [would be] up
there, and finally one of them would be just about to go down. . . .
They'd make it something dramatic, but it was a big deal. With the big
band we were getting some fairly nice dough, and that very thing was
the cause of Bird subsequently [re]joining the band, because one of the
cats was squackin' about the dough. . . .

Gigs like that are the backbone of a band's staying together because
you have to have some dough to hold the cats together. The walkathon
was a big thing, for it must have went on for two to three months. As
far as the band was concerned it was a crucial part of it [getting
started].

Jay McShann: The [walkathon] job lasted two or three months and when
we came out of there we had a heck of a big band. We had, I bet you,
seven hundred head arrangements and maybe two hundred and fifty
written arrangements. . . .

[Head arrangements] was what we called our skull-busters, and I'll
never understand how those guys could remember those heads. . . . Guys
like Bird [Charlie Parker] and John Jackson [tenor saxophone], they were
good at that. I had a bunch of guys with big ears who could play heads.
Those guys doing heads had freedom.[20]

Buddy Anderson: Fairyland Park was the next gig. . . . It was a Johnny
Tumino thing. He engineered the whole thing.

Fairyland Park was Kansas City's largest amusement park, and its best
summertime band job. Gaining this engagement in 1939 was a clear sign
that McShann had made it to the top of the local jazz scene. Jay had
organized some of the region's finest new generation of musicians into a
strong, cohesive group. Aside from Jay and Gene Ramey most of the
bandmembers were either teenagers or in their early twenties.

After Fairyland Park Tumino booked the band on a tour through Missouri,
Kansas, and Oklahoma—thus following in the tradition of earlier K.C. jazz
orchestras who expanded their horizons by playing the Territories. With
the Depression waning by 1939 this was again an option.

Jay McShann: It wasn't very long before we just went out on the
road. . . . We just did a lot of one-nighters. Our first experience was

around the Midwest because we were . . . stationed in Kansas City. . . .
We would go to Columbia [Missouri], to K.U. [Kansas University in
Lawrence, Kansas]. . . . [We] used to play a lot of school dates. . . . That
was the beginning of it. . . .

We had it [the repertoire] all mixed up. We had ballads; we had
swing tunes and jump tunes. We had boogie-woogie [and] we had some
blues. [There] was a variety of numbers in the book because we were
playing a lot of different places, and at that time you had to be able to
play almost everything. . . .

We had a lot of funny experiences, and a lot of experiences that
wasn't so funny, but it is a kick to look back over some of the stuff. A
lot of times we would go in a town to play, . . . like this is Monday . . .
and a guy says, "We had you all advertised for last Monday." . . . So I
would say, . . . "We'll see if we can't get around and get the town advertised, and we'll work this maybe on a forty/sixty basis"[21] or something.
We had experiences like those, too.[22] . . .

Orville Minor: We played almost every college that there was around
here. I mean large colleges: K.U., K. State, O.U. [Oklahoma University],
or any of those near here . . . in the five-state area. . . . College audiences
are different . . . from the average public, local audiences. . . . They're
more interested. . . . We did about a taste of everything they wanted to
hear.[23]

John Tumino: Yeah, shoot, [we] would go up there every night on one-
nighters. We played Tulsa and Oklahoma City. We played Dallas, . . .
Fort Worth, . . . Memphis, . . . Houston, . . . Shreveport, . . . New Orleans.
Every night, man, we had to . . . drive three hundred, four hundred
miles.

By this point the McShann band was well on its way to becoming a truly
excellent group. We know that the ensemble had acquired considerable
polish because during this period the band made its first recordings, albeit
accidentally. On November 30 and December 2, 1939, an eight-piece
subset[24] of the McShann orchestra was invited to broadcast live from a
Wichita, Kansas, radio station. Unbeknownst to the band the broadcasts
were recorded, and surfaced in the mid-1970s. Known as the "Wichita
Transcripts," these are the first recordings of Charlie Parker and demonstrate
a young but exceptionally vigorous small swing band. Both Parker and
Bernard Anderson stand out as soloists, with Parker sounding very much
like Lester Young (tenor sax player for the Count Basie band and a K.C.
idol). They had developed greatly in a short time, but still had a year and

a half of home and road performances before their next, formal, recording session would pave their way to New York and even brighter horizons. By all accounts they also had a wonderful time.

Big Band Sound, Style, and Good Times

Jay McShann: In the big band . . . we used to always try to build for a climax. . . . We would start out with the rhythm section, . . . nothing but the rhythm. And we'd let the rhythm, they might blow for three choruses, before we'd let the rest of the band in. That's to be sure that we had the thing where we wanted it, we wanted to be sure we got the right tempo. . . . These guys sitting there with their horns, after three choruses, they were raring to go . . . and when we do break them in, they hit, see, because they were ready to go. . . . I'd say that was the thing that . . . really made it. . . . They was ready from the gitgo, but we'd sort of wind them up, wind them up with the rhythm section, keep winding them 'till when we turn them loose, why they're ready to go.

Then you see Bird [Charlie Parker], he's right here in the horn section, he set all the riffs on all that head stuff. Then Bernard Anderson and Piggy Minor and Bob Merrill, each one . . . was a good riff-setter in the brass section. . . . Then, whoever comes up for his solo, well he's ready to blow, he wants to get out there and blow. . . . It was a lot of fun, and the guys enjoyed it.[25]

Gene Ramey: We [the rhythm section — piano, bass, drums, guitar] were known as the Twentieth Century Rhythm. In those days Charlie Parker wasn't known [and] the band was featured as a rhythm band. . . . In the Kansas City style the drummer's foot was never supposed to be so loud. . . . The rhythm drummer with the McShann band [was] Gus Johnson. We had it arranged. I played along with the saxophones, the drummer plays the dynamics with the trumpet . . . so that brings out what the trumpet players are playing.

McShann made an important addition to the band while on tour in Texas. Al Hibbler, a blind singer who was later featured with Duke Ellington, approached Jay at their engagement and asked to sing a number with the band. Jay's goodwill got the best of his skepticism, and Hibbler's singing knocked out both the band and the audience. Previously McShann had only been able to display group singing. The absence of a strong lead singer must have been a serious handicap that could now be resolved. Unfortunately for McShann it took Hibbler nearly a year to free himself from a girlfriend who didn't want him to leave. When Hibbler finally got to Kansas City the band had already signed on blues singer Walter Brown, had made its first formal recordings, and was about to leave for New York.

Orville Minor: There's one funny thing I want to tell you about Hibbler. . . . We was in Lincoln, Nebraska. Leanne Rose had a club up there, so Hibbler was with us when we played an engagement up there. [We] went down to a place called the Blue Room . . . and we was having a ball. When it ended up Hibbler and I was sittin' on a lady's front porch. It was hot and we just not thinkin', just hanging out.

Anyway, the window was open, and we could hear somebody snoring. She'd gone to sleep. Hibbler turned and said, "Hey, Piggly Wiggly, I'll be right back." So I'm just sittin' there, enjoying the breeze, and pretty soon I hear tough breathing, and I'd wanted to get that chick myself.

Pretty soon Hibbler came back, and he was saying to himself, "Ahhh," like that, you know. He went in there and scored. . . . When I went in there she began to wake up, got restless, like, "You've been here already." . . .

[Another time] we went to Wichita [Kansas] with Jay's band. Wichita was a rat's nest. It was a wild trip. Everything we did was wild, the women, the wine, everything. It was one of them things you'd never believe.

I remember the time Bird introduced nutmeg to the fellas. He went to the store and got the nutmeg, and all you do is take the nutmeg can and split it open. Don't spill a drop of it, because you'll lose the whole thing. So he opened it, and he gets Pepsi-Cola. You have to have Pepsi-Cola or else, won't nothing happen.

He takes the nutmeg, puts it on his tongue, and you hold your breath because if you don't you'll choke. So he gets the Pepsi-Cola and a half hour from that, you don't know a thing. . . . He feels like he's on a sidewalk and it's a long step down. . . .

Let me tell you what he did at Tootie's Mayfair. We had just started a gig out there. . . . We put on a show one night and Bird got all the whole reed section high on nutmeg. . . . Jay needed a downbeat and didn't hear nobody but the rhythm section and the trumpet. You wouldn't believe this.

Jay himself very seldom gets angry, and he said, "What's the matter guys?" They gave him no reason at all, you know. They'd sit up laughing at each other, man it was really something. The gig was shot. . . .

We had another thing going on [there, too]. Gus Johnson was peepin' over the transom at the women, in the women's rest room. So while Tootie [Clarkin, owner of the club] is racing over trying to keep Gus and them from doing that, from peeping at the women in the toilet, well

Bird is running next door getting nutmeg. Stackin' up the cans. . . . Tootie, he like to threw a gasket. . . .

McShann was going through his role, too, 'cause he takes a taste too much. Hootie[26] gets so high sometimes. . . . One time Jay got too high and he got to playin' . . . and went up to the end of the piano and fell off. . . . The bartender looked up, "What happened to Jay? Look like Jay he done got a little small, ain't he?" And Jay had hit the floor. The band went on playing. . . .

We was still boys, kids you know. . . . It was free, no strings. We just had a ball. That's the reason the band sounded the way it did, . . . we's relaxed. That's the reason we made it to New York. . . . It was just a gang, a brother business.

Buddy Anderson: McShann's was kind of a family-like deal. All the boys was boys together, warm, friendly, everybody was just friends. . . .

McShann's band was [also] more of an individual type thing than most bands at that time. They were all different. Everybody in it was a different thing on the instrument. Nobody was in the same bag, consequently they were pushing toward something unique, not necessarily in or out of any particular groove. The grooves were so varied at that time that it wasn't necessary to be like anybody . . . but as a group we were very together. Everybody just dug everybody, but everybody did their own thing.

The Big Time

As had been true for Andy Kirk's Clouds of Joy with "Until the Real Thing Comes Along" and Count Basie with "One O'Clock Jump," Jay McShann's route to success as a bandleader was through a hit recording. In Jay's case, however, the hit was an anomaly, a small-ensemble blues song featuring vocalist Walter Brown, not at all like the music his big band had worked so long to mold. No matter. With bookings assured, McShann used the hit to introduce his band to jazz audiences.

Jay McShann: Walter Brown started singing with the band about four or five days before we made ["Confessin' the Blues"]. I happened to come into this club one night and I heard Walter singing the blues. . . . I didn't have but half a dollar in my pocket and I went over there to him and I said, "Hey man," give him the half, "sing that, do that blues you did or do another blues or do anything, just sing the blues." Old Brown sang the blues again. So I says, "Say, man, look here, in about three or four days we're going on down to Texas, we want to make some [records], you want to go down with us? . . . We'll do maybe at least one or two blues." He said, "Yeah." I said, "Good." I said, "Now you better give me half of that, give me a quarter back of that money, 'cause that's all I had." He said, "Yeah man. I'll give you half of it back." He said, "Those other cats don't know you give that half dollar no way."[27]

The blues that Walter Brown sang with the McShann band were solidly in the K.C./Big Joe Turner tradition of spontaneous creation, built on a storehouse of well-known phrases, themes, and images. All the band needed was two or three rehearsals to integrate Brown. McShann would indicate which choruses were his, and Brown would weave a blues, sometimes with the assistance of Buddy Anderson or McShann. Within a few days, on April 30, 1941, the band was at the Decca recording studio in Dallas for their first formal recording session, with Walter Brown along as a reserve.

Jay McShann: When we had our first recording session Dave Kapp [owner of Decca Records] recorded us. We had everything set up that we wanted to do, [instrumental] numbers like "Yardbird Suite" and stuff like that. He kept telling us, "Fellows that's good, I enjoy listening to that, but . . . I can't sell it." We [had] been in the studio now about three hours.

He says, "Can you play any blues?" I say, "Yeah" [but] we don't want to play [that]. We were engrossed in one particular thing. . : . We played a boogie-woogie and we noticed he was smiling. So he told us, "Do another blues and I'll take one of those other two [instrumental pieces]." So that is what we did. We compromised and we did another blues, I believe it was "Hootie Blues" and then . . . "Swingmatism" [an instrumental].[28]

Although the band was furious over Kapp's manipulation of their music the result of the session was better than they could have hoped. The second blues song cut on that date, "Confessin' the Blues," was a smash hit, one of the biggest sellers of 1941 and is still considered a blues classic. This assured the band of the long-awaited opportunity to play in New York and to test their skills against the best swing orchestras.

Despite this break the band remained frustrated over their sudden transformation, at least in the minds of record buyers, into a blues band.

Jay McShann: About a quarter of our book was vocals by Walter, while most of the remainder was swinging stuff. When we played dances the audience was surprised we could do anything but back Walter. When we let them have our instrumentals, they went wild.

But Kapp said they [the instrumental songs] wouldn't sell and kept us

recording Walter Brown vocals. If we had recorded a bunch of our originals it might have been different.[29]

John Tumino: After we made the recordings in Dallas, "Confessin' the
Blues" and "Hootie Blues" became big hits in '41, so in October I start
getting calls from different agencies in New York. They heard about the
band and wanted to know who owned it. . . . So the Gale Group . . . said,
"We can get you in here [New York] if you sign an exclusive contract,
and let us book it." Okay. We worked out a deal. I said, "Where's the
first date gonna be?" They said, "The Savoy Ballroom in New York
City." I said, "How the hell are we gonna get there?" "Don't worry
about it, we'll book you all the way up." So they booked us in St. Louis,
Chicago, Pittsburgh. Three days to get there.

[All] one-nighters, so we were going every night. I wanted to see New
York, see what the hell the story was. I heard about them New York
people, move you out fast.

When we got to New York . . . the band was all raggedy looking and
beat, wore wrinkled clothes, all traveling in cars in those days. This guy
named Charles Buchanan, he was the manager of the Savoy Ballroom;
he took a look at this outfit, and he says, "What in the hell have we got
here? This is the raggediest looking band I ever saw in my life! This is
New York City, boy, this isn't Kansas! Goddamned Indians here." . . .

That night they opened at the Savoy Ballroom, and they had Charlie
Parker blowing like crazy. . . . Walter Brown was with the band. We had
two singers, two great singers, and we set that goddamned Savoy Ballroom on fire that night! . . . Jay McShann blew Lucky Millinder off the
stand. It was a great time for Jay. Hell, he had all the stars. . . .

Charlie Parker right away got great publicity. . . . They picked up on
him right away. Of course Al Hibbler got some mention. Naturally, Walter Brown was the big deal at that time 'cause he had the hit record
"Confessin' the Blues". . . . They all got mentioned. It was a great time.

Orville Minor: When we first hit New York . . . everybody was excited,
everybody was scared. I think we all had this conception that this is the
big thing. We've got to show our wares in New York, either do-or-die
thing. . . .

After intermission he [the Savoy's manager] called us all in the corner,
and he said, "You fellas sure got a good band. You're the blowinest raggedy band I've ever heard." We had some Sears and Roebuck suits. . . .

What we did was, . . . it was thirty minutes and thirty minutes—their
[Millinder's] band thirty and our band thirty. . . . We just played ordinary,
average stuff for the first couple of hours. After a while, Lucky went

into his books. We just kinda laid back. . . . So when we went into the books,[30] everybody knew it. While Lucky was on his break some cat went downstairs and told him, "You better get up and see what them Western dogs is doing." . . . By the time Lucky came up the cats is wound up, you know.

Jay McShann: Lucky's band played first because they were on number one, you know. [When] we played the guys kept asking me, . . . "Man, when you going in the books?" I said, "Let's hold it a while." . . . So we kept holding off a while, for at least three sets. . . . After we played our third set [I] got the cats together and said, "Gentlemen, I think we better start getting on the books, because Lucky is shelling out a little bit over there."

So some cat went downstairs . . . and said, "Lucky, we better get upstairs. I don't know what . . . those Western dogs . . . are doing but you better get up there and find out." I guess he come up and he fell right into his book, his heavy stuff, [but] all of his heavy stuff wasn't swinging. . . . His band had some stuff but Lucky wasn't swinging. So . . . as soon as he hit his last note we fell in. This was a thirty-minute number,[31] . . . and the people screamed and hollered for another thirty minutes. That was Lucky's thirty minutes, that he should have been playing, so we had to go right back into it again. We went right back into another thirty-minute [number] and that broke [the house] up. It really did.[32]

Gene Ramey: Lucky Millinder's band sent us a note saying, "We're going to send you hicks to the sticks." And boy, we didn't want to go back to Kansas City, we had dreams and everything. So first we planned on taping the piano keys . . . so when the guys sits down and plays, nothing would happen.

We thought of all these kinds of things. We're going to put tacks on the guy's seats. But then the guys said, "No, these cats might be bigger and badder than we are; then we are going to have to run. . . ."

That McShann band, every band that we caught, we'd blow them out. . . . So they wouldn't never let us play against Basie or Lionel Hampton. . . . We were known as the swingingest rhythm section, the Jay McShann rhythm section, even outplaying Basie. I think the reason is, we played more fast tunes. . . .

[When] we went to New York, all we had written was the first chorus and the last chorus, all the rest of that . . . was nothing but riffs. . . .

Our first broadcast in New York, we started playing "Cherokee." ["Cherokee" was Charlie Parker's showpiece with the band.] It was supposed to have been a fifteen-minute broadcast and the man heard it and

said, "Who is that saxophone player? Let him play." We played forty-
five minutes. Now can you imagine what the old bass player was feeling
like?

Wartime Breaks Up the Band

Gene Ramey: [Savoy Ballroom owner and booking agent Moe Gale] had
corralled all of the black bands . . . [and] when McShann got to New
York, Gale tried to get McShann to sell out to him, and he wouldn't do
it. So then they proceeded to send us out to places . . . where we got in
trouble with the police department, the unions, and everything
else. . . . They did these kind of things to break the band up. So we
hadn't been there [on tour] for six months before guys got disconsolate
and left.

   Gus [Johnson, drummer] and I were the only ones that stayed there.
John Jackson [saxophone] stayed awhile, Bird had stayed, but there was
an effort to break the band up, 'cause all those famous bands, Cootie
Williams, Erskine Hawkins, Lucky Millinder, were working for forty
dollars a week . . . and we got sixteen a night. . . .

   Parker had left us in the fall of '42. . . . [Willie] Cook took him back to
New York and he worked around there until he got with Earl
Hines. . . . I was glad [he left], too, because he was my burden.[33]

John Tumino: In 1942 they started rationing all the gasoline, tires.
Transportation was almost at a standstill. The only way we got on
planes was we made arrangements with the USO to entertain the
troops. . . .

   Each time we'd hit a base we'd kill 'em for all the . . . gasoline
stamps . . . and tires. . . . What killed the ballrooms was the war came
along . . . the bands were losing their men to the war effort and then Jay
finally got drafted, right here in Kansas City [in 1944]. Took him right
from here to Ft. Leavenworth [Kansas], at the Municipal Auditorium.

   They had come in to play a one-nighter. . . . We made a bundle that
time because that was his first time in his hometown after New York
and we had a hell of a turnout. He got nabbed right before he got
through, they took him off the stand. . . . I finally got drafted about a
year later.

Jay McShann: We had been doing a lot of one-night stands, so I kept
missing the draft board because I wanted to take my examination in
New York or California. Those two states were pay-off [states]. [But]
every time we got to New York my papers would be late. . . . I figured I

had it all set in California, [but we] went to California [and] my papers
were still late. . . .

We were going back to New York . . . and did a one-night stand in
Kansas City. We were taking a break [and] during intermission these two
guys came over and told me, "We got to talk to you. This is very important." I said, "Well everything is all right, why don't you get . . . a
little drink or something, [I'll] be right with you." . . . They came back,
said, "We hate to do this but we really got to take you to Leavenworth
[Kansas] right now." I said, "Leavenworth! What is happening in Leavenworth?" He says, "They've got you for immediate induction. They
haven't been able to find you . . . and we have to take you right now."
So I told him, "Okay, give me a chance to find somebody to finish playing." . . . So George Salisbury finished the night out for me, and I went
to Leavenworth. When I walked inside of the gate I was in. . . .

I was in the service . . . for better than thirteen months, and consequently the band broke up right there and then I lost a very good book
[of arrangements]. Someone got it the following morning, but I never
did find the book or . . . uniforms or anything.[34]

Worse than the loss of the book and the uniforms, the continuity of the
band was also lost due to conflicts between Gene Ramey, McShann's designated successor, and the management company.

Gene Ramey: The band was supposed to have been left to me. It had
been agreed. See, I had already run the band when McShann had to go
back for his [physical] exams. . . . But on that last night . . . it was understood that I would have the band, "Jay McShann and His Band." . . .

So we got back there [to Kansas City] but somebody had maneuvered
it around. . . . They wanted me to still manage the band but instead of it
being Jay McShann's band . . . this guy decided it was going to be "Walter Brown and His Band," under the direction of me. . . .

See, Walter Brown was a junkie, [and] how in the world am I going
to get along with a junkie? . . . So I just told him, I wouldn't go.

The whole repertoire was misplaced, 'cause when I quit, all the guys
quit, . . . scattered, and went their different ways.

John Tumino: [After the McShann band broke up] I took Walter Brown
down South with a little band. Walter Brown was well known in all the
black spots. He got nailed in New Orleans. They got knocked, shot
down with a load of pot. Walter Brown got nabbed and the whole band
got put in jail because they had a lot of pot in the station wagon they
were in. We got him turned loose finally. Took about thirty days. . . .

But Jay didn't get the break he should have. The war interfered with everything. We were just a little late gettin' in. . . .
It was tough. It was just pick-up for anything you can, even the nightclubs, everybody. That's why the ballrooms died. . . . It wasn't until 1946 almost the bands started to get together again.

Jay McShann: After coming out of the service I didn't realize that big bands [were] over then, just in that short length of time. See, they had started going to small combos and most of the dance halls were being converted into bowling alleys. . . .
I went back to New York . . . and the guys that was doing the booking told me, "We know you like the big band sound, but I'll tell you, you might as well forget about it for the time being, because everything is going to be combos. . . . We'll go on and book you, but we can get the same thing for a combo that we get for that big band. . . . We just advise you to . . . don't be puttin' no money down the drain on this big band." . . . After three or four months I saw the writing on the wall, . . . and just started using a small combo. . . .
The kids were getting around school age, so I decided that I'd better stop and settle somewhere, . . . so I decided on Kansas City. The kids went to school there, . . . and after [they were] out of school I was back on the road again.[35]

Jay McShann returned to Kansas City and pursued his career there, playing regularly in the region and in local clubs, and continued to improve his skills by attending music school at the University of Missouri, Kansas City. In the mid-sixties he again hit the road and at the present is among the best known and most respected jazz pianists on the international scene, finally enjoying the fruits of a long and distinguished life in jazz.

NOTES

1. Quoted from "Hootie Blues," a 1978 Nebraska ETV production. Used with permission. During his youth Jay's grandmother offered relief from his strictly religious parents. She often asked him to play both religious and secular (blues) music for her on the piano, but at no other time would Jay's parents tolerate his playing secular music in the house.
Jay also heard "hillbilly" music in those days. His father worked in a furniture store that also sold some records, and would occasionally bring home rural fiddle records. While Jay was more attracted to the blues, he still recalls this white mountain music fondly.
2. Quoted from the *Kansas City Star,* February 7, 1986. Copyright *Kansas City Star.* All rights reserved.

3. Some of Jay's early musical "training" came from his sister's piano teacher. Jay would escort her to the lesson and watch during it. One day the teacher went into her kitchen and Jay played the lesson his sister had been struggling to learn. When the teacher discovered that Jay had been learning by osmosis she forbade his coming to any more of his sister's lessons.

Another early musical experience was in high school. A teacher persuaded Jay to play for a pep rally. The rally was a success but the following day Jay was criticized by his teachers for playing improper music. That finished Jay's high school musical career.

4. Quoted from "Hooties Blues," a 1978 Nebraska ETV production. Used with permission.

5. Ibid.

6. Quoted from the *Kansas City Star*, March 16, 1975. Copyright *Kansas City Star*. All rights reserved.

7. Ibid.

8. Quoted from the *Soho Weekly News*, July 26, 1979.

9. "Woodshedding" is slang for secluding oneself to practice. Parker used this job as a chance to remove himself from the K.C. scene and hone his skills.

10. Quoted from "Hootie Blues," a 1978 Nebraska ETV production. Used with permission.

11. Quoted from the *Kansas City Star*, March 16, 1975. Copyright *Kansas City Star*. All rights reserved.

12. At the time Dexter was an occasional correspondent for *Down Beat* magazine. He later became the head of A&R (Artists and Repertoire) for Capitol Records.

13. Quoted from the *Kansas City Star*, February 7, 1986. Copyright *Kansas City Star*. All rights reserved.

14. Tumino ran the Century Room, a large K.C. club, and booked McShann in to follow Harlan Leonard's Rockets.

15. Eighty-five dollars was the wage for the entire band.

16. The excellent work of William Scott often went unrecognized in the shadow of Charlie Parker. As Orville Minor recalls, Scott had a crucial role in shaping the band's sound, and consequently providing the structure for the soloists, including Parker: "Scotty [William Scott], he was the one; he was quite a musician too. It's funny, [I] didn't know much about him . . . person-wise. I went to school with him and everything. He's from Kansas City, Kansas, . . . and he was quite a writer. He never wrote anything from the piano. . . . He'd just sit down and like, write a letter. The majority of Jay's book was arranged from Scotty, unless they were head arrangements. . . . Bird would tear his [own] arrangement up [if] they didn't sound right."

17. Recollections of the name of the Chicago club vary. Both Dexter and Pease reported in 1938 and 1939 that the engagement was at the Off-Beat Club, but McShann has also mentioned the Bandbox and the Three Deuces.

18. Quoted from the *Kansas City Star*, September 30, 1983. Copyright *Kansas City Star*. All rights reserved.

19. Quoted from the *Kansas City Star*, March 16, 1975. Copyright *Kansas City Star*. All rights reserved.

20. Quoted from the *Kansas City Star*, February 7, 1986. Copyright *Kansas City Star*. All rights reserved.

21. The band would agree to split the door receipts with the club owner, with forty percent going to the band.

22. Quoted from "Hootie Blues," a 1978 Nebraska ETV production. Used with permission.

23. Litwak and Pearson, *Goin' to Kansas City*, 42; used with permission.

24. The eight performers were: Orville Minor and Bernard Anderson, trumpets; Bud Gould, trombone; William Scott, tenor sax (replaced for the second session by Bob Mabane); Charlie Parker, alto sax; Gene Ramey, bass; Gus Johnson, drums; and Jay McShann, piano.

25. Litwak and Pearson, *Goin' to Kansas City*, 42; used with permission.

26. "Hootie" is Jay's nickname, coined during McShann's first year in K.C. by drummer Jesse Price and writer Dave Dexter one night when Jay was noticeably "hooted," or drunk.

27. Litwak and Pearson, *Goin' to Kansas City*, 43; used with permission.

28. Quoted from "Hootie Blues," a 1978 Nebraska ETV production. Used with permission.

29. Quoted from the *Kansas City Star*, March 23, 1975. Copyright *Kansas City Star*. All rights reserved.

30. Going "to the books" refers to performing the band's most difficult, and presumably exciting, arrangements.

31. As was typical of the hottest swing orchestras, the McShann orchestra could extend pieces according to the mood of the crowd: "We had . . . six or seven or eight numbers that . . . if we wanted that number to last an hour it would last an hour. We wanted to go forty-five minutes, we could do it. Thirty minutes, fifteen, ten minutes or whatever." (Quoted from "Hootie Blues," a 1978 Nebraska ETV production. Used with permission.)

32. Quoted from "Hootie Blues," a 1978 Nebraska ETV production. Used with permission.

33. Parker's drug abuse had become a serious problem within the band and Ramey usually had the role of "keeper" for Bird.

34. Quoted from "Hootie Blues," a 1978 Nebraska ETV production. Used with permission.

35. Ibid.

16

Kansas City Fade-out: Wartime and the Evolution of Jazz from the Big Bands

The world of the jumping town began to change even before the fall of Pendergast in 1938 and 1939. In 1936 Andy Kirk's Twelve Clouds of Joy made hit recordings, the Count Basie Orchestra left for New York, and the emigration of many stars of a generation of great musicians began.

Just as musicians for twenty years had been "goin' to Kansas City" for employment, creative challenge, and good times, so did the musicians of the late thirties and early forties seek greener pastures. For them, however, the opportunities were in New York, always a home of jazz prosperity and creativity, now dominant as the center of the recording and broadcasting industries, and, to a lesser degree, in Los Angeles for its film and fledgling recording industries. Mary Lou Williams observed this exodus first-hand: "You see, what happened in Kansas City was that John Hammond came to town. He was knocked out by what was happening musically, because he'd never heard such a thing. And he began to get jobs for the musicians. He took all the good musicians out, and it hasn't been good since. It was very beneficial what he did, but it left no one there that anybody could copy or to continue what was happening, because everybody that was playing left."

Kansas City had become an exciting and supportive musical environment and had seen the development of new jazz styles because it was a comfortable and well-situated refuge for musicians during hard times. But most performers greatly missed the flush times of the twenties. Even while reveling in the delights of K.C., most would have traded those good times for something more profitable. Attractive opportunities outside of K.C. began to reemerge in 1936, despite the Depression that still gripped much of the country and the years of drought that devastated the Midwest's economy.[1]

Benny Goodman became the "King of Swing" in 1935, inaugurating a musical craze with his national radio broadcasts. K.C. performers, notably those in the Count Basie Orchestra, were able to capitalize on Goodman's popularity. With their similar but stronger music, they took New York and the jazz world by storm in 1937. In the process they redefined the meaning of "swing." Other Midwestern musicians such as former Blue Devil and Bennie Moten bandmember Hot Lips Page (who left K.C. in 1936) and Oklahoma guitarist Charlie Christian (who joined Benny Goodman in 1939) also established themselves nationally and reinforced the strong influence of the "Western" 4/4 beat, riff-based blues style that characterized the best of swing. To those good enough and bold enough, the New York music center looked very attractive indeed.

Many excellent musicians stayed in K.C. to play in the nightclubs and theatrical revues that still thrived. By 1939 the once roaring club world was quieting down in the aftermath of Pendergast, but jobs were still abundant, pay had improved, and the scene continued, minus many of its strongest performers.

In 1938, however, a new generation of musicians was beginning to emerge. These were performers in their early twenties, the same age the masters of the previous generation—Eddie Durham, Jesse Stone, Lester Young, Buster Smith, Bill Basie, Ben Webster, Dick Wilson, Mary Lou Williams, and many others—had been when they were creating the Kansas City swing style in the heyday of the Territory bands. The new generation was musically sophisticated,[2] and used the swing style as their jumping-off point. They began to stretch conventional boundaries of harmony and melody, and in doing so some of them became the vanguard of performers who led the next major evolution of jazz, to be-bop and other modern styles.

They were well represented among K.C. bands, and the Jay McShann Orchestra had a disproportionate but not exclusive share. Such McShann stars as Buddy Anderson, Gene Ramey, Lucky Enois, and William Scott were matched by saxophonist Tommy Douglas, pianist and arranger Tadd Dameron, and trombonist Fred Beckett as important innovators. Charlie Parker, a McShann bandmember, stood apart as both a performer and trend-setter.

These musicians often found dance bands confining. For all the versatility and power of the riffing big band with a free-rhythmed soloist in front, the total range of harmony, melody, and rhythm was limited. Dancers still dictated the most basic aspects of the music, and a strong beat and relatively straightforward melody were essential. Even star performers soloing in relatively free rhythm were grounded by the orchestra supporting them, and usually continued to "swing the melody," delighting audiences with danceable, accessible jazz.

Not only was playing the same songs seven nights a week often boring, but for the most creative soloists the very size of the dance band was cumbersome. Just as early New Orleans bands realized their musical innovations in cohesive ensembles of four to seven players, and as Count Basie achieved his legendary swing with a nine-piece ensemble in the Reno Club, so did younger K.C. musicians seek to experiment with unconventional harmonies in smaller groups than eleven- to sixteen-piece big bands. The jam session was the traditional arena for this, but even those friendly challenge matches were structured to facilitate "sitting in," and usually limited soloists to a core of simple blues themes and commonly known songs. More complex and technically demanding arrangements required a degree of cohesion that was difficult to achieve in jam sessions.

The frustration of jazz composers and arrangers of the late thirties was great — musical sophistication was increasing, but the big bands that gave musicians a livelihood seemed restricted to playing conventional dance music. Big bands did evolve that could meet the demands of new jazz styles (Billy Eckstine, Earl Hines, Woody Herman, Gerry Mulligan, and Charles Mingus all led "modern" big bands), but most of the creative force of the new generation was focused on small groups. Jazz was moving away from surging dance rhythms to more cerebral delights.

An important element in the story of these musical developments concerns their effect upon jazz as popular (and profitable) music. Several veterans of K.C.'s big-band era believe that modern jazz abandoned the bulk of its audience by leaving dancers behind and becoming a stylized cabaret music. By searching for new musical avenues it became self-conscious and inwardly focused. A massive audience shift then occurred, and rhythm and blues, rock and roll, and country and western filled needs for more listenable, danceable music. Buddy Anderson, Charlie Parker's comrade and trumpet foil for several years, eloquently describes the sorrow and anger he feels for the process that made his music esoteric:

Bird and that movement got to going [and] the cats made an awful mistake, a series of 'em, really. They lost people when they had a chance to carry the people with them. They got too conscious of what they were doing and forgot about what the people need, and dig. Notice, they quit singing. That was the very worst mistake they could've made. They wanted to emphasize just the instrumental and that left them in a hole. . . . Then, of course, that narcotics thing didn't do any good.

They were just too instrumental-minded, in that exhibitionism is really what it was. They played everything too damn fast, or too slow. They didn't use any middle tempos, dance [tempos]. They left out the singing and the dancing. . . .

Then Miles [Davis, trumpeter and bandleader] carried a little influence in turning his back to people and generally ignoring them.[3] Hell, that's not going to help anything.

The cats [now] seem to be really middle-classish, and actually this stuff was more street [music], and cats don't go in the streets anymore. They don't seem to have contact with people, and that seems like where you catch your different moods, is from the people, and then play it back to them.

It seems to be getting a little sterile, by the cats not getting with the people. They ought to get out there and get with them to really enrich themselves with the understanding of what's happening, so that they can tell the people something they want to hear.

The wartime economy coupled with a musicians' union strike against the recording and broadcast industries helped speed these changes in jazz and end the era of big bands traveling from dance hall to crowded dance hall. Jazz was going through an evolution—away from dance halls and toward other venues—that would fundamentally change the position of jazz in popular culture, eliminate much of its previous audience, but assure that it remain dynamic. Jazz continues on the path of experimentation and change that Charlie Parker led in the forties, and is still a boldly creative and beautiful music.

The Evolution of Style—Roots of Be-bop

Charlie Parker: Be-bop is what I brought from Kansas City. What I play I learned in my Mother's woodshed back home.[4]

Gene Ramey: Generally speaking the Kansas City jazz you played with the freedom, but you didn't go too far with the solos. When they used to come on the air [the Count Basie band's radio broadcasts from the Reno Club] and Prez [Lester Young] was starting to blow, . . . he was so definite, so swinging, that everybody was trying to get home to hear that radio program. I used to call him up the next day and say, "Man, I think you come out with a new note or something."

He's the first one that started what they later started calling be-bop. Then it was called "running out the key." You had no key signature. You would probably start out playing in the key of B, but he might wind up playing in the key of F. Just running his cycles.

So now this is what Bird and I started doing. The two of us used to practice that. . . . I found that this is the only thing that I could do to keep him from doing the thing [using heroin]. I'd get his eye, I'd say, "Man, let's go somewhere and jam." He'd forget about it [heroin] right away. . . . I didn't have any ideas for him, but it was just enough to get him away, and we'd jam day and night. . . .

There was a guitar player, . . . his name was Efferge Ware. . . . He had been with Harlan Leonard's band for a while . . . but he would show us how the cycles would work, and how there's no such thing as a bad note, if you know how to get out of that hole, you know.

We would sit down and try that. . . . All I did was just play the straight rhythm, straight chords, and let him go [play] wherever he wanted to, . . . as long as he got back home [to the original chord and key signature] in time. . . . Efferge might have gotten his stuff from some of those teachers like [Jack] Washington [baritone and alto sax player for Bennie Moten, Jesse Stone, and Count Basie], but there was another great man in Kansas City named N. Clark Smith [and] all those guys over there in Kansas City went to school [under him].

The End of the Big-Band Era

Much of the musical change that was occurring in the late thirties and early forties (which Buddy Anderson saw as destructive of the jazz audience) can be seen as an inevitable progression. Economic forces, however, accompanied the artistic changes. A dance hall tax, the recording ban effected by the American Federation of Musicians from August 1942 until December 1943, the absence of dance partners due to the war, and wartime gasoline rationing all contributed to the demise of the big band as America's dominant musical entertainment.

When the war ended, both the economic and musical environments had fundamentally changed. Most of the big bands had disintegrated and few regrouped. Club owners realized that much smaller ensembles could also draw good audiences, at much less expense, and the most inventive musicians were drawn to more modern jazz styles, most of which were tailored to small groups.

The sum of these changes was that jazz was no longer popular dance music, and in Kansas City all the major bands had left town for better prospects in either New York or California. After World War II the jazz mainstream played concert and cabaret music for a limited audience of aficionados, and Kansas City was no longer a center of creativity.

Eddie Barefield: In 1941 the government put a tax on all dance halls, about a twenty percent tax. So all of the dance places closed up . . . except the Savoy Uptown, and maybe the Roseland [in New York]. All over the country, these dance pavilions closed up because the crowds refused to pay this twenty percent.

So for ten years people didn't dance, until they started playing the rock music and it started getting popular, and they started to dance again.

Buddy Anderson: The [big] band as a holding together thing must have a gig, a job, preferably a stationary one [like] at a ballroom. [But] this is something that is gone now. It might be a little difficult for a young person to realize because they didn't actually dig 'em, [but] there used to be dance halls.

That left with World War II. Nightclubs in their lavishness left because of World War II. . . . There was a breakdown in all bands at that time. . . . They were just all falling apart, and any excuse is as good as another as to why things like that actually happen.

Wartime Experiences

Following the bombing of Pearl Harbor in December 1941, many jazz musicians of draft age were thrust into a military environment that was racially prejudiced and rigidly segregated. Nonetheless, wartime service was benign for some. Orville Minor and Buck Clayton were able to continue performing, Minor in a military band, Clayton both in service bands and moonlighting in periodic recording sessions in New York. For many others, however, the experience was more like a prolonged nightmare.

The somewhat special status that these performers had enjoyed as civilians in cities, living in a world of nightclubs and dance halls apart from conventional society, was gone. Their considerable sophistication was not only unappreciated, but was often a handicap, leading some to regard the musicians as arrogant and therefore requiring particularly strict discipline to force conformity. Some individuals were emotionally shattered by the experience.

While the experience of black musicians in military service is a minor footnote in the history of World War II, it was one of several watershed disillusioning events in black American life. Duke Ellington eloquently described the frustration of that time: "We find ourselves today struggling for solidarity. But just as we're about to get our teeth into it, our country's at war and in trouble again, and as before we, of course, find the black, brown, and beige right in there for the red, white, and blue."[5]

Orville Minor: I left the [Jay McShann] band because of the Navy thing. Uncle Sam was chasing me around, [and] I had to give in. . . .

We [the band members] were going off into different directions. Some of the guys didn't even know that they were inducted, and some of the guys went to the board and didn't even pass. I got into the Navy accidentally. There was supposed to have been a doctor that was supposed to go, and the man says, "You're the one, you replace the doctor." I stayed naked for two days. That was a dilly. . . . I got up there in the Great Lakes and [spent] two more days in the nude. They finally decided to put a suit on me, and then I got in the band. We had sessions every day. Clark Terry [trumpeter] was up there. They had three bands up there, and they had trumpet players from everywhere. . . . It was just like a ball all day.

We'd get up in the morning . . . and everybody would get their horns out, get to blowing 'till about nine o'clock.

Buck Clayton: I stayed with Basie seven years, until '43. Then I got called into the army. They put me right out here in New Brunswick [New Jersey] in a band and I had to play all kind of ceremonies. . . . When the soldiers were leaving, getting on the boat, we had to be down there playing at the pier while they're marching. Sometimes [we'd] be down there playing for seven and eight hours for all these soldiers getting on the boat. When the war was over we had to go down there and play "They All Got Off." I got out fairly late, in '46, after they was all back, because I went in late. . . .

I'd made records while I was in the army. . . . There was vocalists that asked me [to]. Dinah Washington or whoever. . . . I wasn't supposed to do it, but anyway I made a lot of records. I started making more money in the army than I made with Basie, and I was writing music for different bands.

Herman Walder: I stayed in the service seventeen months. Man, if anybody hated to go to the army, it was Herman. Telling everybody else what to do, all that. I ain't gonna like that, taking no orders.

My son was already down there, at Ft. Leonard Wood [Missouri]. I didn't know where they was sending me, and I get up one of them hills, got that dust and cinders falling in your face, and he [my son] was the one calling the roll. . . .

We'd go on a twenty-five mile hike; I was thirty-seven, and a grandfather then, and twenty-five-year-olds was falling down like flies. But everytime we got that ten-minute break, I'd set down against a tree, with my full field pack and all. My son was running around there chasing butterflies.

Ernest Daniels: Then the war broke out, and I was ducking, I was trying to get a defense job. I figured if I got a defense job, I wouldn't have to go to [the] service. The first job I could get was outside. It was in the fall of the year, so it started getting cool. I was working nights [playing in bands], so I quit the job. . . .

[Then] I went to a steel company. . . . I worked one day. That's the hardest job I ever had. I didn't even go after my money. I was unloading a boxcar . . . [and] I was afraid I was going to hurt my hands. . . .

The next job I went to the bomber plant, where they'd make the B-29. They had one job left, and that was working on the ramp. I said okay. I didn't really know what a ramp was.

I'd been playing music for practically all this time . . . [and] I started going to work [in the factory] at five in the morning. . . . I had a coat on, my shoes shined, had a white shirt, and everything. Finally they came up and they brought me a sack, a burlap sack, and a stick with a nail in it. Then he said, "I want you to clean up the ramp, get all the cigarette butts and paper and so forth." . . .

I knew a lot of people there, and there was a lot of women working at the bomber plant. This kind of hurt my ego, see, because I'd been playing around the clubs [and] I was more or less in demand . . . for once. . . . We were playing three different places in one night. That had never happened to me before. . . . I stayed there about four weeks. My ego was pretty hurt.

So I quit the bomber plant . . . and I still was drafted because I was quitting defense jobs.

Buddy Anderson: While I was with the group at Tootie's [Mayfair Club, with Charlie Parker], I got greetings from the government to report for physical examinations for the war. They wasn't jiving, man. I had to make it to Ft. Leavenworth. When I came back, right around Thanksgiving time, and went to go back to the gig, the cat [Leonard Enois, who led the band at Tootie's Mayfair] acted very funny and cold, until I just was through with the gig. . . . I was let go. Why, hell, I couldn't help going to see about being inducted, anybody ought to get some consideration on that, but nevertheless that was the feeling, and rather than try to buck it, I just went on and cut [out].

Charles Goodwin: I left to go to the army, March the thirteenth, '41. I did twenty-seven months. . . . I was thirty-five when I went in, and I had been living a soft life. I went to Camp Lee, Virginia, I done my basic training there, and I was shipped to Hattiesburg, Mississippi, which, at that time, was the end of the world. . . . Boy, I never did run across people like that before in my life. I stayed there for eighteen months. I couldn't get out of there. I asked to go overseas. I didn't want to be around these people. They're not educated. I didn't know any place like this existed in America. . . .

I think they did this for a purpose, sent the black music men down South, to break us up. It was a tough go, too. . . .

Eddie Tompkins, another kid [who] used to play with Jimmie Lunceford, got killed there. He was an officer, . . . a first lieutenant, and he got killed on the infiltration course. . . . He was a fabulous musician. . . .

They treated us servicemen like we was lower than a dog, [the] black servicemen. You couldn't do anything right.

Lester Young's War

Among the most notable musical casualties of the war was Lester Young. Before the war, Young was an internationally recognized giant of the jazz saxophone, a kind, gentle, quiet man with an oblique wit and speaking style. These were coupled with a dependence on marijuana and alcohol. Soon after being drafted into the army he was found with marijuana and barbiturates, court-martialed, and sentenced to a military prison. Upon his dishonorable discharge and return to the jazz world he was a changed man, withdrawn and often sullen, with his musical brilliance dulled. He continued to be a major jazz attraction until his death in 1959, but was never again a stunning innovator.

The following excerpts from Young's court-martial and appeal records provide some illumination of the gulf that existed between him and his officers, contributing to his imprisonment and subsequent emotional decline, and of the prevalence of marijuana and narcotics in the prewar jazz world.

Excerpts from Lester Young's Testimony at his Court-martial, February 16, 1945:

QUESTION: Why did you start taking them [drugs]?
ANSWER: Well, sir, playing in the [Count Basie] band we would play a lot of one-nighters. I would stay up and play another dance and leave and that is the only way I could keep up.

Q: Any other member of the band . . . take them?
A: Yes, all that I know.

Q: Did . . . the draft board . . . know you had this habit of taking habit-forming drugs?
A: Well, I am pretty sure they did, sir, because before I went to join

the army I had to take a spinal [tap] and I didn't want to take it and
when I went down I was very high and they put me in jail and I was
so high they took the whiskey away from me and put me in a padded
cell and they searched my clothes while I was in the cell. I was in that
day and the second day they took me upstairs and this is the fifth camp
I have been on and so. . . .

Q: What do you mean by [saying] that you were pretty high? Do you
mean because of the whiskey?
A: The whiskey and the marijuana and the barbiturates.

Q: Did you tell . . . the board that inducted you that you
took . . . habit-forming drugs?
A: Yes, sir.

Q: Now if you do not take these drugs, smoke these things, does it
affect you in any way physically?
A: Yes, sir, it does. I don't want to do anything; I don't care to blow
my horn and I don't care to be around anybody.

Q: Could you do this training here if you left them alone?
A: No, sir.

Q: Why?
A: Because I tried it, sir, I tried it, truthfully.

Q: Have you had any of these drugs in the last few days?
A: Haven't, not since I have been in the stockade now.

Q: Feel pretty nervous now?
A: I think about it all the time.[6]

**From a U.S. Army Report: Data for First Clemency Consideration [for
release from military prison], October 30, 1945:**

General Prisoner: Lester W. Young

Inducted: September 30, 1944

Age: 35 5/12

Offenses: AW [Article of War] 96, Wrongfully have in his possession
habit-forming drugs (marijuana and barbiturate), January 30, 1945.

Sentences: 1 year. . . Sentence expires December 15, 1945.

Date Adjudged: February 16, 1945.

Sentence: To be dishonorably discharged from the service, to forfeit all pay and allowances due or to become due, and to be confined at hard labor, at such place as the reviewing authority may direct, for one year. . . . It is noted that the subject has never been subjected to disciplinary training and evidence of his continued use of drugs is based largely on his own statements. In view of these facts together with the possibility that his undesirable traits may be corrected by proper treatment and disciplinary training it is recommended that the sentence be approved, but execution of the dishonorable discharge be suspended until his release from confinement. . . . The United States Disciplinary Barracks, Ft. Leavenworth, Kansas, is designated as the place of confinement, but pending further orders the soldier will he held at the Post Stockade, Ft. McClellan, Alabama.[7]

While Young's fate was not typical of jazz musicians in the military, it was a tragically extreme example of the cultural clash that sometimes occurred.

NOTES

1. The U.S. agricultural economy had been in generally poor shape since the early 1920s. Low prices and rising capital costs were tremendously aggravated in the Midwest by the Dust Bowl, which followed several years of unusually dry weather. Soil conservation programs were virtually nonexistent. The first great dust storm occurred in April 1934. The worst year of the storms was 1937, when strong Canadian winds blew dry topsoil off the Great Plains and darkened skies in New York, Washington, and London. Nationally, the effects of social welfare programs and gradually returning economic prosperity had begun to be felt by 1934/35, but much of the nation experienced a seriously depressed economy until World War II.

2. In the twenties and early thirties only a few jazz musicians were on the level of musical sophistication of Eddie Durham, Jesse Stone, Mary Lou Williams, or Buster Smith. All four arranger/composers recall difficulties with fellow musicians who couldn't easily hear or read harmonies beyond three parts, forcing the arranger to either double one of those parts or to painstakingly teach the fourth, fifth, and sixth harmony parts to them. Even then the bandmembers rarely played in tune. These common limitations effectively restricted the range of innovation possible in most bands. But by 1938-40, musical skills had progressed. More musicians were hearing and experimenting with the underlying chords in songs. What Buster Smith, Lester Young, Coleman Hawkins, and Louis Armstrong had done individ-

ually as soloists, young arrangers were trying to do in the ensemble, and their soloists wanted to reach even farther.

Some of the first generation of Midwestern arranger/composers kept in step with the new age. Eddie Durham continued to provide material for the new musicians, and was among the outstanding arrangers through the mid-1940s. Mary Lou Williams often anticipated the most advanced modernists through the early 1950s, but a young school, including Tadd Dameron, Charlie Parker, Thelonious Monk, and Dizzy Gillespie, predominated.

3. Anderson is referring to Miles Davis's unfortunate behavior before audiences: In addition to being one of modern jazz's most brilliant composers and performers, he is noted for such habits as failing to appear for concerts, turning his back to the audience for entire performances, and playing only for moments and then leaving the stage.

4. Quoted by George Hoefer in 1949.

5. These remarks were made by Ellington in his introduction to "Beige," the second segment of the "Black, Brown, and Beige" suite, during a concert at Carnegie Hall, January 23, 1943 (*The Duke Ellington Carnegie Hall Concert #1*. Prestige Records, P-34004E, 1977).

6. This material was obtained through the Freedom of Information Act from U.S. government records. It is the official transcript of Lester Young's court-martial, February 16, 1945.

7. U.S. government records. Official transcript of Lester Young's first clemency consideration, October 30, 1945.

17

The Great Innovators of Kansas City Jazz: Buster Smith, Lester Young, and Charlie Parker

The sound and style of Kansas City jazz survived World War II, but the vitality was gone. Most of the big bands had disintegrated, and the jazz mainstream was small-group cabaret and concert hall music. Many of its style-makers were Kansas City veterans, the most notable Charlie Parker. Other Kansas City musicians stayed with dance music and moved toward rhythm and blues and rock. Much of the early power of R & B came from the same strong rhythm-and-riff foundation that powered the greatest K.C. bands of the thirties. Jay McShann, Walter Brown, Wynonie Harris, and particularly Big Joe Turner brought the K.C. drive to rhythm and blues. In modern jazz, however, solo instrumentalists were the primary carriers of the Kansas City heritage.

Soloists were the stars of the music. They attracted fans and fellow musicians to hear them seek new musical dimensions and achieve ever greater expressiveness. Soloists have been a hallmark of the music since Buddy Bolden and Louis Armstrong helped to create jazz in New Orleans. Ever since, soloists have been key figures in moving jazz into new styles.

Among the great early instrumentalists who led major stylistic change were Earl "Fatha" Hines, who redefined the jazz piano, Coleman Hawkins, the tenor saxophone, and Eddie Lang, the guitar. Each of these masters set a standard to be challenged. Subsequent instrumental stars sought to develop new sounds that would surpass these models and serve as new bases for other musicians.

Few musicians entered this company of trendsetters, although many Kansas City-era musicians were brilliant imitators. Oran "Hot Lips" Page featured trumpet and vocal styles that were patterned after Louis Armstrong. Pete Johnson's great boogie-woogie and jazz piano, while ideal accompaniment for Big Joe Turner and also outstanding in its own right, was of a well-established style and did not break major ground. Some other K.C. musicians, however, were originals with important impact on the music. Recognizing their contribution is essential to understanding fully the significance and impact of Kansas City jazz.

Buster Smith and Lester Young were K.C.'s great saxophone innovators of the thirties. Smith is a largely unsung hero, with a reputation mostly among fellow musicians and devotees of Kansas City jazz. He deserves more recognition, as he strongly influenced Charlie Parker by stretching the harmonic dimensions of the alto saxophone and using a lightning-fast, "dancing" style that anticipated and inspired Parker's.

Young, also a major influence on Parker, used a light, breathy style that was a dramatically different approach to the tenor saxophone than the virile gutsiness of Coleman Hawkins (a St. Joseph, Missouri, native and, briefly, a member of one of Jesse Stone's early jazz bands). Young also swung powerfully, but obliquely, always suggesting the strong underlying rhythm. In this way, and with his inclination to experiment with unusual intervals and chord progressions, he was a trendsetting modernist.

Charlie Parker was, after Louis Armstrong, the second genius of jazz, profoundly influencing all the musicians who followed him, leading fundamental change in concepts of song structure and melody, playing with creativity, force, and beauty that are unsurpassed. Important aspects of Parker's style and brilliance were outgrowths of his Kansas City jazz heritage. An equally important element of his genius, however, was purely personal. As with Armstrong, the stylistic framework for Parker's music was familiar (in his case it was the blues and K.C. swing), but the special part that took his art beyond that of his contemporaries was his alone.

Buster Smith

Buster "Prof" Smith is, with Eddie Durham and Jesse Stone, one of the musical "heroes" in this book. Fellow musicians remember him with regard approaching reverence not only as a gifted arranger and composer but, most notably, as a truly extraordinary performer on both alto saxophone and clarinet. His legend as a performer is heightened by the extreme scarcity of his recordings. In addition he is among the most appealing personalities of the Kansas City jazz story—a quiet, self-effacing, witty man who rarely went out of his way to achieve prominence.

When Howard Litwak and I interviewed Smith in 1977 in Dallas we found him to be almost shy, but extremely gracious, although his long-time dental troubles made his speech difficult to understand at first. The story he told not only greatly expanded our understanding of the Blue Devils and the development of the Count Basie band but also gave another poignant capsule story of a rural musician's development into a master performer. Buster's history, as did that of Eddie Durham or Jesse Stone, offers rich descriptions of the kinds of paths that led to K.C. and its brilliant, exuberant music.

Buster Smith: We lived ten miles out from Ennis, Texas, out in the country, my daddy was farming there. Every Saturday he would bring us to town, to eat hamburgers and drink red soda water. . . . Blind Lemon [Jefferson, blues guitarist, singer, and recording artist] would be up there in the colored restaurants playing guitar in the evenings. . . . I was crazy about the music. We had an organ and I was playing it, but my mother said, "You're going to the devil," and got rid of the organ. I had a couple of uncles played old guitars and things, and I'd get an old guitar and pluck on 'em. . . . I loved blues. . . .

On a Saturday we'd go on to town, shopping, you know. . . . I saw an old clarinet laying in the window, it was all raggedy and everything, old A-clarinet. They let me have it for $3.50. . . . I had heard 'em before with the boys playing them on the Ringling Brothers show when they came down to Ennis. [My mother] said, "If you pick me three, four hundred pounds [of cotton] every day next week I'll let you buy that." So, man, I was rustling cotton. . . . I was about nineteen [thus dating this story to 1923]. . . . So I bought it and all that week I was blowing that thing, trying to make it say something, and I ran 'em all away from the house. . . . In about a week's time I commenced to getting something out of it. . . .

[Later on] I got a three-piece band, started playing them chop houses around there. . . .

I didn't do much jamming. I always had to get music ready for the band. I didn't stay out too many nights. My old lady would want me to come on home. . . .

Basie and them, all them started that [nickname of mine]. You see, I smoked a cigar all the time, and they called me "Professor," writing music and smoking a cigar. That's why they called me "Prof."

Druie Bess: He'd eat up clarinets, he plays so much clarinet. . . . I liked his clarinet better than his saxophone. He played so much saxophone, and arranged for the band [the Blue Devils] too.

Raymond F. Howell: He was a clarinet player right straight from the heart, oh boy. . . . Buster was tops. . . . Lester Young learned a whole lot of clarinet [from Buster].

Don Albert: Buster, I thought he was the *one*. The bands he was in, he always set the head [arrangement]. He was the outstanding musician. There wasn't anybody who could touch Buster! Bus wrote the song that Count Basie uses as his theme song ["One O'Clock Jump"]. Count Basie stole it from him.

John Hammond: Buster Smith didn't think Basie would make it [be successful] so he refused to come East [when Basie embarked on his first tour to New York].

Buster Smith: [After not going East with Basie in 1936] I [thought] I had to do something for myself and I made me up a band, got Charlie Parker and a bunch of boys in there, got twelve pieces . . . and then Lucille's Paradise wanted me to work up there. I couldn't hire the whole band, [so] I got half.

So Crook [guitarist and singer Charles Goodwin], . . . he was in the band. . . . I got him and Charlie Parker and about six of us was playing up there every night. I think we was off one or two nights. During them nights I would take the big band out on some of them club dates, social functions, like that. . . . But I used Charlie in both bands.

Orville Minor: Charlie Parker . . . could play something and make it sound just pretty. He knew what to do. He'd pick the right notes. But when he first started playing, nobody wanted to hear him. They couldn't understand what he was doing. In fact, he never played [much] until Buster Smith got to him. . . .

Down in the Bottoms [the Missouri River bottoms of Kansas City] there's a place called the Antlers Club. Buster Smith had got a band, it was about five or six of us, and he used to tell Charlie, "Don't rehearse on my bandstand." Bird had his ears open so much, that he wanted to steal everything that everybody was doing, particularly what Smith [did].

That's the source of all the knowledge. Anytime we'd get to intermission, here'd come Buster Smith, would sit down to the piano and play everything . . . that he did in the arrangements . . . and Bird would pick it up. . . . This is one of the things that prompted Charlie to be a better musician. When that job ended, they went down in the Ozarks,[1] and when Charlie Parker came back from the Ozarks he was a different musician.

Buster Smith: Then I went down to the Antlers Club, down there by the packing houses, with eight pieces. And [then] I left Charlie [Parker] and Odell West heading the band, I said, "I'm trying to get to a bigger place where I can use a big band. I'm going all the way to New York."...

I finally ended up with Don Redman's band.... Pete Johnson and Joe Turner was down there working at the Cafe Society, so they wanted me to make a record with them. I had to go on down and get my horn out of pawn, hadn't blowed it in five months, and we made that [song] called "Cherry Red."

John Hammond: I made one record with Buster and Lips [Page] and everything, Joe Turner's "Cherry Red," as they both happened to be in town at the same time. It was marvelous, marvelous.

Buster Smith: I had saved up a little bankroll [after touring with several bands, including Benny Carter's]... and I said, "I think I'm going back to Texas." I had lost my father and I couldn't even be there, to see him put away.... I stayed there about four months. [Then I] went on back to New York, stayed on there about a year, saved up another bankroll and went on down there [Dallas, Texas] and opened me up a restaurant, and organized an eight-piece band, ... built it on up to thirteen pieces, playing all them little shows around here.

Buster Smith stayed in Dallas, leading many local bands, and maintaining a strong if purely local reputation. In time, his need to play piano and to arrange combined with dental problems caused Smith to give up saxophone and clarinet entirely. On last report he still lives in Dallas, playing occasionally, and going fishing. Since the death of his old friend Ernie Williams, Smith may now be the real "last of the Blue Devils."

Lester Young

Lester Young was among K.C.'s greatest, best loved, and best known musicians. He was the most popular soloist in Count Basie's big band, and later was heard widely in both recordings and on tours. He left many superb recordings as a legacy that gives ample evidence of his art. Among the highlights of his career were scores of masterful vocal/saxophone duets with his friend Billie Holiday and an appearance in Gjon Mili's film *Jammin' the Blues* that shows something of his unique style as well as his music.

Like Buster Smith, Young was a brilliant clarinetist as well as a saxophonist (but tenor rather than alto). His career was extremely successful, except for a brief, humiliating stint with Fletcher Henderson's orchestra, and his previously described (chapter 16) army service. Despite his successes, however, he was always withdrawn, and his last years were deeply unhappy. The following accounts, however, stress his musical development, and the delighted surprise experienced by his contemporaries when they encountered his beautiful and often startlingly innovative music.

Gene Ramey: Lester Young was born in Louisiana [actually Woodville, Mississippi, August 27, 1909; the family moved to New Orleans when Young was a child], but his family came down from Minnesota. It was a band made up of family. His sister was a great alto player [and] I think his father and mother played musical instruments.

There's a funny story about when Prez was a drummer, and they asked him why he stopped playing drums. He said, "Man, everynight, by the time I got my drum packed, the chick I'd been checkin' out had cut out with somebody else." So he says that's why he stopped playing drums, so he could get there first.

Buddy Tate: I knew him when he played alto and his sister played tenor. They came down to my hometown [in Texas]. They played on a carnival. His daddy was the leader of the band.

Druie Bess: When Lester Young came in [the Blue Devils] it was just terrific. Lester come in in 1931, I think. [Actually it's more likely that Young joined the Blue Devils in early 1932.] I never will forget it.

It was upstairs in a joint, [he was] playing, and [Walter] Page says, "Who's that fast saxophone?" He was playing "After You've Gone" and he was making breaks [of] four bars, sometimes it was eight bars.

Page said, "I'm going to get that saxophone player." We had just drove up there [to Minneapolis], jumped out the car, and ran upstairs. . . . They had intermission and he got ahold of Lester. Lester was bothered with asthma [then]; he didn't drink nothing.[2]

He says, "I can't go [with you], I have to ask my wife." He had a little, heavyset woman. Said, "I'm doing pretty good up here; I don't want to get out no kind of way." They talked to him and talked to him, and we was working out of Minneapolis anyway, and Page got him into the band. . . .

He was in the band about two years, and every time he played he played something different.

Buddy Tate: In the later years he was with King Oliver [important New Orleans cornet "king" and the bandleader who brought Louis Armstrong to Chicago from New Orleans] in Tulsa, and I was with a chorus line-type show. Victoria Spivey. Somewhere during '33, '34.

I remember one time, I woke Prez up . . . in this hotel, the finest hotel in the world for blacks, in Tulsa, Oklahoma. They had a big baby grand . . . in the lobby there . . . and we'd go in there and jam all day. . . . It went on and on. I says, "I'll wake him [Lester] up and bring him down here and see if he's really playing as much as they say, since he's [now] on tenor [saxophone, Tate's instrument]."

I'll never forget it. I'll never forget those sounds. . . . Man, he jumped up and put his clothes on and grabbed his horn and came down there and he started playing, man. He played so much, all I could do was just put my horn over in a chair and listen to this. I'll never forget that. . . .

He was something else, exciting. He had so many beautiful ideas, and he made them just as fast . . . as it come. He was just executing them and making everything. . . .

In [March] '34 Coleman Hawkins was playing with Fletcher Henderson and he was leaving to go to London and work with Jack Hylton's band, so his notice was in and Fletcher was looking for a tenor player.

He came to Kansas City and Herschel [Evans], Ben Webster, and Lester were in Kansas City. They carried him out that night, and when they jumped on it there, he's going to choose which one he wanted. His choice was Lester out of the three. . . . Basie and them asked me if I'd join, and I took his place [with Bennie Moten's orchestra]. . . .

When he came in, they gave him a hard time in the band, everybody but Fletcher. Fletcher knew he had a lot to offer. He paid some dues in the band; they treated him cool. Some of the guys would turn their back . . . and they wouldn't help him [learn] some of Hawk's [Coleman Hawkins's] arrangements.

Prez told me this himself, "Man," he said, "They treated me so cool." Fletcher's wife used to take him downstairs in the basement and put one of Hawk's records on. She said, "This is where it's at, baby. Can't you sound like this?" . . .

[So] Lester came back to Kansas City. He didn't make it [with Fletcher Henderson] because of his sound, this cool sound of his hadn't gotten through. They wanted a big sound like Hawk had. If you didn't have that sound in those days they didn't recognize you as a tenor player.

John Hammond: Smack [Fletcher Henderson, Hammond's friend and client] . . . was in a terrible spot about getting a saxophone player to replace Hawkins. I paid Fletcher to bring Lester Young in.

Fletcher was auditioning for the Cotton Club, it was about five o'clock in the afternoon, and I listened to Lester Young. I just couldn't believe my ears, it was so wonderful.

That was the first time I'd heard [Lester] and I looked and saw horrified faces in the rest of Fletcher's band, because he didn't sound like Hawkins. Fletcher was weak, you know, . . . and backed down.

Lester then was staying with Mrs. Henderson. Fletcher had a beautiful Stanford White house at 139th Street [in Harlem], and Leora, Fletcher's wife, was telling Lester he should be playing like Hawkins. She would play old Hawkins records, and this burned Lester up. So he went back to Kansas City.

I actually don't think he played more than about three gigs with Fletcher, one-nighters, and they brought Ben Webster in to replace him, which was the sound they wanted. I think he [Ben Webster] was drinking even then, so he was replaced by Chu Berry, who was perfect for the Henderson band.

Eddie Durham: Lester [in his early career] never stayed with a band. They didn't keep him, because they were all looking for tenor tone, and he didn't fit good. The tone was kind of sharp all the time.

So, in Basie's band, I'd use his horn to advantage. I layed him next to those altos [saxophones]. Could never get him on the bottom. I'd keep him laying right between the tenor and the second alto. That's what the C-melody [saxophone] used to be used for, and that made the reed section balance out. He sounded more like the altos than he did the tenors [and] that left the tenor a good opening. Jack Washington was on that baritone [saxophone] and it worked out fine.

Lester was a good balance, and if you're going to keep playing sharp, I'd find a way to play a chorus and start a note sharp.

Orville Minor: They had a duel one morning when Coleman Hawkins came to town. I think they were down to the Subway [Club] when they was havin' it. He and Prez got into this thing, and Coleman had to leave after a while, 'cause he was going to St. Louis, his mother was sick, that was his excuse, you know. But Prez was gettin' to him. He really was. . . .

It was just an experience being with those guys up there. They played so many things. Prez used to come down to the Barley Duke [a club where Minor played], and he and Margaret ["Countess"] Johnson [K.C. pianist reported to have been Young's lover for several years] would exchange ideas. She would write down everything he would play. Would tell him every chord he played. . . .

I asked him how he played, what style he played. He said he never played the same passage the same way twice. If you listen to some recordings you found out that this is where Charlie Parker gained a lot of ideas.

John Hammond: I brought down Benny Goodman at one point to Pennsylvania [where Lester was playing with Count Basie]. Benny was so impressed by Lester Young [that] he gave him his clarinet on the spot. The first and last time that Benny's ever done that. Poor Lester had a terrible little metal clarinet, but he could still play wonderful clarinet.

Young continued to enjoy wide recognition for being among jazz's foremost instrumentalists for many years. His career entered a long decline, however, when he entered military service. After being court-martialed for use of marijuana and narcotics (see chapter 16), Young was sentenced to a year of hard labor in military prison. After his release Lester Young moved to California. In 1946 he began to work with producer and entrepreneur Norman Granz's "Jazz at the Philharmonic" shows, including several overseas tours. During this period New York was his most frequent base. He was very active through the late fifties, leading his own small groups and recording often. His health after leaving the military was poor, and he began to drink more heavily. Young died March 15, 1959, in New York at the age of forty-nine.

Charlie Parker

Charlie Parker was an extraordinary artist who led tremendous change in jazz music through his artistic power, but who also led himself down a self-destructive spiral of dissolution. His life and music were extreme and they gave him a romantic image that he probably fostered.

The following accounts trace Parker from his early performances through his apprenticeship at the feet of K.C. masters, particularly Buster Smith, his emergence as the leader of a whole new jazz movement, be-bop, and his increasingly frequent descents into heroin-induced degeneracy. Parker was loved and loathed, admired and scorned, but was always first and foremost a musician of remarkable dedication, skill, and invention. He stood apart from his contemporaries on so many musical levels that it is difficult to grasp today his impact then.

These tales are told by some of the musicians who knew him best — Buck Clayton was on the bandstand with Basie when Bird was most humiliated; Orville Minor was his friend and colleague; Gene Ramey served as his father figure and protector for many years; Buddy Anderson was thought by many to have been Parker's only K.C. contemporary who could keep up with him musically; Jay McShann was the bandleader who provided Parker's springboard to greatness; John Tumino was the long-suffering band manager who had to get Parker from the bar and the needle to the stage; Buster Smith was, with Lester Young, one of the two great musical influences on Parker; Mary Lou Williams was not only a great pianist and innovator herself but also kept a "salon" in New York that offered Parker and his fellow modernists a comfortable place to share ideas; Charles Goodwin was of an older K.C. generation who saw Parker roar through the city.

They recall the growth of a great musician whose influence is still deeply felt. Even now, more than thirty years after his death, "Bird lives" is a cry for inspiration from a departed master that is still heard. Bird's legacy will continue to excite and inspire new generations.

Buck Clayton: Charlie Parker was just another guy playing sax [when I first heard him in Kansas City]. . . . They wouldn't even let him come on the stand [in Kansas City]. . . . He didn't break loose until after he got here [to New York].

Orville Minor: He could play something and make it sound just pretty. He knew what to do; he'd pick the right notes. But when he first started playin', nobody wanted to hear him. They couldn't understand what he was doing. . . .

It began when Bird was giggin' all over town. . . . Anybody he could play with, you know [he did]. Go out in the park and play all night and all day, gettin' hisself together.

Gene Ramey: We had a little band called Oliver Todd and His Hot-Ten-Tots, and that's when I first met Bird. This is a Kansas City, Kansas, band, and we had a battle with Bird's band, a Missouri band.

We was all high school kids except me. Then I think Bird was four-teen years old. [He] couldn't play, and was mad about it too. In that respect he was just an evil, spoiled kid. You'd go over to him and say, "Hey Bird, how you doing?" He might call you all kinds of them names. . . .

When we had started rehearsing and practicing everyday, [he] went into that jam session with Basie and them, and they rang the bell on him.[3] He was utterly disgusted.

"These guys can't do nothing like this to me," you know. He felt that if he did make a mistake, it's all right [and he] could blow as long as he want to. But they stopped him. They wouldn't call you aside and show you where you did wrong, but they would stop you if you were messing up the whole jam session.

When Basie went to New York and made those first Jones and Smith records [the first recordings of the Basie band, in October 1936], that's all he needed. He took the records and he went up into the country with George E. Lee's band [to gain experience and improve his skills].

Buster Smith: Charlie Parker was in my band [when I went to New York to find other work]. I was gone so long, seven months, and hadn't sent back for him so he came up there to see what I was doing, what was going on. He hoboed up there. Came up there and stayed in my [house], slept in the bed in the daytime and my wife and I slept in the bed at night. . . .

He'd go out trying to play around with them boys but he was new in town and they wouldn't let him blow too much. . . . The man around the corner ran a little old saloon and Charlie would go and clean up there after they close at night. That's where he made a little money to survive on.

Jay McShann: He [Charlie Parker] played the blues. If you listen closely, anything that he played, if it was a ballad, Bird played the blues. . . . He played the blues regardless how much technique he had. . . . Bird was one of the greatest blues musicians in the world. . . .

When Bird was just learning how to play, . . . before he got his stuff together, he would pull [out] his horn and . . . just run it up and down. I mean, he knew his instrument backward. Every time you would see him he would have his horn on his arm, and probably have the . . . exercise book. . . . In jamming he [would play] his exercises. It wasn't really saying too much then. But finally he got his exercises down. He would run one chord into the other and put a meaning along with it. When he got that, [there] wasn't no stopping Bird, because by having that knowledge, knowing his horn backwards, and then having a little blues experience that he had heard practically all his life . . . there was no stopping him. . . .

He was one of those types of guys that . . . gets himself together [musically], just overnight. . . . I can remember [when] we used to rehearse the big band, and Bird told me, "Man, this little cat you got on first alto [John Jackson] is just reading rings around me. . . . I'm sick of it. . . . That makes me look bad. . . . I'll tell you what I'm going to do. I'm going in the woodshed for about a couple or three days, so if I'm not at rehearsals don't pay it no mind 'cause I'll be woodshedding. . . . Whatever music you come out with . . . if I don't play it right . . . you can fine me." I said, "Well we got about three new pieces we're going to be rehearsing on for the next three days." He says, "If I don't play it why don't you just let me know and then you fine me whatever you think."

So sure enough. We played a date down . . . in Manhattan [Kansas], and we had been rehearsing on these three new pieces I guess three, four, five days. Bird comes in there and put that music up there and went through that music better than anybody that had been rehearsing.

He sat up there and looked over [at me] and . . . gave me that sign. That type of cat, you know.[4]

Orville Minor: There were only three things that Bird really did. Things come in threes. Eat food first, then it was a toss-up between the habit and the horn. The women were just a side, a little accessory. . . .

Every time we'd get ready to go out of town, Bird had to go down to Mom's [a well-known K.C. drug dealer]. That's where he's scoring all the time, see, and he would pawn his horn or anything. He had to go to Mom's . . . just to get high. . . . He was always talkin' about Mom's. . . .

[But] he was like a brother. I mean, we'd fight for each other. We wouldn't let nobody else intervene if we thought it was going to be disastrous to us, if we needed something, if we were hurting for this or that. . . .

As wild as Bird was, he was just for anything, you know. . . . Like he and [Harold] Bruce [trumpet player with the McShann band] were living together. That was the act going on. They got into a fight. Bird [was] fooling around with some girl, and he wanted to bring her around to the crib [room]. And that wasn't to be, as far as Bruce was concerned. When he'd get drunk he'd go into his other side [homosexuality]. . . . They had a relationship. They were living together in Wichita. . . .

[Another time] we went into a restaurant one night, and Jay [Mc-Shann] ordered something. Whatever it was, Bird said, "That looks good," and got his fork and went on and helped hisself. . . .

When he was around he was always looked to as the bad child, always into something. Everybody was doin' the ordinary thing. He had to be doing something different. We would wonder why he would do this, but he had a point every time. . . . It's a search for knowledge. . . . He would always be trying to put two and two together.

But he was a leader and he set all the riffs. A lot of the time we went on a job, we didn't have no music, it was his head arrangement. . . .

He was more than a[n ordinary] person. . . . He'd get on the bandstand and he get to playin' his horn, he was just like a soaring thing all the time. If you make a wrong note, he would turn around and look at you. You just had the feeling his eyes were on you anyway, because he heard it.

Buddy Anderson: Bird dug Buster Smith and Prez [Lester Young, as musicians], although he didn't do a whole lot of talking about either one of them, . . . but it [Bird's music] didn't strike me personally as being anything absolutely new. I did come to know for sure [later] that he was an extraordinary musician. . . .

It [be-bop] really didn't get formulized 'till I met up with Dizzy [Gillespie], although it was already going. Dizzy and them had something out East already going by then. . . .

When we first met Dizzy he was in town with Cab Calloway. Orville [Minor], and Gene Ramey, myself dug that Diz was a different kind of cat than we were used to seeing, funny sound, you know. . . . Dizzy went to doing all this funny stuff and Orville and I [also trumpeters] got very interested in him. . . .

We met Dizzy at the intermission and we told him we were sessioning after the gig if he wanted to make it. He said he did, and we told him where, which was at Nineteenth and Vine, in a place called the Kentucky Barbecue.

Dizzy showed up, and Chu Berry [tenor saxophone star with Calloway] too. . . . They blowed the walls down, but for some reason Charlie Parker didn't show up that night at all, and that wasn't like him, because he was *there* regardless. They could be doing nursery rhymes even, he was there, evermore. . . .

The next day, I came down on the street and I met Dizzy right there at that same spot again. I was telling him about Bird, and sure enough, Charlie showed up. . . . He had his alto in a case. It was what you call Momma-made. It wasn't a case, it was a sack. It was made out of this army stuff, . . . and he'd take his little saxophone and carry it under his arm. . . .

We went up to the Foundation [American Federation of Musicians Local 627, now a private club called the Mutual Musician's Foundation]. That's actually where it happened. . . . There was a piano there, and dog shit too. The president of the local . . . kept his hunting dogs up there. . . .

We went upstairs, and Dizzy played piano. He didn't play trumpet at all. He just wanted to hear us play . . . and he dug it. . . . Dizzy is definitely his own man, but Bird was the master spokesman.

John Tumino: Charlie Parker was always broke every morning. He was hocking his instrument every day to get the bread to get the stuff [heroin]. And I'd have to go and get the money, get the horn, and put him to work the next night, and make him promise not to hock it before he gets to work.

Jay McShann: Bird was . . . an individual, you know. . . . The guys that were in the band at that time, everybody didn't try to play like Bird, but they would always find things that Bird did that they could use with what they were doing. . . .

There was one guy that really surprised us, that was the alto saxophone player [John Jackson]. Quite naturally it's got to rub off on him 'cause he's sitting right there with Bird every night. . . . I'd always keep

Bird on third alto and solos. That's on the [written] music. This other guy on first going to be playing the [melody]. Then when we were playing head tunes I put Bird on first and the other guy on third, . . . and this gives the other guy a chance to do some blowing too. But he loved to hear Bird blow, so he'd give Bird most of his solos anyway. . . .

We made a Pabst Blue Ribbon [beer] broadcast one night and Bird was late getting there. . . . Bird come in just as they had got into the first number ["Cherokee," Parker's signature tune], but he was out in the hall, you see, couldn't get in. He was standing out looking through the windows. And J. J. played Bird's solo note for note. [Later] Bird said, "Man, don't ever give this cat none of my solos no more. . . . Give it to the tenor player, the trumpet, anybody but him, don't give him my solos."

The cat had sat there and it rubbed off on him. . . . If it says something to you, if you hear it and it moves you, it's gonna rub. . . . The musicians grabbed it right quick, but . . . even the musicians hadn't heard nothing like what Bird was doing.[5]

McShann also recalled that Ben Webster[6] was an early convert to Parker's genius. He passed the word to other musicians that Parker was someone they ought to hear. Webster was scoffed at for praising this unknown musician, but soon after he noticed that many of New York's best performers were coming to hear Parker, and hiding to avoid Webster's jibes.

Orville Minor: Bird's thing was exhibitionism. It was just phenomenal. Played fifteen choruses and none of them the same, in New York. I never heard anybody execute that way. . . .

Bird was wild [too]. . . . [Walter Brown] and Bird got into a fight in the Savoy Ballroom. That's the reason we didn't get a chance to get back. It was the afternoon . . . broadcast, and Bird had done something, and Walter Brown came over to the Savoy Ballroom bathroom angry about it. First thing he did, he took a swing at Bird. Before you knew, everybody was grabbing. Imagine that, this was a broadcast [and] we had to go on. . . . Bird couldn't play because the man had hit him. . . .

We were in Detroit, playing in [the] Paradise Theater, and I recall . . . in the middle of this first number, Bird walked out, he didn't even have his shoes on, to play something, and hit one note. Just stood there . . . too stoned.

Fred Culliver took his arm, automatically [they] cut the light off. . . . People were wondering what in the world was going on. That was supposed to be a solo. Of course, McShann wanted to go through the floor. Somebody picked it up [after that], me or somebody else.

Buddy Anderson: That element [drug addiction] didn't come up until the end [of the McShann band]. I think that was the reason McShann let them [Parker and Harold Bruce] go mainly. He got loaded one night in Detroit, in the Paradise Theater. . . .

Bird got so loaded till he was damn near paralyzed, and when it came time for his solo, he had already took off his shoes, and he was just sittin' there, dead as a kink. . . .

When it came time [for his solo] he finally struggled up, I'm sitting right there behind him, and headed for the mike. But it was a big stage, and it was a little walk out there. . . . He took two steps forward and one step back, and the people [went], "Boooo, he's loaded."

I guess Johnny Tumino and Mac [Jay McShann] just decided that [after that] . . . rather than [have Parker] cast too much influence on the band, they'd . . . let him go.

Gene Ramey: I think he got the habit because he didn't learn how to cope. He couldn't fit into society, 'cause evidently his mother had babied him so much, that he thought that he was expecting that from everybody else in the world.

Buddy Anderson: I think it was '43 . . . after I left McShann I came directly back to Kansas City. Several of us left McShann at the same time, including Orville [Minor and] . . . Little Joe Baird, trombone. Bird [had] got fired out of the McShann band, which he resented very bitterly. . . . It was just sort of a breakdown in bands at that time. They all were breaking down. . . .

Leonard Enois formed a group and he got Bird too. . . . Then we [Charlie Parker, alto saxophone; Anderson, trumpet; Leonard Enois, guitar; Winston Williams, bass; Sleepy Hickox, drum; and Eddie "Little Phil" Phillips, piano] went to Tootie's [Mayfair Club] and that's where we formed this thing that the cats later came to say was the first be-bop band. Bird was writing for the band, and he was just accepted as the honorary co-leader.

[Be-bop] was a step forward, technically speaking. It brought the cats up, and I'm amazed at what these young cats are doing now. I mean, they're doing the impossible [musically].

Mary Lou Williams: Charlie Parker was such a giant, he probably listened to a lot of people. . . . Bud Powell was at my house every day, Bud Powell and Thelonious Monk, [to] write music in New York, in the forties and fifties.

It was maybe about eight or nine of 'em, Dizzy Gillespie, Charlie Parker, Tadd Dameron, Klook [Kenny Clarke], Oscar Pettiford, and a drummer used to play with Billy Taylor, J.J. Johnson, he changed the trombone. It was about ten of 'em. I'd play with 'em, but mostly they'd write a tune, come to my house, like "Ruby My Dear," and things, " 'Round About Midnight." [I'd say], "No, don't phrase it like that, do it like this."

I got off my job at four o'clock in the morning. We met outside the door, maybe I'd go by Birdland or someplace, pick 'em up. I'd go home, buy foor for the Frigidaire; I learned so many dishes to cook, to put everything together. . . . And we used to play and jam. . . . Ideas were flowing, and maybe somebody'd go over to the piano and start playing. We never asked 'em to play anything.

Charles Goodwin: What a lot of people didn't know about Charlie Parker [was] money meant nothing to him. Clothes meant nothing to him. He said many a time that the only thing that he had in his mind was to "continue to eat, and play my horn."

Charlie came here [back home to K.C.] in the fifties. It wasn't too long before he passed on. One of the guys paid him $250 a week in a small tavern. Well, he needed every dime he could get him. . . . What Charlie would do, he would go to some place and get in a jam session and send after some money, and still wouldn't show. This is the kind of person he was. He was a great musician but not reliable.

John Tumino: Charlie Parker, he'd beg you out of house and home. He was good at it. He never had a dime to eat anyway. He spent it all for whatever he could get. [The] only time he was tough and hard to do business [with] was when he was hurting [from heroin withdrawal]. Then he became unbearable. But he'd give you everything he had to pay you back. But he had a bad disease there and it took everything he made. If he'd make $100 he'd spend $110. . . .

It was a continual hassle with Charlie Parker, all through the war, all through the time we went to New York, and the guy stayed broke, made a lot of money, killed himself. He died young, he died mighty young.

Gene Ramey: [I took care of Charlie] even after he got on Fifty-second Street [in the late forties], and he was working with Diz [Dizzy Gillespie]. I was working up the street there with Ben Webster's group, and Diz would bring him right to me.

On this day, he'd been drinking rum, too. The cops told me, "Now don't let him go to sleep. If you do, he's dead." We got on the subway, and he wanted to sit down, and I have to make him stand up. I had to walk him . . . home.

I got home, my old lady was swearing that I was out with somebody, but sometimes it'd be daylight when I got home.

Just before he died, in '55, I was working at the Apollo Theater with Sonny Stitt [alto saxophonist whose playing style is strongly patterned after Parker's]. This is Christmas time, [and] Bird came up, he had on a black formal overcoat, it was expensive. He had on some Indian moccasins. He had on socks, but he had on just a tee shirt [under the coat], and he asked Sonny Stitt to loan him a horn. Sonny was the leader of the band there, so he had four saxophones, including the baritone. Sonny told him, "I can't do it." . . .

He came over to me, and I gave him some money. [He] went around to the bar and had a few drinks, and we went back onstage to do the next show. All of a sudden we heard a crash. . . .

There was a man and his wife, that did a thing like birds, . . . that was their act. They were in the process of dressing and Bird made a mistake and broke through their window. The lady screams, but by the time I got up there, [Joe] Schiffman [manager of the club] had come back there too. Bird had gotten the fire ax off the wall and was going to kill Schiffman. . . . Said, "I'm going to kill you. Been making all us black guys suffer."

I finally had to get him calm, get him out of there, . . . gave him some more money. He went around to the bar. At that time, this bar, they had three-for-one drinks. He went around, and instead of taking his money to buy, he's standing up by all the guys, and while the guy was talking he'd reach and get one of their drinks.

The guy told me, "You better come around and get Bird, somebody gonna kill him." I went around and I had to almost fight him to get him around there. He told me, "You think you're my father, don't you? I'll break your head. Don't bother me. I'm getting along all right. If somebody want to kill me, let them kill me."

Charlie Parker made jazz history by leading the way to modern jazz styles and forms after he left Jay McShann. In informal sessions at Minton's Play House and Monroe's Uptown House in New York he joined with Dizzy Gillespie, Thelonious Monk, Kenny Clarke, and others to reshape the music. In the forties and fifties his performances were legendary for their invention and beauty. Parker's fame was such that New York's best-known jazz club of the fifties, Birdland, was named for him. A life of extreme physical self-abuse took its toll on March 12, 1955. The official cause of death was heart failure, but a fifteen-year addiction to heroin and alcohol was the true cause. Charlie Parker was thirty-four years old.

NOTES

1. Parker left his job with Buster Smith at the Antlers Club to join George E. Lee's band on a summer engagement at a resort in the Missouri Ozarks in 1938. Parker used his spare time to practice the lessons Smith had taught him, and returned to K.C. a formidable musician.

2. During his decline, Young was noted for heavy drinking. At this time, however, it was apparently not yet a problem.

3. Jo Jones threw a cymbal to the stage as a scornful gesture to get Parker off the stage.

4. Quoted from "Hootie Blues," a 1978 Nebraska ETV production. Used with permission.

5. Ibid.

6. Webster was among K.C.'s most prominent saxophonists, and had played with most of its major bands, including Andy Kirk and Bennie Moten. When the McShann band first arrived in New York in 1941 Webster was the featured tenor saxophone for Duke Ellington, probably the most prestigious reed position in jazz.

18

Kansas City Jazz Today

The jazz scene in Kansas City declined abruptly in the late 1930s, but nightclubs continued to be active through the early 1960s, when urban renewal and racial conflict finally obliterated K.C.'s black downtown,[1] the center of the scene. Most of that area literally vanished, to be replaced by low-income housing, highways, playgrounds, vacant lots, and derelict buildings. Scattered clubs and barbecue and soul-food restaurants are the remnants of a jumping town.

There never was, however, a complete diaspora after the heyday. Many fine musicians from the thirties had made K.C. their permanent home, and jazz performers continued to stop off while on the road, often for extended periods. However, the spark and the necessary critical mass of creative performers were gone. K.C. was never again to be an exotic city with a legendary aura fueled by the glowing accounts of musicians who happened by or sought it out. Nor was it to again produce new sounds that would inspire jazz musicians everywhere and lead to fundamental changes in the direction of jazz style.

Many elements contributed to this decline. Musicians and club owners most often blame the legislation of early closing hours (1 A.M.) in the forties as the death blow. There is some truth to this complaint, as liberal, or unregulated, club hours both allow for much greater income for club owners (thus helping to justify employing musicians), and provide greater potential for the informal late-night jam sessions that prove so productive for jazz creativity.

The broader reforms that followed Pendergast's demise probably had an even stronger cooling effect. Although gambling was always illegal, the laws were rarely enforced in Pendergast's day, and slot machines as well

214

as dice, card, and roulette tables were important revenue producers for clubs. Even more important as a revenue source was alcohol (and, peripherally, marijuana and narcotics). During Prohibition it is likely that high mark-ups on liquor sales provided clubs with most of their profit and thus helped to sustain the jazz scene.

Illicit prosperity was not unique to the twenties and thirties, however. Kansas City had also enjoyed the economic fruits of being a "wide-open" town since the 1890s when cattlemen and merchants, flush with cash from business activities, found themselves in a town offering many pleasures. Prostitution, gambling, and alcohol were freely accessible, often in clubs that featured jazz musicians to draw the crowd, and were all part of the milieu of the brash neo-frontier town. By the beginning of World War II both agriculture and vice were fading as supports of K.C.'s economy.[2]

Kansas City's energy and sensuality, much of it rooted in widespread vice, had obvious negative aspects. Tom Pendergast, in addition to being the most dominant urban boss in American political history, was also among the most thoroughly corrupt. Tom's ambitions, greed, and apparent addiction to gambling led him inevitably into the arms of K.C.'s Mafia. While music was being indirectly supported, there is no question that large sectors of the population were systematically exploited for the gain of Pendergast and his cronies. Much of Pendergast's political strength derived from the poor — black, Italian, and Southern white — who received better treatment from his ward-based paternalistic welfare system than from K.C.'s rival laissez-faire Republicans. But the support from the poor waned by the mid-thirties when Roosevelt's New Deal superseded and surpassed Pendergast's system, which rapidly became anachronistic.

Reforms were inevitable in this environment and Pendergast's conviction for tax evasion accelerated the process. When America returned from war to prosperity in a much more mobile society, the geographic, political, and economic forces that had made Kansas City a major regional hub no longer held sway. In fact K.C. was on its way to becoming a jazz backwater as popular music evolved away from it — dance halls closed, jazz bands left dancers behind, and simpler, small ensembles took their place with R & B, country, and, eventually, rock. Kansas City retained musical talent, energy, and, sometimes, a jazz audience, but it was no longer a musical oasis where the most gifted musicians in the country looked forward to meeting the challenges of swinging K.C. comrades.

Jam sessions continue to characterize K.C. jazz. Living through peaks and valleys of local popularity, the city's musicians have never lost the spirit of jamming or their appreciation of the education, stimulation, and entertainment it offers. Currently, several clubs feature jam sessions that allow for genuine experimentation and informal sharing of ideas. (Even in New York, the center of the jazz world since the early twenties, such sessions are rare and often found only in private clubs or homes.) Kansas City also continues to produce gifted jazz musicians who play music in styles that carry traces of their city's heritage. Guitarist Pat Metheny, saxophonist Bill Perkins, and trumpeter Mark Pinder have emerged in recent years, but have migrated elsewhere, usually to New York. Many of the finest musicians who remain in K.C. began their careers in another era, and cannot carry the heritage indefinitely.

If there is a tragedy in Kansas City's decline as a jazz center, or if there are lessons to be learned, they have to do with the failure of a city and region to recognize the value of its indigenous artistic heritage, to understand the forces that permit it to prosper, and to try to nurture them.

Kansas City jazz grew first in a wide-open cow town and later during Tom Pendergast's corruption-ridden regime. Both circumstances led to a relatively free flow of large amounts of cash and a tolerance of an active nightclub world. No one rationally seeks the return of Pendergast-era conditions, but focused civic energies could lead to freer cash flows into the club world, and this could in turn have a galvanizing effect on the city's artistic life. New Orleans has accomplished this to a degree through promotion of the French Quarter and events such as the annual Jazz and Heritage Festival.[3]

Even so, New Orleans's French Quarter is an imperfect model, and has long been a tourist attraction for more reasons than jazz. However, nearly all cities with a distinct cultural heritage have similar potential in some neighborhoods, even after suffering through an urban renewal process that so often demolishes the bedrock of local history. Kansas City's equivalents are found in its old Missouri and Kansas black downtowns. Both are still relatively intact and periodically the focus of revival efforts.

Recently, these revival efforts have been strong. Attention is being focused both on K.C.'s jazz heritage, with museums, exhibit spaces, and archives proposed, and on support for contemporary musicians in the city with concert programs. There is ample justification for a suitable civic tribute to its musical heritage, and there are many musicians from both the prewar and modern eras who merit greater support. We can only hope that current efforts succeed in providing new bases for a continuing heritage of fine music. Even if the best work of many local jazz supporters is only partly successful, it is certain that both survivors from the heyday and their descendants will continue to carry on the spirit of the jumping town. As they do, Kansas City will be reminded that it produced some of the hottest, most interesting music in the world, and that for nearly twenty years it was the liveliest town around.

Big Joe Turner with the Jay McShann All-Star Band, May 1980. These jazz greats performed together in concert before a battle of bands held to celebrate the opening of "Goin' to Kansas City," an exhibit at the Kansas City Museum, Kansas City, Missouri. *Left to right:* Jay McShann (piano), Paul Gunther (drums), Joe Turner (vocals), Claude "Fiddler" Williams (violin), Eddie "Lockjaw" Davis (saxophone). (Courtesy of Mary Brumback)

Members of the Mutual Musician's Foundation, May 4, 1980. On the fiftieth anniversary of the opening of Kansas City's black musicians' union local its members gathered for another photograph, illustrating a musical "scene" that was still vibrant but very different from the one a half-century before. (Courtesy of Jerry Eisterhold)

NOTES

1. Kansas City's black downtown was relatively well defined. On the west, Troost Avenue was the recognized demarcation between the black and white worlds. Cleveland Avenue was the approximate easterly border, and Twelfth and Twentieth Streets framed the south and north.

2. K.C. was the hub of a vast agricultural distribution network. Before World War II this distribution tended to be centralized, and K.C. was rich in stockyards and granaries. After the war a slow shift to localized storage and processing began, thus robbing the city of some of its economic base.

3. Although New Orleans has a partly justified image as the home of jazz, its status as the heartland of jazz is somewhat contrived. The original New Orleans jazz world largely disappeared after 1922 and all the original generation is long dead. In contrast, the Kansas City—or Chicago or New York—jazz culture has many outstanding veterans living and performing locally.

Appendix A

Chronology

Much of this chronology originally appeared in *Goin' to Kansas City*, the 1980 exhibition catalog. It is included in the present volume, with permission, to enable the reader to place the Kansas City jazz era in the context of other contemporary musical, political, and historical events.

1899   Publication of Scott Joplin's "Maple Leaf Rag" and "Original Rags." Publication of Charles L. Johnson's "Doc Brown's Cake Walk."

1903   Publication of James Scott's first rag, "A Summer Breeze—March and Two Step."

1909   Organization of Theatre Owners Booking Association (TOBA), the black vaudeville circuit.

1912   First publication of a blues song, W. C. Handy's "Memphis Blues."

1917   Original Dixieland Jass Band makes first jazz recordings (Jan. 30); United States enters World War I (Apr. 6).

1918   Bennie Moten, Bailey Hancock, and Dude Lankford (B. B. and D.) play first jobs. World War I ends (Nov. 11).

1920   Prohibition begins (Jan. 16); Mamie Smith records "Crazy Blues," first vocal blues recording (Aug. 10).

1921   Coon-Sanders Nighthawks make first recordings (Mar. 24). Recession of 1921 deflates prices of farm products.

1923   Louis Armstrong makes first recordings with King Oliver's Creole Jazz Band (Apr. 6). Jelly Roll Morton makes first recordings (June 23). Bennie Moten Orchestra makes first recordings (Sept. 23). Coon-Sanders Nighthawks begin extended residency at Hotel Muehlebach.

1924   Paul Banks, K.C. pianist, makes only recording.

1925   Reform charter approved by K.C. voters (Feb. 24). Phil Baxter and the
        Texas Tommies make first recordings (Oct. 24). Louis Armstrong makes first
        recordings as leader (Nov. 12).

1927   Jesse Stone and the Blue Serenaders make only recordings (Apr. 27). George
        E. Lee Singing Novelty Orchestra makes first recordings (Oct. 11).

1928   Troy Floyd Orchestra makes first recordings (Mar. 14). Alphonso Trent
        Orchestra makes first recordings (Oct. 11). Bennie Moten Orchestra records
        "South," which becomes a national hit (Nov. 9).

1929   Stock market crash (Oct. 29). Andy Kirk's Twelve Clouds of Joy make first
        recordings (Nov. 9). Walter Page's Blue Devils make only recordings (Nov.
        10).

1931   Lloyd Hunter's Orchestra makes only recordings (Apr. 21). Red Perkins
        Dixie Ramblers make only recordings (May 5, 6).

1932   Coon-Sanders Nighthawks make last recordings (Mar. 24). Dow Jones In-
        dustrial Average hits all-time low of 41. Franklin D. Roosevelt elected
        President (Nov. 8). Bennie Moten Orchestra makes last recordings, including
        "Moten Swing" (Dec. 13).

1933   F.D.R. closes banks nationally (Mar. 6). K.C.'s Union Station Massacre (June
        17). Prohibition ends (Dec. 5).

1934   K.C.'s Bloody Election (Mar. 27). First major dust storm of Dust Bowl era
        (April).

1935   Bennie Moten dies (Apr. 2). Count Basie moves into Reno Club.

1936   Andy Kirk's Twelve Clouds of Joy record "Until the Real Thing Comes
        Along," which becomes a national hit (Mar. 11). John Hammond hears the
        Buster Smith/Count Basie Barons of Rhythm at Reno Club. Lester Young
        makes first recordings with Jones-Smith, Inc., a small group from Basie's
        band (Oct. 9). Basie holds farewell dance and leaves K.C. (Oct. 31). Wide-
        spread vote fraud in K.C. election (Nov. 3).

1937   Count Basie Orchestra makes first recordings (Jan. 21). Worst year of dust
        storms. Japan invades China (Aug. 11).

1938   Germany invades Austria (Mar. 11). Pete Johnson makes first recordings
        (Dec. 24). Joe Turner makes first recordings (Dec. 30).

1939   Tom Pendergast pleads guilty to income tax evasion charges and is sentenced
        to sixteen months in jail (May 22). Oklahoma City-born guitarist Charlie
        Christian makes first recordings with Benny Goodman (Oct. 2).

1940   Harlan Leonard's Rockets make first recordings (Jan. 11). Citizen's Reform Ticket triumphs in K.C. election (Apr. 21). Charlie Parker makes first recordings with a small group from Jay McShann's Orchestra (Nov. 30).

1941   Broadcasters ban ASCAP songs (Jan. 1). Jay McShann Orchestra make first studio recordings, including "Confessin' the Blues," which becomes a national hit (Apr. 30). United States enters World War II (Dec. 8).

1942   McShann band defeats Lucky Millinder in a battle of the bands at New York's Savoy Ballroom (March). American Federation of Musicians recording ban begins (Aug. 1).

1944   Jay McShann drafted.

1945   Charlie Parker makes first recordings with trumpeter Dizzy Gillespie (Feb. 29).

Appendix B

Brief Biographies

The following biographical notes appear in the oral histories with the first appearance of a speaker. They are gathered here to serve as a convenient reference. Each entry includes the following information where known: birth date, birthplace, death date, place of death, musical specialty, career highlights.

DON ALBERT (Albert Dominique). Born 8/5/1908, New Orleans, Louisiana. Died January 1980, San Antonio, Texas. Trumpet, bandleader. Performed in New Orleans and then with Alphonso Trent and Troy Floyd in Texas. Led his own bands through the 1940s, continued to be active as a trumpeter in San Antonio through the late 1970s.

BERNARD "STEP-BUDDY" ANDERSON. Born 10/14/1919, Oklahoma City, Oklahoma. Trumpet and piano. Performed with Leslie Sheffield, Jay McShann, Benny Carter, Billy Eckstine, and Roy Eldridge and led own group. Early be-bop trumpeter and musical companion of Charlie Parker. Currently active in Kansas City as pianist and bandleader. Author of "Sufferin' Cats," an unpublished history of modern jazz.

EDDIE BAREFIELD. Born 12/12/1909, Scandia, Iowa. Saxophones, clarinet, arranger. Featured with many bands including Bennie Moten, Count Basie, Cab Calloway, Zack Whyte, Don Redman, Benny Carter, and Duke Ellington.

BILL "COUNT" BASIE. Born 8/21/1904, Red Bank, New Jersey. Died 4/26/1984, Hollywood, Florida. Originally a drummer. Toured with TOBA road shows from 1924 to 1927, when the Gonzelle White show disbanded in Kansas City. Played piano in local clubs and the Eblon movie theater until joining Walter Page's Blue Devils in 1928. Joined Bennie Moten's Orchestra in 1929 and formed his own band, with Buster Smith, upon Moten's death in 1935. Continued to lead his big band until his death in 1984, with a brief interruption to lead a nine-piece band between 1950 and 1952.

DRUIE BESS. Born 7/24/1906, Montgomery City, Missouri. Trombone. Played with minstrel shows, including Harvey Minstrels and Herbert's Minstrels, and jazz bands, including Jesse Stone's Blue Serenaders, Chauncey Downs's Rinkey Dinks, and Walter Page's Blue Devils. Among the most proficient trombonists of the era.

WILBUR "BUCK" CLAYTON. Born 11/12/1911, Parsons, Kansas. Trumpet and arranger. First worked professionally in California with several bands, then traveled with Teddy Weatherford's band to Shanghai, China, where they played from 1934 to 1936. After returning, Clayton stopped by K.C. on his way to New York, met Bill "Count" Basie and joined his band, replacing Hot Lips Page who had already left for a solo career in New York. Clayton remained with Basie until 1943 when he was drafted into World War II. With Basie's band he was noted for both his ensemble and solo work, particularly with Lester Young and Billie Holliday. He remained very active upon his return from military service until dental problems led him to retire. Clayton was inspired to return to music by hearing Orville Minor play trumpet (without teeth) in 1975, and continued to be active until his second (and presumably final) retirement from performing in the early 1980s. Still active as an arranger.

ERNEST DANIELS. Born 1911, Little Rock, Arkansas. Drums. Moved to Kansas City in 1925. Played in local bands until joining Harry Dillard's WPA band in 1934. Active through the 1970s.

HERMAN DAVIS. Former Kansas City, Missouri police officer and detective. Active in organized crime investigations, including that of the Kefauver Commission.

LAWRENCE DENTON. Born 2/11/1893, Heartville, Missouri. Clarinet, arranger, bandleader. Active in Kansas City jazz in 1920s, toured widely. Co-founder of Kansas City's black musicians' union, Local 627 of the American Federation of Musicians.

EDDIE DURHAM. Born 8/19/1906, San Marcos, Texas. Guitar, trombone, arranger, and composer. Performed and arranged for many jazz orchestras, including the Walter Page Blue Devils, the Bennie Moten Orchestra, the Count Basie Orchestra, Jimmy Lunceford, Glenn Miller, Jan Savitt, and Artie Shaw. Pioneer electric guitarist.

RALPH ELLISON. Born Oklahoma City, Oklahoma. Author and critic. Also a musician and resident of Oklahoma City during the twenties.

BERNARD GNEFKOW. Born c. 1900, Kansas City, Missouri. Became a judge of election in 1924, kept the honorific title of "Judge" the rest of his career. Political worker and recipient of patronage jobs until 1932 when he became Tom Pendergast's personal secretary, where he remained until Pendergast's conviction. Became a justice of the peace in 1943, and chairman of the Jackson Democratic Club (the rubric for the Pendergast machine) after the death of Jim Pendergast, Tom's nephew.

CHARLES GOODWIN. Born 10/26/1903, St. Joseph, Missouri. Died 1/3/1983, Kansas City, Missouri. Guitar and vocals. Active in many Kansas City bands, including George E. Lee, Thamon Hayes's Rockets, and, most recently, the Art Smith K.C. Jazz Band.

SAM GRIEVIOUS. Born c. 1905. Reeds and Booking agent. Performed in many Omaha bands, including Ted Adams and Dan Desdunes.

JOHN HAMMOND. Born 12/15/1910, New York City. Died 7/10/1987, New York City. Critic and producer. A member of a socially prominent and wealthy family, Hammond began writing jazz criticism in 1931, producing jazz concerts in 1932 and jazz records in 1933. From that time he was among the most influential and most respected figures in jazz, blues, and rock production, aiding the careers of hundreds of musicians.

WALTER HARROLD. Born c. 1908, Omaha, Nebraska. Drummer. Active in Omaha and on the road. Performed with many bands, including Lloyd Hunter and Nat Towles.

TORRENCE "T." HOLDER. Born c. 1898, Muskogee, Oklahoma. Died 1979, Muskogee. Trumpet. Performed with several bands, notably Alphonso Trent. Reputed to play the "sweetest horn in Texas." Organized and led the Twelve Clouds of Joy until 1928 when the band deposed him for mismanagement. Continued to lead and perform actively through the 1970s.

RAYMOND F. HOWELL. Born c. 1910, Kansas City, Missouri. Drums. Original member of Chauncey Downs's Rinkey Dinks in Kansas City in 1924; joined Jap Allen in 1929, and the Blue Devils in 1931. After their break-up he continued to play in and around Kansas City through the early seventies.

JIMMY JEWELL. Born c. 1914, Omaha, Nebraska. Club owner and booking agent. Father owned the Dreamland Hall, Omaha's finest black club, which Jimmy took over in 1930. Continued to operate the hall for many years, and booked acts around Omaha.

HUGH JONES. Born 1/23/1910, Pine Bluff, Arkansas. Trumpet. Performed with many Territory and show bands, including June McCarr's Ragtime Steppers, Drake and Walker's Review, the Bronze Mannequins, and Jimmie Lunceford.

PARRIS "DUDE" LANKFORD. Born c. 1894, Kansas City, Missouri. Drums. Played in local parade and school bands until joining Bennie Moten's first band, B. B. and D., in 1917. Performed with Moten until 1922 when he went on the road with various vaudeville, circus, and carnival troupes.

CLARENCE LOVE. Born 1/26/1908, Muskogee, Oklahoma. Violin, piano, saxophone, bandleader. Led successful bands in Kansas City, Oklahoma, and Texas for many years. Still performs occasionally.

HENRY McKISSICK. Born 3/18/1900, Kansas City, Missouri. Died 10/14/1984, Hot Springs, Arkansas. Ward boss in the Second (predominantly black) Ward, first under Cas Welch and then with the Pendergast machine.

JAY "HOOTIE" McSHANN. Born 1/12/1909, Muskogee, Oklahoma. Piano and vocals. Toured Southwest with Al Dennis and Eddie Hills, then moved to Kansas City in 1937. Organized first band in 1938, enlarged to big band proportions in 1939. Gained national prominence with blues hit "Confessin' the Blues," sung by Walter Brown, in 1941. Currently active nationally and internationally.

ORVILLE "PIGGY" MINOR. Born 4/23/1912, Kansas City, Missouri. Trumpet. Active in many Kansas City bands, including Jay McShann, Oliver Todd, and Dee Stewart. Currently active in K.C.

EDNA MINTIRN. Born c. 1912, Kansas City, Missouri. Singer, dancer, and entertainer. Performed in many K.C. and Chicago clubs through the 1940s.

SAM PRICE. Born 10/6/1908, Honey Grove, Texas. Piano and vocal. Played with many bands, including Alphonso Trent, then performed widely as a single and as a bandleader. Many recordings. Currently active in New York and Europe.

GENE RAMEY. Born 4/4/1913, Austin, Texas. Died 1984, Austin. String bass. Active in many bands, including Oliver Todd, Jay McShann, Ben Webster, Coleman Hawkins, Charlie Parker, Dizzy Gillespie, Miles Davis, Lester Young, Count Basie. Featured on many recordings.

WILLIAM SAUNDERS. Born 1909, Arkansas. Saxophones and flute. Played extensively around Kansas City, notably with Bennie Moten and Bus Moten, and as one of the Four Tons of Rhythm.

ROY SEARCY. Born 1913, Moorhead, Mississippi. Piano and vocal. Active in Kansas City since 1942 as solo performer and bandleader. Heads the Jason Royce Searcy Foundation, which accepts contributions and donations.

BUSTER SMITH. Born 8/26/1904, Ellis County (near Dallas), Texas. Saxophones, clarinet, guitar, electric bass, piano, arranger. Prominent band member, bandleader, and arranger. Performed with many bands, including the Blue Devils, Bennie Moten, and Count Basie (co-leader of the Buster Smith-Count Basie Barons of Rhythm). The most influential Midwestern alto saxophonist of the era and a major influence on Charlie Parker.

JESSE STONE. Born 11/16/1901, Atchison, Kansas. Piano and arranger. Led the Blues Serenaders, arranger and performer with T. Holder and Andy Kirk's Twelve Clouds of Joy, George E. Lee, Thamon Hayes's Kansas City Rockets, and for many recording sessions, including with Joe Turner. Generally considered to be, along with Buster Smith and Eddie Durham, among the most influential composers and arrangers of Midwestern jazz in the twenties, thirties, and forties.

GEORGE "BUDDY" TATE. Born 2/22/1913, Sherman, Texas. Tenor saxophone, clarinet. Performed with many bands including Gene Coy's Black Aces, T. Holder and Andy Kirk's Twelve Clouds of Joy, Nat Towles, Count Basie, Lucky Millinder, and Hot Lips Page. Extensive recordings. Continues to be very active international performer and recording artist.

MYRA TAYLOR. Born c. 1922, Kansas City, Missouri. Vocalist. Featured singer with the Harlan Leonard band, particularly for "I Don't Want to Set the World on Fire." Still active performer, mostly in Europe.

JOHN TUMINO. Promoter and booking agent. Managed and booked several bands, notably Jay McShann, Harlan Leonard's Rockets, and Julia Lee.

HERMAN WALDER. Born 4/2/1905, Dallas, Texas. Alto saxophone. Prominent performer and arranger in Kansas City with many bands, including George E. Lee, LaForest Dent, Thamon Hayes, and Harlan Leonard. Widely regarded as an important early influence on Charlie Parker.

BOOKER WASHINGTON. Born 4/9/1909, St. Charles, Missouri. Trumpet. Featured with the Bennie Moten Orchestra and Thamon Hayes's Kansas City Rockets. Remained active in Kansas City through 1983 with Art Smith's Kansas City Jazz Band.

JERRY WESTBROOK. Born 2/2/1904, Westpoint, Mississippi. Piano and vocals. Active in Kansas City in the twenties and thirties. Achieved considerable local prominence by being the first black performer to have local radio broadcasts. Continued to perform with the Little Jerries through the late 1970s.

CLAUDE "FIDDLER" WILLIAMS. Born 2/22/1908, Muskogee, Oklahoma. Violin and guitar. Performed with many bands, including Alphonso Trent, T. Holder and Andy Kirk's Twelve Clouds of Joy, George E. Lee, Count Basie, and Jay McShann.

ERNIE WILLIAMS. Born 6/8/1904, Winston, North Carolina. Died 1/27/86, Kansas City, Missouri. Drums and vocals. Performed widely, including three years with a show in Shanghai, China; directed and sang for the Blue Devils and Harlan Leonard's Rockets. Featured in the 1980 film "The Last of the Blue Devils."

MARY LOU WILLIAMS. Born 5/8/1910, Atlanta, Georgia. Died 5/28/81, Durham, North Carolina. Piano and arranger. Learned to play in Pittsburgh, Pennsylvania, and began performing professionally at age four. Went on the road as a pianist in 1925. Married saxophonist John Williams in 1927. Became pianist for the Twelve Clouds of Joy in 1929. Immediately achieved prominence. Recognized as being among the outstanding pianists and arrangers in jazz history, and among the pioneer modern jazz stylists. Active as a performer and teacher until her death in 1981.

Appendix C

Selected Discography

Many of the best available recordings of Midwestern jazz are either foreign, from specialty labels, or no longer in print. Such cases are noted, respectively, with one, two, or three asterisks.

Recordings: 1920s–1950s

Anthologies

Boogie Woogie, Jump and Kansas City. Many performers, including Pete Johnson. Folkways 2810. °°

Big Band Jazz. Many performers, including Count Basie and Bennie Moten. The Smithsonian Collection of Recordings R 03030.

From Spirituals to Swing. Count Basie, Pete Johnson, Hot Lips Page, Charlie Christian, et al. Vanguard VSD 47/48.

International Association of Jazz Record Collectors, Vol. 6. Lloyd Hunter, Red Perkins, et al. IAJRC-6. °°

Rare Bands of the Twenties. Alphonso Trent, Mary Lou Williams, et al. Historical HLP-3. °°

St. Louis Jazz, 1925-1927. Jesse Stone. Herwin 114. °°

San Antonio Jazz. Don Albert, Boots and His Buddies, et al. IAJRC-3.°°

The Smithsonian Anthology of Classic Jazz. Includes Scott Joplin, Jelly Roll Morton, Louis Armstrong, Bennie Moten, and Count Basie. R 025.

Territory Bands 1927-1931. George E. Lee, Blue Devils, et al. Historical HLP-26. °°

Territory Bands 1929-1933. Alphonso Trent, et al. Historical HLP-24. °°

Basie, Count

The Best of Count Basie. Recorded 1937-39. MCA2-4050E.

Blues by Basie. With Jimmy Rushing. Columbia PC-36824.

Count Basie at the Famous Door, 1938-39. Jazz Archives JA-41.

The Count Basie Orchestra: 1944. Circle 60. °°

The Count Basie Orchestra: Savoy Ballroom 1937 (with Billie Holiday). Archive of Folk Song 318.

The Count at the Chatterbox (1937). Jazz Archives JA-16.

Good Morning Blues. MCA2-4108.

One O'Clock Jump. CSP JCL-997.
Showtime. MCA2-2-4163.
Super Chief. Columbia CG-31224.

Christian, Charlie
Charlie Christian. Archive of Folk Music, Jazz Series, FS-219.
Charlie Christian with the Benny Goodman Sextet and Orchestra. Columbia
   CL-652.
Charlie Christian with the Benny Goodman Sextet, 1939-41. Jazz Archives JA-
   23.
Charlie Christian with Dizzy Gillespie, Thelonious Monk, and Don Byas. Archive
   of Folk Song. 219E.
Solo Flight. Columbia CG-30779.

Johnson, Pete
Boogie-Woogie Mood (1940-44). MCA 1333.

Kirk, Andy
Andy Kirk: Instrumentally Speaking (Recorded 1936-1942). MCA-1308.
*Andy Kirk's Twelve Clouds of Joy "Live" from the Trianon Ballroom in Cleveland
   (1937).* Jazz Society AA 503. ° °
The Best of Andy Kirk. MCA2-4105.
Lady Who Swings the Band. MCA 1343.
The Territories, Volume 1. Arcadia 2006. ° °

McShann, Jay
Early Bird. Spotlite 120. ° °
The Early Bird: Charlie Parker. MCA 1338.
Jay McShann, Charlie Parker: Early Bird. RCA Black and White FXM 17334. °
Kansas City Piano. Decca DL 9226. ° ° °
K.C. in the '30s. Capitol T1057. ° ° °
New York: 1208 Miles, 1941-43. Decca DL 9236. ° ° °

Moten, Bennie
Bennie Moten's Kansas City Orchestra, 1923-1929. Historical HLP-9. ° °
Bennie Moten's Kansas City Orchestra, Volume 2 (1928-1929). RCA Black and
   White Volume 80. °
Bennie Moten's Kansas City Orchestra, Volume 3 (1929). RCA Black and White
   Volume 99. °
Bennie Moten's Kansas City Orchestra, Volume 4 (1929-1930). RCA Black and
   White Volume 112. °
Bennie Moten's Kansas City Orchestra, Volume 5 (1929-1932). RCA Black and
   White Volume 130. °
The Complete Bennie Moten, Volume 1 & 2 (1926-1928). RCA Black and White
   PM 42410. °
Count Basie: Kansas City Style (Recorded 1929-32). RCA AFM1-5180.

Page, Hot Lips
Feelin' High and Happy. RCA Vintage. °°°
Joe Guy and Hot Lips Page: Trumpet Battle at Minton's. With Charlie Christian.
 Xanadu 107. °°
Sweets, Lips, and Lots of Jazz. With Count Basie. Xanadu 123. °°

Parker, Charlie
Bird/The Savoy Recordings (Masters). Savoy 2201.
Birth of the Bebop: Bird on Tenor 1943. Stash ST-260.
Charlie Parker: Complete Savoy Studio Sessions (1945-48). 5-Savoy 5500.
Charlie Parker: Encores (Recorded 1944-48). Savoy SJL-1107.
Charlie Parker: Encores Volume 2 (Recorded 1944-48). Savoy SJL-1129.
Charlie Parker: First Recordings! Onyx 221. °°
Charlie Parker: Takin' Off, with Dizzy Gillespie (Recorded 1945-46). Hall
 620E. °°
Charlie Parker: The Very Best of Bird. Warner Brothers 2WB 3198 or J5A 3198.
Complete Charlie Parker on Verve. Recorded 1946-54. 10-Verve OOMJ-326877.

Rushing, Jimmy
The Essential Jimmy Rushing. 2-Vanguard T 65/66.
Going to Chicago, Jimmy Rushing's All-Stars. Vanguard VRS 8518. °°°
Jimmy Rushing: Listen to the Blues. Vanguard 73007.

Turner, Joe, and Pete Johnson
Big Joe Turner: Boss of the Blues (Recorded 1956). Atlantic SD-8812 or CS-8812.
Big Joe Turner: Early Big Joe: 1940-1944. MCA. °°°
Have No Fear, Big Joe Turner Is Here. 2-Savoy SJL-2223.
Jumpin' the Blues. Arhoolie 2004.

Williams, Mary Lou
Mary Lou Williams: Asch Recordings (1944-47). 2-Folkways 2966. °°
Mary Lou Williams (1944-46). Stinson 24 or 8T-24 or CA-24. °°
Mary Lou Williams. Folkways 2843. °°

Young, Lester
Charlie Christian & Lester Young: 1939-1940. Jazz Archives JA-42.
Charlie Christian: Lester Young Together Again. Jazz Archives JA-6. °°°
The Kansas City Six and Five: The Commodore Sessions. Columbia Special
 Products 14937 or Commodore XFL-14937.
The Lester Young Story, Volume 1. Columbia CG 33502. °°°

Recordings: 1960s–1980s

There are many worthy contemporary recordings by K.C. alumni, including:

Barefield, Eddie
Indestructible Eddie Barefield. Famous Door 113. °°

Basie, Count
Count Basie and Big Joe Turner: The Bosses. Pablo 2310709.
Count Basie, Joe Turner, and Eddie "Cleanhead" Vinson: Kansas City Shout.
   Recorded April 1980. Pablo D2310859.
Kansas City 5. Pablo T 2312-126.
Kansas City 6. Pablo 2310-871.
Kansas City 7 (Recorded July 1962). MCA 29003.
Trio (First Time!). Pablo 2310712 or K10712.

Clayton, Buck, and Buddy Tate
K.C. Nights. 2-Prestige 24040.

Hamilton, Scott, and Buddy Tate
Back to Back. Concord J 85.
Scott's Buddy. Recorded 1980. Concord J 148.

Humes, Helen
Helen Humes and the Muse All-Stars, with Arnette Cobb, Buddy Tate, Eddie
   "Cleanhead" Vinson. Recorded 1979. Muse 5217.

McShann, Jay
Confessin' the Blues. Recorded 1971. Black & Blue 33.022. °°
Goin' to Kansas City. Master Jazz 8113. °°
Jay McShann: After Hours. Recorded 1977. Storyville 4024.
Jay McShann: The Big Apple Bash. Atlantic 90047-1 or 90047-4.
Jumpin' the Blues. Black & Blue 33.039. °
Kansas City Hustle. Sackville 3021. °°°
Kansas City Joys. Sonet 716. °°
Kansas City Memories. Black & Blue 33.057. °
The Last of the Blue Devils. Atlantic SD8800. °°°
McShann's Piano. Capitol T.2645. °°°
Man From Muskogee. Sackville 3005. °°°
Tribute to Fats Waller. Sackville 3019. °°°

Price, Sammy
Sammy Price: Fire. Class. 106. °°
Sammy Price and His Musicians, 1944. Circle 73. °°

**Smith, Art (Band includes Herman Walder, Charles Goodwin, Booker Wash-
   ington, and Ben Kynard)**
K.C. Jazz Lives! Sound Recorders. °°
Once Again, Kansas City Jazz on 12th Street, USA. Cavern Sound. °°

Tate, Buddy
Buddy Tate: Hard Blowin', Live at Sandy's. Recorded 1978. Muse 5249.
Buddy Tate and the Muse Allstars. Recorded 1978. Muse 5198.
The Great Buddy Tate. Recorded 1981. Concord J 163.

Turner, Big Joe
Big Joe Turner and the Roomful of Blues: Blues Train. Muse 5293 or MC- 5293.
Everyday I Have the Blues. Pablo 2310818.
Singing the Same, Sad, Happy, Forever Blues. Pablo 2310883.
Things that I Used to Do. Pablo 2310800.

Williams, Mary Lou
Black Christ of the Andes. Mary 101. °°
Mary Lou Williams and Don Byas. GNP 9030.
Mary Lou Williams and Cecil Taylor: Embraced. Recorded April 1977. 2- Pablo
  L2620108.
Mary Lou Williams in London. GNP 9029.
Mary Lou's Mass. Mary 102.
My Mama Pinned a Rose. Recorded 12/77. Pablo 2310819.
Zodiac Suite. Folkways 32844.
Zoning. Recorded 1974. Mary 103.

Selected Bibliography

Baxter, Derrick. *Ma Rainey and the Classic Blues Singers*. New York: Stein and Day, 1970.

Blesh, Rudi. *Shining Trumpets: A History of Jazz*. 2nd ed., rev. Roots of Jazz Series. New York: Da Capo, 1975.

Blesh, Rudi, and Harriet Janis. *They All Played Ragtime*. Rev. ed. New York: Oak Publications, 1971.

Brown, A. Theodore, and Lyle W. Dorsett. *K.C.: A History of Kansas City, Missouri*. Boulder, Colo.: Pruett Publishing Co., 1978.

Charters, Samuel. *Jazz: New Orleans 1885-1963*. 1963. Reprint. Roots of Jazz Series. New York: Da Capo, 1983.

Charters, Samuel B., and Leonard Kundstadt. *Jazz: A History of the New York Scene*. 1962. Reprint. Roots of Jazz Series. New York: Da Capo, 1981.

Chilton, John. *Who's Who of Jazz: Storyville to Swing Street*. 4th ed. New York: Da Capo, 1985.

Collier, James L. *The Making of Jazz: A Comprehensive History*. Boston: Houghton Mifflin, 1978.

Collins, Lee. *Oh, Didn't He Ramble: The Life Story of Lee Collins As Told to Mary Collins*. Edited by Frank Gillis and John W. Miner. Urbana: University of Illinois Press, 1974.

Courlander, Harold. *Negro Folk Music, USA*. New York: Columbia University Press, 1963.

Dance, Stanley. *The World of Count Basie*. 1980. Reprint. New York: Da Capo, 1985.

————. *The World of Swing*. New York: Da Capo, 1979.

Dexter, Dave. *Jazz Cavalcade*. 1946. Reprint. Roots of Jazz Series. New York: Da Capo, 1977.

————. *Playback*. New York: Billboard Publication, 1976.

Dorsett, Lyle. *The Pendergast Machine*. New York: Oxford University Press, 1968.

Driggs, Frank. "Kansas City and the Southwest." In *Jazz*, edited by Nat Hentoff and Albert McCarthy, 189-230. New York: Da Capo, 1975.

Driggs, Frank, and Harris Lewine. *Black Beauty, White Heat: A Pictorial History of Classic Jazz, 1920-1950*. New York: Morrow, 1982.

Ellington, Duke. *Music Is My Mistress*. New York: Da Capo, 1976.

Ellison, Ralph. *Shadow and Act*. New York: Vintage Books, 1972.

Esquire's World of Jazz. New York: Crowell, 1975.

Feather, Leonard. *The Encyclopedia of Jazz.* New York: Horizon, 1960.

Gillespie, Dizzy, and Al Fraser. *To Be or Not To Bop.* New York: Da Capo, 1985.

Gitler, Ira. *Swing to Bop.* New York: Oxford University Press, 1985.

Hadlock, Richard. *Jazz Masters of the Twenties.* New York: Macmillan, 1974.

Hentoff, Nat, and Albert McCarthy, eds. *Jazz.* New York: Da Capo, 1975.

Hester, Mary Lee. *Going to Kansas City.* Sherman, Tex.: Early Bird Press, 1980.

Horricks, Raymond. *Count Basie and His Orchestra.* 1957. Reprint. New York: Greenwood, 1972.

Jackson, George Pullen. *White and Negro Spirituals, Their Life Span and Kinship.* New York: J. J. Augustin, 1943.

Jasen, David A., and Trebor Jay Tichenor. *Rags and Ragtime: A Musical History.* New York: Seabury Press, 1978.

Keil, Charles. *The Urban Blues.* Chicago: University of Chicago Press, 1966.

Litwak, Howard, and Nathan Pearson. *Goin' to Kansas City.* Museum exhibit supplement. Kansas City, Mo.: Mid-America Arts Alliance, 1980.

Lomax, Alan. *Mister Jelly Roll: The Fortunes of Jelly Roll Morton, New Orleans Creole and "Inventor."* 1950. Reprint. Berkeley and Los Angeles: University of California Press, 1973.

McCarthy, Albert. *Big Band Jazz.* New York: G.P. Putnam's Sons, 1974.

————. *The Dance Band Era.* London: Spring Books, 1971.

Marquis, Donald. *In Search of Buddy Bolden: First Man of Jazz.* New York: Da Capo, 1980.

Martin, Asa. *Our Negro Population.* Kansas City, Mo.: Franklin Hudson, 1913.

Milligan, Maurice. *The Last Waltz.* New York: Scribners, 1948.

Murray, Albert. *Stomping the Blues.* New York: McGraw-Hill, 1976.

Nathan, Hans. *Dan Emmett and the Rise of Early Negro Minstrelsy.* Norman: University of Oklahoma Press, 1962.

Oliver, Paul. *The Story of the Blues.* Radnor, Pa.: Chilton, 1969.

Ostransky, Leroy. *Jazz City: The Impact of Our Cities on the Development of Jazz.* Englewood Cliffs, N.J.: Prentice-Hall, 1978.

Placksin, Sally. *American Women in Jazz, 1900 to the Present: Their Words, Lives, and Music.* New York: Putnam, 1982.

Porter, Lewis. *Lester Young.* Boston: Twayne, 1985.

Ramsey, Frederic, Jr., and Charles Edward Smith. *Jazzmen.* New York: Harcourt Brace, 1939.

Reddig, William. *Tom's Town.* New York: Lippincott, 1947.

Reisner, Robert. *Bird: The Legend of Charlie Parker.* New York: Da Capo Press, 1973.

Rose, Al, and Edmond Souchon. *New Orleans Jazz: A Family Album.* Rev. ed. Baton Rouge: Louisiana State University Press, 1985.

Russell, Ross. *Bird Lives!* New York: Charterhouse, 1973.

————. *Jazz Style in Kansas City and the Southwest.* 1971. Reprint. Berkeley: University of California Press, 1982.

Schaefer, William J., and Richard B. Allen. *Brass Bands and New Orleans Jazz.* Baton Rouge: Louisiana State University Press, 1977.

Schiedt, Duncan. *The Jazz State of Indiana.* Bloomington, Ind.: Duncan Schiedt, 1977.

Schuller, Gunther. *Early Jazz*. New York: Oxford University Press, 1968.

Schuller, Gunther, and Martin Williams, eds. *Big Band Jazz: From the Beginnings to the Fifties*. The Smithsonian Collection of Recordings Series. Urbana: University of Illinois Press, 1983.

Shapiro, Nat, and Nat Hentoff, eds. *Hear Me Talkin' to Ya*. New York: Dover, 1966.

_____. *The Jazz Makers*. New York: Rinehart, 1957.

Smith, Willie (The Lion), and George Hoefer. *Music on My Mind: The Memoirs of an American Pianist*. 1964. Reprint. New York: Da Capo, 1975.

Southern, Eileen. *The Music of Black Americans*. New York: Norton, 1971.

Stearns, Marshall, and Jean Stearns. *Jazz Dance: The Story of American Vernacular Dance*. New York: Schirmer, 1979.

Stewart, Rex. *Jazz Masters of the Thirties*. 1972. Reprint. The Roots of Jazz Series. New York: Da Capo, 1980.

Tirro, Frank. *Jazz: A History*. New York: Norton, 1977.

Toll, Robert. *Blacking Up*. New York: Oxford University Press, 1974.

Waldo, Terry. *This Is Ragtime*. New York: Hawthorn Books. 1976.

Williams, Martin. *The Jazz Tradition*. Rev. ed. New York: Oxford University Press, 1983.

_____. *The Smithsonian Collection of Classic Jazz*. The Smithsonian Collection of Recordings Series. New York: Norton, 1973.

Young, William H., and Nathan B. Young. *Your Kansas City and Mine*. Kansas City, Mo.: William H. and Nathan B. Young, 1950.

Index

239

Note on the Author

NATHAN W. PEARSON, JR., has long had a personal and professional interest in jazz, history, and American culture. His B.A. and M.A. degrees in music were earned at Wesleyan University where his master's thesis was an oral history of the life and times of Texas songster Mance Lipscomb. As an ethnomusicologist, Pearson worked with the Folklife Programs of the Smithsonian Institution, the American Folklife Center of the Library of Congress, the Folk Arts Program of the National Endowment for the Arts, and many state and local groups. With Howard Litwak, he was awarded a National Endowment for the Humanities Youthgrant in 1976 to support research on Kansas City jazz. The two collaborated on several related projects in Kansas City, culminating in their co-direction of a major traveling museum exhibit on Kansas City jazz produced by the Kansas City Museum in 1980. Pearson is currently a management consultant with McKinsey and Co. in New York City, where he continues to be involved in ethnomusicological and folkloric projects, and to enjoy jazz.

Books in the Series *Music in American Life*

Early American Music Engraving and Printing: A History
of Music Publishing in America from 1787 to 1825
with Commentary on Earlier and Later Practices
Richard J. Wolfe

Sing a Sad Song: The Life of Hank Williams
Roger M. Williams

Long Steel Rail: The Railroad in American Folksong
Norm Cohen

Resources of American Music History: A Directory of Source Materials
from Colonial Times to World War II
D. W. Krummel, Jean Geil, Doris J. Dyen, and Deane L. Root

Tenement Songs: The Popular Music of the Jewish Immigrants
Mark Slobin

Ozark Folksongs
Vance Randolph; Edited and Abridged by Norm Cohen

Oscar Sonneck and American Music
Edited by William Lichtenwanger

Bluegrass Breakdown: The Making of the Old Southern Sound
Robert Cantwell

Bluegrass: A History
Neil V. Rosenberg

Music at the White House: A History of the American Spirit
Elise K. Kirk

Red River Blues: The Blues Tradition in the Southeast
Bruce Bastin

Good Friends and Bad Enemies: Robert Winslow Gordon
and the Study of American Folksong
Debora Kodish

Fiddlin' Georgia Crazy: Fiddlin' John Carson, His Real World,
and the World of His Songs
Gene Wiggins

America's Music: From the Pilgrims to the Present,
Revised Third Edition
Gilbert Chase

Secular Music in Colonial Annapolis: The Tuesday Club, 1745-56
John Barry Talley

Bibliographical Handbook of American Music
D. W. Krummel

Goin' to Kansas City
Nathan W. Pearson, Jr.